Indian Lives

INDIAN LIVES

Essays on
Nineteenth- and Twentieth-Century
Native American Leaders

Edited by
L. G. Moses and Raymond Wilson

University of New Mexico Press
Albuquerque

Design by Milenda Nan Ok Lee

Library of Congress Cataloging in Publication Data

Main entry under title:

Indian lives.

Bibliography: p.
Includes index.
1. Indians of North America—Biography. 2. Indians of North America—Government relations. 3. United States—Biography. I. Moses, L.G. (Lester George), 1948- II. Wilson, Raymond, 1945-
E89.I43 1985 973'.0497 85-1188
ISBN 0-8263-0814-7
ISBN 0-8263-0815-5 (pbk.)

First edition

Contents

Illustrations

To Ian, Bronwen, and Raymond Nathan

Introduction

In 1962 the American Indian Chicago Conference met on the campus of the University of Chicago. More than five hundred Indians representing ninety tribes and bands expressed their desire, embodied in the "Declaration of Indian Purpose," to maintain their identity as Indians and their right to choose what they considered to be appropriate aspects of the dominant culture.[1] Most Indians then—and today—did not want to relinquish their identity as Indians. Rather, they insisted on retaining ethnic distinctiveness and preserving their cultural heritage.

As the decades of the 1960s and 1970s would prove, however, American Indians had to struggle to preserve their ways. In the quickening atmosphere of social rebelliousness during those decades, American Indians shouted at other Americans such variegated slogans as "self-determination," "Red Power," and even "God is Red." So extraordinary were the many changes of the previous twenty years that Alvin Josephy, Jr., would write in 1982 that Indians "have regained a pride in their identity as Native Americans and as members of tribal groups. In a burst of resurgent nationalism, they have shed the inhibitions and shame of conquered peoples and, strengthened by their own revitalized cultural heritages, have turned against governmental paternalism and injustices perpetrated by their fellow Americans."[2]

In 1980 the U.S. Census enumerated 1,418,195 Indians, of whom at least 700,000 were living on reservations. Whereas only a few hundred had been attending college in 1960, two decades later Indians numbering in the thousands were attending colleges and universities. Male and female Indians alike were entering the professions in ever larger numbers, one of the indices of success recognized within the dominant culture—or as Josephy wrote, "not a few have acquired national and international reputations in their professions."[3]

By the 1980s, tribes had also won significant settlements either through the long-lived Indian Claims Commission, now defunct, or in the U.S. Court of Claims. On the surface at least, such awards provided belated recognition that treaties between sovereign "nations," however diminished that sovereignty might be for one of the signatories, had been violated unconscionably. Tribes long disestablished, or "vanished"—to use an appropriate word—had regained federal recognition of their tribal status. And during an administration largely remembered for political scandals, American Indians had at last heard a president, Richard Nixon, proclaim the inherent right of self-determination and repudiate the policies of "liberation-termination." However noble the sentiment when it first bore results during the overcharged Cold War atmosphere of the 1950s, "liberation" of the first Americans produced typical results—non-Indians stealing Indians' lands and resources.

Although the paean about cultural dynamism and nationalism over the last twenty-odd years is justified, more than two centuries of mutable federal policies resound in discord; the government's willingness to abide by the principle that "the utmost good faith shall always be observed toward the Indians" has been more honored in its breach than in its reality. Statements uttered early in 1983 by James Watt, then Secretary of the Interior, about the "failure of socialism" on the reservations and the consequent need to liberate Indians from governmental meddling are echoes from the past. Vigilance as to their own rights and responsibilities is as important today for American Indians as at other times in their histories. Great also, one may assume, is the need for effective leadership to meet the challenges and demands of the present and the future.

A troublesome question recurs, however—leadership by whose criteria? If we mean solely that leadership which is recognized and honored within the context of mainstream American society, great varieties of leaders are excluded. Even few tribal chairmen, for example, are known beyond their own reservations, and certainly they are among the more prominent American Indian leaders. Outside the political sphere, American Indian leaders in art, literature, science, medicine, education, and other professions of high status are celebrated as individuals of talent and ambition and occasionally held out as "aspirational images" upon whom other Native Americans can ruminate. Yet, at the same time, the impression is created that these men and women of fame and influence had to overcome what for most people would have been insuperable difficulties. Are we then to conclude, quite wrongly, that they have succeeded despite great cultural disadvantages? To make such a conclusion is to invite the same attitudes that made it possible in the first place to destroy wantonly the very cultures that have been praised for their vital achievements despite the odds.

Perhaps there is something unique in native cultures that sustains the leader in his rise to prominence. The image of the American Indian living in two worlds occurs frequently in Native American biography. Josephy used it in *The Patriot Chiefs* as have other historians during the last two decades. Certainly the idea reinforces the view that American Indians are indeed unique. But as scholars of immigration would doubtless contend, immigrants also have lived in two worlds, the one from which they emigrated and the other to which they journeyed. Unlike the immigrant minorities, however, American Indians have unique claims upon the laws and conscience of the nation. As original inhabitants—and this designation can be extended to native Hawaiians and Alaskans in the broadest definition of Native American—they have been accorded a singular status. The individual cultures of American Indians have been preserved, despite the intentions of their adoptive parents, through this special status and in special environments set aside from the rest of the nation. It is on the reservations that Indian cultures are most obviously preserved. As historians of immigration have demonstrated, immigrant communities largely disappear once ties to the old country are broken. Without constant revitalization immigrants begin to walk the road to assimilation. American Indians, especially those born on the reservations, are more likely to be nurtured in the cultures and languages of their ancestors; on the reservations they meet for the first time the culture of other Americans. Perhaps, instead of using the image of the American Indians as peoples living in two worlds, it is better to suggest that American Indians live in a complex world of multiple loyalties. The strength of their individual cultures often contributes to how successful they will become in the world of the dominant culture. Native American leadership—and not just in the restrictive political sense—is the most visible means for making such judgments.

The American Indian leaders in this study have responded as persons of multiple loyalties. Although there has been a tendency to judge their successes and failures by criteria borrowed from the dominant culture, it is worthwhile remembering, as each of the contributors here suggests, that each regarded himself or herself as an Indian and was recognized as such, and that this identification helped to shape his or her responses. All tried to preserve what he or she considered to be the strengths of his or her heritage—even Charles Curtis, in his most roguish stance, saw in his great-great-grandfather White Plume a capacity for greatness, a capacity which traditionalists probably lamented. Maris Pierce labored in behalf of the preservation of the landbase of the Senecas, for without their land the people would be set adrift in a world removed from their ancestors; Nampeyo dug into the earth around First Mesa and found the inspiration for an artistic renascence that celebrated both past and present; Susan LaFlesche Picotte, in her reformer's zeal, ministered to the health needs of her people so that Omahas might not perish from the earth; Henry Chee Dodge fought for the rights of Navajos in the midst of the complex political realities of his day; Charles Curtis worked to remove the vestiges of what he saw as barbarism so that other Indians might be transformed through the process of assimilation, and like most self-made men he praised too much his creator; Luther Standing Bear extolled his heritage in the arena, on celluloid, and on the printed page, and proclaimed that if given the chance he would raise all Americans to be Indians; Minnie Kellogg strove to reassert communalism as the best means to preserve her culture and at the same time provide an adjustment to the pressures of modern society; and Peterson Zah, as tribal chairman of the largest Indian tribe on the largest reservation in the United States, saw in 1982 the need to bring into greater coincidence traditionalism and progressivism, the life of the hogan and the life of urban, industrial America.

All of these remarkable men and women attest to the vitality and panoply of Indian cultures. They did not live in two worlds, but in one world of great complexity that challenged, sustained, and sometimes destroyed them, but never removed their "Indianness."

The question "Who is an Indian?" is laden with difficulty and uncertainty.[4] American Indians are generally regarded as a unique branch of the human family possessing wide varieties of cultural expressions, origins, and traditions. It is the variety of Indian cultures that has hampered efforts to treat Indians as a single, undifferentiated group. Historians and social scientists have often struggled to bring meaning and understanding to what the non-Indian community views as "the Indian." Generalizations about the nature of "Indianness" have broken down when the particularities of tribal existence have been noted. Then too, Indian history has been written largely from the non-Indian point of view; consequently the perspective of the non-Indian, as Vine Deloria and Clifford Lytle have explained, does not always coincide with the view from the reservation.[5] Because perceptions regarding the relative importance of events may differ markedly between the observer and the observed, those traditions that shape Indian perceptions of the world may be overlooked or misunderstood.

From a primarily cultural perspective of Indianness then, customs and traditions most readily distinguish Indians from other people—customs and traditions which have survived in the minds and lives of Indians today and which have been jealously preserved over several centuries of contact with non-Indians. There are also other methods of recognizing Indianness.

An Indian, Wilcomb Washburn has written, may be identified according to his or her relationship to the legal system of the United States. All Indians today are citizens, but those Indian citizens who are members, ex-members, or descendants of Indians having recognized tribal status possess rights and obligations that are distinct from the rights and obligations of non-Indian citizens. But consider, for example, a "full-blood" Indian who has ended or abandoned his tribal membership and has no claim to benefits or obligations deriving from tribal association. He is, for legal purposes at least, not an Indian. On the other hand, if a person is accepted as an Indian by tribal authorities and by the governmental agencies dealing with tribal authorities though his "Indian" ancestry may be slight or tenuous, he is, nevertheless, legally an Indian.[6] Thus the legal definition of an Indian in the United States is likewise more closely related to cultural rather than to biological criteria. If the person looks upon himself as an Indian, and if he lives within an "Indian" cultural community, and if an Indian social or legal entity accepts him as such, then that person is normally regarded as an Indian. It matters little if he can prove that his ancestors lived in America before Columbus.

Answers to the question "Who is an Indian?" may also incorporate "racial" criteria, most often specified on the basis of an acceptable quantum of Indian "blood." Both terms, *race* and *blood*, are emotionally charged and have scant meaning for the science of human genetics. Rather they are commonly used (and therefore ill-defined) terms by which people assign one another to categories of assumed biological differences. Very often these differences are imagined to be evident in physical appearances but can also include alleged moral, intellectual, and psychological differences. This "folk" usage, as Karen Blu has described it, merges unscientific ideas about biology with observed and sometimes enforced social differentiation and discrimination.[7] The social facts of racial classification must not be confused with the biological or genetic facts. There is no widely accepted taxonomy of biologically defined races of humans, either for the natural or the "social" sciences. Further, it cannot be assumed that a person's physical appearance importantly reveals either his genetic heritage or his social classification.[8]

"Blood," according to Blu, is "the mystical medium that transfers from parent to child physical characteristics and the moral, intellectual, and psychological qualities linked to them." This notion has not been appreciably affected by scientific evidence from modern genetics and evolutionary biology. In folk biology, "blood" links parents and children and it is used as an idiom with which to talk about kinship as well as race. In its most insidious usage "blood" can be regarded as a substance that is either racially pure or racially polluted.[9] In its most common usage relating to Indians, it refers to their presumed degree of Indianness.

In recent years there have been serious questions and complaints about when and under what circumstances the Department of the Interior will place Indian lands in trust when the land has been purchased by an individual Indian, the tribe, or the federal government. In regulations that became effective October 20, 1980, the Interior Department enumerated those occasions when the government would agree to accept land in trust status for individuals and tribes. The department defined "Individual Indian" as: (1) any person who is an enrolled member of a tribe; (2) any person who is a descendant of such a member who was, at the passage of the Indian Reorganization Act of 1934, physically residing on a federally recognized Indian reservation; and (3) any other person possessing a total of "one-half or more degree of Indian blood of a tribe."[10] Except for this last requirement, the emphasis is historical and cultural rather than racial.

It is probably impossible therefore to assert absolutely who is an Indian in the United States today, though certain general statements can be made. First, it is obvious that the federal government's definition of Indianness is not a true definition but is instead a description of the people served by the Bureau of Indian Affairs (BIA). Also, a purely racial definition of Indianness cannot be applied operationally in the United States so long as the Mexican-American population is, in many ways, at least as "biologically" Indian as that population served by the BIA.[11] And finally, a purely "cultural" definition of Indianness is itself hard to apply in those instances where persons of full-blood tribal descent, living an Anglo-American style of life in non-Indian urban settings are regarded in practice as still being Indian because of their physical characteristics, former tribal affiliation, or self-definition as Indians.

Jack D. Forbes has suggested that it is perhaps better to describe the different kinds of Indians who reside in the United States solely on the basis of their tribal or group affiliations. The problem of stating who is an Indian, given all the contradictions, would be in great measure eliminated. This method of identification would conform to usages in other parts of the world. For example, the Mong of Southeast Asia are not called Mong Asians or Mong Vietnamese. Dropping the designation "Indians," Forbes has argued, would make matters less difficult. "If a person belongs to the Shawnee Tribe he is, in fact, a Shawnee (provided . . . that he is accepted by other Shawnees as a Shawnee) regardless of his ancestry. He may not be a Shawnee 'Indian' but he is a Shawnee person."[12] Persons of mixed tribal ancestry, such as a Cherokee-Quapaw, could then become the true hyphenated Americans. Discarding the term *Indian*, however, would not be met with enthusiasm by all Indian groups.

It is accurate to suggest that there were no "Indians" present in 1492 when Columbus arrived in the New World. Ironically, the many attempts of colonial and later national governments to destroy the indigenous peoples of the Americas, whether through warfare or programs of assimilation, actually helped to create American "Indians." In these years of heightened ethnic consciousness the designations *Native American* or *Amer-*

ican Indian can be as much a source or pride as tribal identity. Those persons who regard themselves as members of individual tribes may, nevertheless, also regard themselves as equal members of an identifiable ethnic group with a common heritage. Much of that heritage represents their relations over the centuries with non-Indians.

In 1971 Hazel Hertzberg published her study of modern Pan-Indian movements. In *The Search for an American Indian Identity*, she analyzed the growth of a wider Indian identity and found that, until the end of the nineteenth century, Indian response to white encroachment was largely tribal but on occasion included some loose, regional, intertribal groupings. It was not until the Progressive Era of this century, however, that a number of organized movements arose nationally and championed a common Indian interest and identity as distinct from strictly tribal interests and identities. These organizations, according to Hertzberg, stressed accommodation to the dominant society, and drew membership largely from acculturated "mixed-bloods" who, through their own experiences, had found much of value in both Indian and white worlds. They tried to create an identity that drew from both. She labelled these persons as "people in transition."[13]

Vine Deloria, Jr., on the other hand, has defined "Pan-Indian" as "a label used [by anthropologists and sociologists] to paste over the efforts of Indian tribes to organize for effective political action."[14] Pan-Indian for Deloria represented the efforts of disparate tribal groups to combine out of self-interest and lobby for larger "Indian" interests. In the years since World War II a number of organizations have been founded whose membership rises or falls in manic swings according to the nature of threats to Indian communities and the willingness of Indian "ethnic groups" to assert a larger and wider identity. Such organizations as the National Congress of American Indians (of which Deloria was once executive director) and the American Indian Movement (AIM) are only two such modern Pan-Indian organizations that have defined "Indianness" in a larger context, and frequently as "Us" against "Them" where *them* represents most frequently governmental threats to the Indians' land base, resources, or privileges.

Pan-Indian identity has also been important for persons of mixed ancestry who have had little, if any, contact with a traditional culture. It allows those persons to express an identity otherwise not well attested to by a reservation experience or the use of an indigenous language.[15] Pan-Indianism is a way to affirm an Indian identity for people who lack the traditional mechanisms for holding themselves together—formal organizations like a tribal government, explicit membership criteria, and distinctive cultural traits.[16]

Since the 1970s, social scientists have shown great interest in the role played by "ethnic identity" or "ethnicity" in their analyses of political behavior and cultural dynamics in the United States.[17] Whereas ethnicity once referred almost exclusively to immigrant groups of the late nineteenth and early twentieth centuries, in recent years definitions have become so broad, and in many instances so ambiguous, as to include such agglomerations as towns, religious sects, and even fraternal organizations.

According to popular perceptions, ethnic groups are made up of people who share common interests and are capable of acting in concert on the basis of those interests. Common interests may include nationality of ancestors, language, "race," "blood," religion, historical events, or any combination of elements. In the term *ethnicity*, Werner Sollors has written, "the double sense of general peoplehood . . . and of otherness (different from the 'mainstream' culture) lives on."[18]

American Indians have increasingly been identified as "ethnic groups," combining folk imagery of race with other ideas of "grouphood." For Edward Spicer, using a neutral term *ethnic group* to describe Indians has additional advantages. Like Forbes, he would prefer to drop the term *Indian* because of its imprecision. In his definition of Indian ethnic groups he means "a number of people who share a particular Indian group name and other symbols of a common historical experience unique to those who use the group name." Such an identity includes the use of language, customs, and beliefs. "However, because of assimilation processes, it may be that the language is replaced and only the historical experience . . . and the group name remain of the Indian heritage. Nevertheless, the sense of identity among members of culturally assimilated groups may be very intense as a result of alienation from whites."[19]

In such definitions—and there are many others—group identity is self-conscious, self-expressed, and persistent. Individually and collectively, American Indians have been pressed during the last two centuries to give up their distinctive identities, tribal as well as "Indian," by the assimilationist policies of federal and state governments. Yet despite all the efforts, American Indians retain their separate identities.

Perhaps, in the end, only Indians themselves can answer with any authority or precision the question "Who is an Indian?" Indians are the ones who know more than others the often unarticulated assumptions that sustain and set apart Indian groups from other Americans. Louis W. Ballard, a Cherokee-Quapaw, has remarked: "[I]t seems somewhat strange when Indians say they don't want to be white people, when at the same time they are fond of using modern day conveniences. However, one of the characteristics of the Indian, and I suppose of many cultures like that of the Indian, is to select what he can use—and make it 'Indian' in the use of it."[20] N. Scott Momaday has said that "an Indian is an idea which a given man has of himself and it is a moral idea, for it accounts for the way in which he reacts to other men and to the world in general. And that idea, in order to be realized completely, has to be expressed."[21] Joe Sando, the Jemish historian, has written that "having Indian blood or claiming Indian ancestry does not make an Indian according to Pueblo values; one has to be an active participant in Indian life."[22] Indian identity, or "Indianness," may only be understood in the way Indians perceive themselves in relation to the rest of the world and how those perceptions shape their actions. The idea of Indianness, therefore, must not only be expressed but lived. It is in the living of the identity that the identity is realized.

The varieties of Indianness and complexities inherent in it, are often best found in American Indian biography. Biography is essential to the common identity of any ethnic group. It also enlivens human interest in a culture's legendary heritage.[23] In the many studies of American Indian leaders, leadership, and personalities, historians have focused considerable attention on those persons who have defied the alien governments and who have sought to preserve through warfare their separate cultures. These leaders, sometimes quixotic and heroic, have been the subjects of numerous individual biographies. Their heroism and patriotism inspire admiration; their tragedies inspire pity and terror. Alvin Josephy used patriotism as the theme of his compilation of nine biographical sketches. The persons he wrote about in *The Patriot Chiefs* represented the " 'good and brave men,' . . . Nathan Hales, George Washingtons, and Benjamin Franklins." Their biographies, arranged chronologically as well as geographically, conveyed a "narrative outline" of much of American Indian history. Resistance, Josephy explained, was a logical, indeed patriotic, response to oppression. There were, however, no women included among the greats. This should not be regarded as criticism of Josephy but rather as testimony to the passage of time and the changes in popular perceptions since *The Patriot Chiefs* first appeared. In fairness to Josephy, he acknowledged that "there were many other Indian leaders of heroic stature," even sometimes among the collaborators, the "good Indians" of the whites, who "recognized the inevitabilities of historic situations and tried peacefully to find paths to security for their peoples." These men, for all their stature, nevertheless accepted rather than resisted the changes wrought by colonial and national governments.[24]

R. David Edmunds relaxed the rules of admission into the pantheon of Indian heroes though, again, heroines were conspicuously absent. In Edmunds's *American Indian Leaders: Studies in Diversity*, various authors contributed biographies that expanded upon Josephy's theme of patriotism in both tribal and mainstream American society. The selections included warriors, collaborators, and acculturated professionals. Edmunds, as his subtitle suggested, avoided generalizations about the nature of American Indian leadership. It is not that ethnic leadership as a subject defies generalization, but rather that the patterns of leadership among Indians have yet to be sufficiently explored, let alone explained.[25]

Margot Liberty's edited volume on *American Indian Intellectuals* provided an original approach in biographical studies of Native Americans. It represented an effort to bring together short biographies of some of the outstanding North American Indian intellectuals of the nineteenth and early twentieth centuries, citing their contributions to the discipline of anthropology. Some of the persons contributed little—for example, Charles Eastman (Santee) and Sarah Winnemucca (Paiute)—to the development of anthropological scholarship; nevertheless, they provided, according to Liberty, "awareness of lifeways precious because they were unique."[26]

To these more elaborate studies of historic American Indian leaders can be added the several biographical directories and dictionaries. As Frederick J. Dockstader has written, "we know a great deal about some tribes, and almost nothing of others; we also know in depth of the careers of some individuals, and know very little about others."[27] In many instances, the lack of information about certain leaders is due to the absence of reportage by outside observers. Then too, we will never know anything about some leaders. The records of their deeds do not exist; the memories of their contributions are no longer recalled. Other leaders we may know too well, and perhaps not at all, because biographies have often been based on repetitious accounts copied from earlier writings of questionable accuracy and authenticity.

Works which form more of a "Who's Who" in native North America have their origin in the two-volume *Handbook of American Indians North of Mexico*, edited by Frederick Webb Hodge. The handbook began inauspiciously as an "in-house" project of the Smithsonian Institution's Bureau of Ethnology. Known for years informally as the "Tribal Synonymy," it was the collective work of bureau personnel who wrestled with a "confusion of nomenclature perplexity"—a myriad of names borne by various tribes at various times throughout the colonial period. It represented one of the first steps in the organization of ethnological information in the United States, the larger goal of the Bureau of Ethnology. Once the data were organized, or so John Wesley Powell and his colleagues believed, the bureau would then provide the government with scientific principles to advance a humane Indian policy. The bureau's reach, however, escaped its grasp. In time, the original synonymy was transformed into a "cyclopedia," and later still into the handbook which, when issued as two volumes in 1906 and 1911, represented a distillation of work at the bureau for more than a quarter century, as well as the then current research of scholars around the country. Included in the alphabetical listing of tribes, myths, religious ceremonials, and many other aspects of American Indian cultures, were short biographies of famous Indians written from field notes, wherever possible, but also from an exhaustive search of French, Spanish, Dutch, and English colonial records and books. The bureau finally published the handbook largely to impress Congress with its practical research and to forestall further reductions in the bureau's operational budget. Ethnological research at the bureau seemed never to end. The handbook's usefulness, however, went well beyond public relations. Although it has since been superseded by an even more ambitious, multivolume project carried out under the auspices of the Smithsonian Institution, scholars still make use of the original Hodge edition. One of its best features was its ease of use as a ready reference work for American Indian history and ethnology.[28]

Usefulness as an organizing principle has inspired other compilers of directories. Frederick J. Dockstader's *Great North American Indians: Profiles in Life and Leadership* contains biographies of three hundred "individuals . . . clearly of Indian ancestry," organized chronologically rather than alphabetically. Dockstader hoped that his work would improve the reading consciousness of the literate public in the realm of Native American history, serve the general reference needs of scholars, and guide readers to further research.[29] Like Josephy, Dockstader also suggested that readers who began at the beginning and diligently read through to the end without skipping to better known persons would find a narrative in pastiche of Indian-white relations; they would "encounter a fresh approach to understanding the problems which confronted both peoples during resettlement of North America.[30]

To those purposes outlined by Dockstader and others, Marion Gridley would add another. The long-lived editions of *Indians of Today* have saluted the outstanding contributions of American Indian leaders—all at least one-quarter Native American—to their people and to the United States. It was the hope of Gridley that the individual achievements of Indian leaders and their successes in their tribes as well as in American society in general would serve as "aspirational images" for younger Indians.[31]

In contrast, the present volume expands the literature of American Indian biography. Its theme is maintaining Indian identity—being an Indian—during times when it proved difficult to do so, from the early nineteenth century down to the present. Popular ideas of what it is to be an Indian have undergone significant changes. "Indianness," observed Josephy, "may be many things, and mean something different, to different persons—the possession of certain cultural traits, blood relationships, beliefs and values, or a membership on a tribe's roll."[32] As the contributors to this volume have aptly demonstrated, Indianness is a complex concept. Indeed, some Indians used their Indianness either to help their people, to help only themselves, or to help both their people and themselves.

The selection of these eight prominent individuals, three of whom are women, is in no way exclusive or representative of the various Indian cultural areas. We recognize that other cultural areas provide additional subject for study. These eight were chosen because their lives demonstrate a world of multiple loyalties and the complexities and uniqueness inherent in living as Indians. Maris Pierce used his knowledge of law on behalf of Iroquois property rights. Nampeyo created "Indian" art that would be recognized and celebrated by other Americans. Susan LaFlesche Picotte, while revering her heritage, nevertheless embraced assimilation, believing it to be the only means for the Omahas, and by extension all Indians, to survive with dignity in a world not of their making. Henry Chee Dodge's life mirrored the strength and resiliency of his people who prevailed, despite a period of exile, and adapted and grew into the largest Indian "nation" in the United States. Charles Curtis, far from finding his Indianness a liability, capitalized on his ethnic heritage and, for well or ill, became the first and, thus far, only "Indian" vice-president of the United States. Luther Standing Bear championed through his writings the rights of traditionalists to live their cultures. Minnie Kellogg spoke of herself as an "Old Indian" adjusted to a modern world but insisted that Indian values must be preserved if the nation were to survive. And finally, Peterson Zah, in his leadership of the Navajo Nation, voiced the timeless concern of American Indians who have tried to preserve their distinctive cultures and, at the same time, to meet the challenges of the modern world.

The eight persons whose biographies are retold in the pages that follow have had to adapt to a dominant culture which sometimes demanded of them abandonment of distinct and traditional attributes of their cultures; they were told to be other than what they were, whether Seneca, Hopi, Omaha, Sioux—or "Indian." The problems faced by these men and women varied according to historical circumstance, though each tried to create a world that allowed Indians to be Indians according to his or her particular vision.

Notes

1. Joan Ablon, "The American Indian Chicago Conference," *Journal of American Indian Education* 2(1962), pp. 17–23.

2. Alvin M. Josephy, Jr., *Now That the Buffalo's Gone: A Study of Today's American Indians* (New York, 1982), p. xiii.

3. Ibid.

4. Wilcomb E. Washburn, *Red Man's Land, White Man's Law: A Study of the Past and Present Status of the American Indian* (New York, 1971), p. 163.

5. Vine Deloria, Jr., and Clifford M. Lytle, *American Indians, American Justice* (Austin, Tex., 1983), p. 1.

6. Washburn, *Red Man's Land, White Man's Law*, pp. 163–64.

7. Karen I. Blu, *The Lumbee Problem: The Making of an American Indian People* (Cambridge, England, 1980), p. 6. We have relied on Blu's valuable discussion in chapter 7 (pp. 200–235) which includes such subheadings as "The 'Lumbee Problem' and American Ethnicity" and "Ideas of 'race' and 'ethnic group' in America."

8. Ibid., p. 23. For biologists, a race is a relatively isolated breeding population within a given species. The isolation of the population, whether geographical or social, has resulted in the development of gene pools or gene frequencies that distinguish it in minor ways from other populations in the same species. Biologists disagree about just which populations constitute races and how those boundaries between them are to be drawn. Physical anthropologists as well maintain that there is no acceptable biological taxonomy of human races; rather they view "race" as a social classification that does not necessarily mirror biological divisions. More significant are the ways people assign one another to racial categories and then how they behave on the basis of those socially defined categories.

9. Ibid.

10. Department of Interior Regulations, vol. 25, *Code of Federal Regulations*,

Part 120a.2, "Definitions." A fourth category is also designated for purposes of land acquisitions outside the state of Alaska where "Individual Indian" also means a person who meets any of the three criteria and where "tribe" includes any Alaska Native Village or Alaska Native Group which is recognized by the Secretary of the Interior as eligible for the social programs and services from the BIA.

Section 120a.2b defines "tribe" as "any Indian tribe, band, nation, pueblo, community, rancheria, colony, or other groups of Indians, including the Metlaktla Indian Community of the Annette Island Reserve. . . . 'Tribe' also means a corporation chartered under section 17 of the Act of June 18, 1934 (48 Stat. 988; 25 U.S.C. 477) or section 3 of the Act of June 26, 1934 (49 Stat. 1967; 25 U.S.C. 503)."

11. See the discussion in Jack D. Forbes, *Native Americans of California and Nevada* (Healdsburg, Calif., 1969), pp. 122–24, 126, 127.

12. Ibid., p. 127.

13. Hazel W. Hertzberg, *The Search for an American Indian Identity: Modern Pan-Indian Movements* (Syracuse, 1971), p. 324.

14. Vine Deloria, Jr., *We Talk, You Listen* (New York, 1970), p. 85.

15. George L. Hicks, "Separate But Similar: Adaptation by Two American Indian Groups," in George L. Hicks and Philip E. Leis, eds., *Ethnic Encounters: Identities and Contexts* (Belmont, Calif., 1972), p. 81.

16. Harold R. Isaacs, "Basic Group Identity: The Idols of the Tribe," *Ethnicity* 1(1974), p. 15.

17. See the extensive bibliographic analysis in Werner Sollors, "Theory of American Ethnicity, or: '?S Ethnic?/TI and American/TI, De or United (W) States S SI and Theor?' "*American Quarterly* 33 (1981), pp. 257–83. In 1970, historian Rudolf J. Vecoli called attention to "Ethnicity: A Neglected Dimension of American History," and in 1979 he published a survey on "The Resurgence of American Immigration History" in which he noted the significant increase in books, articles, and dissertations about the roles of race, nationality, and religion in American history. See Rudolf J. Vecoli, "Ethnicity: A Neglected Dimension of American History," in Herbert J. Bass, ed., *The State of American History* (Chicago, 1970), pp. 70–88; and "The Resurgence of American Immigration History," *American Studies International* 17(1979), pp. 46–66.

18. Sollors, "Theory of American Ethnicity," pp. 260–61. Anthropologist George De Vos has defined an ethnic group as one that is "self-consciously united around particular cultural traditions." George De Vos, "Ethnic Pluralism: Conflict and Accommodation," in George De Vos and Lola Romanucci-Ross, *Ethnic Identity: Cultural Continuities and Change* (Palo Alto, Calif., 1975), p. 9. For Abner Cohen, a British anthopologist, an ethnic group shares "patterns of nor-

mative behavior" and forms part of a larger population, interacting with people from other groups within a social system. "The term ethnicity refers to the degree of conformity by members of the collectivity. . . . [W]hat matters sociologically is what people actually do, not what they subjectively think or what they think they think." Abner Cohen, ed., *Urban Ethnicity* (London, 1974), pp. ix–x. One definition stresses culture whereas the other stresses "normative behavior" in action.

19. Edward Spicer, "American Indians," in Stephen Thernstrom, ed., *Encyclopedia of American Ethnic Groups* (Cambridge, Mass., 1980), p. 64. Sociologist Martin Doornbos has written that persons usually acquire their identities from at least two different sources, one being the ethnic group to which they belong and the other being the sense of solidarity that devolves upon the group as it finds itself alienated or cut off from mainstream society. Martin Doornbos, "Some Conceptual Problems Concerning Ethnicity in Integration Analysis," *Civilisations* 22(1972), pp. 263–84. In the first instance the group defines itself and in the second, boundaries between groups reinforce contrasts. Boundaries may be either symbolic or physical. Spatial isolation in rural areas, as is the case with most Indian reservations, can slow acculturation and protect group identity from alien influences. See Amy Peterson Royce, *Ethnic Identity: Strategies and Diversity* (Bloomington, Ind., 1982), p. 7, and Milton M. Gordon, *Assimilation in American Life: The Role of Race, Religion, and National Origins* (New York, 1964), p. 78.

20. Louis W. Ballard, "Cultural Differences: A Major Theme in Cultural Enrichment, " *Indian Historian* 2(1969), p. 6.

21. Quoted in *Indian Voices: The First Convocation of American Indian Scholars* (San Francisco, 1970), p. 49.

22. Joe Sando, *Nee Hemish: A History of Jemez Pueblo* (Albuquerque, 1982), p. 217.

23. John A. Price, *Native Studies: American and Canadian Indians* (Toronto, 1978), p. 69.

24. Alvin M. Josephy, Jr., *The Patriot Chiefs: A Chronicle of American Indian Resistance* (New York, 1961), p. xiv.

25. R. David Edmunds, ed., *American Indian Leaders: Studies in Diversity* (Lincoln, Neb., 1980), pp. vii–xiv. The varieties of Indian leadership and the difficulties inherent in the subject are explored in Robert F. Berkhofer, Jr., "Native Americans," in John Higham, ed., *Ethnic Leadership in America* (Baltimore, 1978), pp. 119–49 and Walter L. Williams, "Twentieth-Century Indian Leaders: Brokers and Providers," *Journal of the West* 23(1984), pp. 3–6.

26. Margot Liberty, ed., *American Indian Intellectuals* (St. Paul, 1978), p. 1. See also Raymond Wilson, *Ohiyesa: Charles Eastman, Santee Sioux* (Urbana,

1983), and Gae Whitney Canfield, *Sarah Winnemucca of the Northern Paiutes* (Norman, 1983).

27. Frederick J. Dockstader, *Great North American Indians: Profiles in Life and Leadership* (New York, 1977), p. 1.

28. *Twenty-Second Annual Report of the Bureau of American Ethnology* (Washington, D.C., 1904), p. xi, and *Twenty-Fourth Annual Report of the Bureau of American Ethnology* (Washington, D.C., 1907), pp. xxiv–xxvi. Congress added the word *American* to the title of the Bureau of Ethnology in 1894. See also Curtis M. Hinsley, Jr., *Savages and Scientists: The Smithsonian Institution and the Development of American Anthropology, 1846–1910* (Washington, D.C., 1981), pp. 156–58, 282–83, 286–89.

29. Dockstader, *Great North American Indians,* p. 4.

30. Ibid.

31. Marion E. Gridley, ed. and comp., *Indians of Today* (New York, 1971). See also Harry Waldman, et al., *Dictionary of Indians of North America* (St. Clair Shores, Mich., 1978), especially the introduction by Marion E. Gridley, "Problems of American Indian Biography," pp. 5–9.

32. Josephy, *Now That the Buffalo's Gone,* p. 78.

1

Maris Bryant Pierce

The Making of a Seneca Leader

H. A. Vernon

Indians figured prominently in wars that resulted from rival European imperial ambitions as, especially in the eighteenth century, Spain, France, England, and eventually the United States vied with one another for supremacy in North America. Whenever Indians held the balance of power between competing colonial nations, their ways of life were least threatened—least threatened, that is, if they happened to be on the winning side. Once native groups lost their ability to play off one European power against another, with their numbers dwindling as the Euroamerican population increased, they had to submit either through diplomacy or force of arms to the whims, policies, and prejudices of the majority.

The Six Nations, or League of the Iroquois, in New York—Seneca, Cayuga, Onondaga, Oneida, Mohawk, and, after 1712, the Tuscarora—are frequently cited as masters of the play-off policy. For most of the eighteenth century, down to the period of the American Revolution, the Iroquois maintained their power and independence, which kept the colonies nearest to them watchful and respectful. The Six Nations bartered their neutrality or aid with, first, the Dutch in the seventeenth century, and later with the English, on the one hand, and the French, on the other, depending on which side provided the most concessions or presents, signs in Iroquois cultural terms—and, by extension, in most Indian groups—of true friendship and allegiance. However, with the defeat of the French in the

Seven Years' War, the play-off policy came to an end, with only a brief renaissance during the American Revolution. Although undefeated in the field, the Iroquois had largely sided with the British, the losers in the Revolution as far as the Americans were concerned. Afterward, the Iroquois faced the demands of the new United States. Most of those demands, made continually for more than a generation, pertained to the surrender of Iroquois lands. The Six Nations' power to resist militarily the assaults on their culture had been broken. In the two decades following the close of the Revolution, the Iroquois experienced considerable cultural decay.

About 1800, a Seneca sachem (a hereditary leader, of whom there were fifty in the council of the league) named Handsome Lake beheld visions in which he learned how the Iroquois might restore their culture. Handsome Lake, brother of the Seneca leader Cornplanter, traveled between the nations' villages, bringing his message of peace, sobriety, and cultural renewal. His visions and revelations became the basis of a religion. Although aboriginal in origin, the religion of Handsome Lake contained many elements of Christianity, and in the generations that followed, those who practiced it incorporated additional Christian elements into the traditions.

Handsome Lake, like many other American Indian messianic leaders, stressed the centrality of land to culture. He enjoined his followers to retain their lands. Yet demands for Iroquois lands increased in the first five decades of the nineteenth century, reaching a high point in the 1840s, the decade of Indian Removal. Maris Bryant Pierce (1811–1874) devoted much of his life to the fight to preserve Iroquois lands. As an acculturated Seneca, he used his considerable talents to fight for Iroquois property rights through methods and means adopted from the larger society. Pierce is representative of that group of Native Americans who emerged in the nineteenth century with an understanding of the realities of the modern world while simultaneously preserving an identity with their traditional cultures. Pierce never took up arms against the dominant culture. Always a realist, he could be dismissed as a collaborator with white America. But in his struggle to retain the lands of the Iroquois, sometimes against hopeless odds, Pierce showed himself to be well within the tradition of other Iroquois patriots.

The life of Maris Bryant Pierce, like that of his contemporary, General Ely S. Parker, spanned the critical years of Seneca treaty negotiations, land loss, tribal political reorganization, and missionary influences. As a man who learned to live in the dominant culture, Pierce served his people well, especially during their loss of independence. This essay examines his education as preparation for Iroquois leadership and his role in the Treaty of Buffalo Creek.

Despite certain generalizations about their ineffectiveness, a few Native American students returned to their societies to provide for their people creative leadership and commitment to Indian sovereignty. Pierce was a case in point; yet unlike Handsome Lake, Cornplanter, Red Jacket, and Governor Black Snake, his accomplishments have gone unrecognized. In order to understand what made him a major figure in Seneca history, it is important first to explain the conditions affecting his people during the nineteenth century.

Like the other members of the Six Nations Confederacy, the Senecas, or "Guardians of the Western Door," suffered greatly during the years of the American Revolution. The punitive expedition of General John Sullivan in 1779 had destroyed most of the Seneca settlements in the Genesee country, driving many Senecas farther northwest to Niagara and other areas of western New York.[1]

After the American Revolution, the Seneca Nation still preserved the major portion of their tribal lands. It was at this time, however, that white pressures for Indian lands increased. By 1797, the Mohawks had left their valley to settle on a small strip at St. Regis, on the St. Lawrence River; the Oneidas, Onondagas, and Cayugas had abandoned their traditional lands except for small parcels in central New York; and the Senecas had given up all lands east of the Genesee. The Senecas, nevertheless, still retained sizable tracts west of the Genesee where hunting grounds and old settlements were located. At Buffalo Creek, for example, there existed whole villages of Senecas joined by refugee Cayugas, Onondagas, and Tuscaroras.

It was in 1797, however, that the Treaty of Big Tree deprived the Senecas of most of their remaining lands in western New York. Robert Morris, a financier of the American Revolution, had held the legal right to buy these western tracts, and he had hoped to build a fortune on speculation in frontier real estate. Morris was at this time bankrupt and, in need of cash, he sold his preemptive rights to the Holland Land Company, a union of Dutch bankers. Morris and his son, Thomas, negotiated the company's purchase of Seneca lands through pressure, threats, and bribery, which was much the same method used later in the treaty of 1838. Stores of all kinds were laid in to persuade the Senecas to sell. Included in these were 750 gallons of whiskey, calculated to last thirty days, and to be dispensed at the rate of 25 gallons a day, but only after the treaty had been signed.[2]

Bribery, promised private annuities, and subversion of some Seneca chiefs and leading Seneca women finally induced the nation to sell their remaining lands for one hundred thousand dollars. Eleven reservations were created which encompassed existing villages in a total land area of 311 square miles, or about 200,000 acres. The sale price, divided equally among about fifteen hundred Senecas then in New York State, provided each with an annuity of less than four dollars a year.[3] By the Treaty of Big Tree the Senecas accepted reservations aptly described by Anthony Wallace as "slums in the wilderness"; from an estimated original sixty-seven towns and settlements ranging over a vast area, the Senecas now lived in isolated settlements separated by the intervening farmlands and fences of newly arrived white settlers.[4]

It was on one of these settlements—the Allegany Reservation—a tract of forty-two square miles, that Maris Bryant Pierce was born in 1811. He attended a Quaker primary school as a child and was later sent to Fredonia Academy.[5] Later still, he transferred to another academy in Homer, Cortland County, after which he spent some time in Rochester. While in Rochester, he was converted to Christianity by the Presbyterian church. His precollege studies ended in a school located in Thetford, Vermont, following which he was admitted to Dartmouth College.[6]

During these years, the Pierce family appears to have moved closer to Buffalo, and the Buffalo Creek Reservation, or *Dyosyowan*. Pierce came to regard the reservation, which lay some five miles from the city, as his home until its abandonment in 1845. John Tawse, secretary of the Society in Scotland for Propagating Christian Knowledge, described the reservation in the 1830s as prosperous and progressive. According to Tawse, he

> saw their fields under very respectable cultivation, and bearing good crops. They had exchanged their original rude wigwams [*sic*] for comfortable houses, with barns and offices attached to them, scarcely if at all inferior to those of the whites, and some of the houses have little plots or gardens in front kept in good order. . . . All these marks of improvement surprised

us; we did not expect to meet with a state of such high comparative civilization.[7]

At *Dyosyowan* Pierce's father, John, lived on the fertile farmlands, bordered by valuable stands of timber; lands which were later coveted and acquired by the Ogden Land Company.

While relatively little is known of Pierce's earliest years, his Seneca name, *Ha-dya-no-doh* ("Swift Runner") survived.[8] Following his conversion to Christianity, Pierce, at the age of twenty-five, was sponsored by the Society in Scotland for Propagation of Christian Knowledge to enter Dartmouth College in 1836. This evangelical Christian society had been founded in 1709 by Scotch Presbyterians. The society established missions among the Mohawks, the Oneidas, and the Delawares of New Jersey during the eighteenth century.[9] By 1800, their mission work included some Senecas, among them the Pierce family. Part of the rationale of the society for sending Pierce to Dartmouth may have come from their belief that Indians working as missionaries among their own people might succeed where whites had failed.[10] As far as the society was concerned, Pierce, a promising young Seneca from western New York, possessed the intelligence and skills to enter a well-established white institution of higher learning.

Pierce was not the first Native American to enter college in New Hampshire. Reverend John Sargeant had established an all-Indian school at Housatonic in 1748, followed by Eleazar Wheelock's school in 1754. But Wheelock believed that Indians should associate with English youths in a mixed school, and should be removed entirely from native influences.[11] From this school, later named Moor's Charity School in honor of its benefactor, Dartmouth College eventually emerged. Dartmouth was founded in 1769 in Hanover, New Hampshire, where Wheelock had been offered both land and capital. As president, Wheelock drafted Dartmouth's first charter. Its mission was to educate "Youths of the English, and also the Indian tribes of this land in reading, writing, and all . . . Liberal Arts and Sciences.[12] Educating English youth, however, remained a subordinate part of Wheelock's educational plans; he hoped instead to attract large numbers of Indians to the new institution. Despite his vision of an Indian liberal arts college, Dartmouth graduated only three Indians in the eighteenth century and eight in the nineteenth, of whom Maris Pierce was one. As a college graduate, Pierce was in a sense among the elite, for during most of his lifetime he enjoyed the benefits deriving from a college education and sustained contacts with prominent whites. These advantages enabled him to deal effectively with some of the problems facing the Seneca Nation in the nineteenth century.

Despite his earlier experiences in the world of white education, Pierce's enrollment at Dartmouth in 1836 marked a rather drastic and perhaps traumatic change in his way of life and daily routine. First years in college are often difficult under the best of circumstances; Pierce found himself in an environment quite different from that of his early education, and the Dartmouth yearly calendar at this time may have proved baffling even to whites accustomed to the complexities of mainstream American society.

At this time, and throughout the presidency of the Reverend Nathan Lord (1828–65), the following college calendar prevailed. The fall term began about September 1, and ran until November 25; this was followed by a seven-week vacation (until about January 24), after which a winter term of seven weeks began. During the winter term, those students who were teaching were not required to be in residence. The spring term started about March 21 and lasted until commencement on the last Wednesday in July. The spring session was punctuated by two weeks of vacation in May. After commencement, a four-week vacation ensued until the beginning of the new fall term.[13]

In his first two years at Dartmouth, Pierce took courses designated as "languages and mathematics," yet he himself refers to having attended daily lectures in mineralogy and chemistry accompanied by experiments. Perhaps his interest in mineralogy was stimulated by the pools of oil located on the Oil Spring tract just north of the Allegany Reservation.[14] Oil had long been used by the Senecas for a variety of medicines. Other classes he attended consisted of anatomy, and lectures on opium and alcohol intoxication. Yet studies in the humanities, and the physical and biological sciences did not preclude work in the social sciences, for Pierce reports having studied Jean-Baptiste Say's *Political Economy*.[15]

During Pierce's years at Dartmouth, the marking system was based on a scale of one to five, with one representing the highest achievement. His transcript for his freshman year indicates a rather pedestrian performance, yet this may be due to the necessary adjustments to college life and routine; some improvement was made in his sophomore year, which he ended with a 2.8 average. In any event, his final two years in college were marked by much better academic work. President Lord remarked that Pierce "had finished his course in college very honorably." Elsewhere, Lord described Pierce as "intelligent, pious, stable, and a good scholar."[16] John Tawse, of the Scotch society, was also pleased with Pierce's college work, and observed that he "is altogether as interesting a young man as ever I saw, and I trust from his talents, his sound principles, and the knowledge he has acquired, he will prove a great blessing to the Nation of Indians to which he belongs. . . ."[17] Thus, it appears that Pierce's qualities of leadership were apparent to educational and religious leaders with whom he had occasional contacts at campus gatherings.

While studies occupied much of his time, Pierce still found opportunity for recreation. In the late 1830s, diversions at Dartmouth often consisted of forays into the surrounding areas and picnics in the countryside. On one excursion, a group of young men and women, including Pierce, visited Enfield, New Hampshire, where a Quaker village was located. A picnic, followed by boating on a lake occupied the group on this occasion. Pierce remarked that he had a "jolly time"; although accompanied by a white woman named Miss Thompson, whom he described as "lively and agreeable," he had not expected to have an especially good time. The group had been sociable, and had shown "good sense." Yet Pierce followed this statement in his diary with the remark that "there was something unpleasant said which might as well or better not to have been spoken," but he does not elaborate upon it.[18] It could be conjectured that perhaps some derogatory remark had been made about his being an Indian.

On another occasion, the Dartmouth College phalanx, a primitive ROTC, held a muster on the college green, and Pierce carried the standard, as he had done the previous year. The group marched to Norwich, Vermont, where they saluted a Captain Partridge, who made a short speech and treated the company to a glass of wine.[19]

As Pierce's final year drew to a close, graduating seniors were assigned topics on which they were to speak at commencement; understandably, Pierce's assignment was "The Destiny of the Aborigines of America," a subject in which he expressed great interest. Unfortunately, there is no record of what Pierce said in his commencement speech, but there is ample evidence that his years at Dartmouth were filled with a concern for the fate of the Seneca Nation, that of the Six Nations, and for that matter, of all Native Americans.

Dartmouth's rigorous academic calendar had worked to Pierce's advantage. It allowed him time away from the campus to promote the cause of the Six Nations, particularly the Senecas, before white audiences. It also permitted him to go, on occasion, to Washington to work for legislation beneficial to his people.

Loss of Seneca lands had begun with the Treaty of Big Tree in 1797, and it was during Pierce's sophomore and junior years that the infamous Treaty of Buffalo Creek was signed between the Ogden Land Company and the Senecas. Previously, in 1810, the Holland Land Company had sold its preemptive rights to the Seneca reservations to the Ogden Land Company, and soon pressure was brought on New York Indians to sell their reservations. By a treaty of August 1826, the Senecas sold all five of the Genesee reservations, most of Tonawanda, about one-third of Buffalo Creek, and one-fifth of Cattaraugus for the sum of 48,260 dollars. The Senecas lost 86,887 acres at the selling price of about 55 cents per acre.[20] Because this treaty was never ratified by the United States Senate nor proclaimed by the president, the Senecas in later years claimed the treaty to be invalid.

During the next twelve years, from 1826 to 1838, further pressure was applied to the Senecas to induce them to vacate their reservations and to remove west of the Mississippi to lands in Kansas.[21] Through bribes, threats, and misrepresentation, certain Senecas designated as leaders of the tribe signed the Treaty of Buffalo Creek in 1838, which included a statement that the Senecas leave their reservations and emigrate to Kansas.[22]

The general provisions of this treaty stipulated, in Article 2, that the several New York tribes, Senecas included, would be moved to territories west of Missouri into lands amounting to 1,824,000 acres. According to Article 4, the New York Indians were assured that "the lands secured to them by patent under this treaty shall never be included in any State or Territory of this Union."[23]

Schedule C, appended to the treaty, dealt specifically with the Senecas, whose population, in a census of 1837, was estimated to be 2,309. This section provided that the Senecas sell all reservations which they then occupied for the sum of 202,000 dollars to Thomas L. Ogden and Joseph Fellows of the Ogden Land Company. These reservations included: Buffalo Creek in Erie County, 49,920 acres; Cattaraugus in Erie, Chatauqua, and Cattaraugus Counties, 21,680 acres; Allegany in Cattaraugus County, 30,469 acres; and Tonawanda in Erie and Genesee Counties, 12,800 acres. The Senecas gave up 114,869 acres at the bargain price of about 17.58 cents per acre. Title to the Seneca lands was to be transferred to "Thomas Ludlow Ogden and Joseph Fellows, their heirs and assigns, to their proper use and behoof forever, as joint tenants. . . ."[24] Despite the fact that only sixteen Seneca chiefs out of a total of ninety-four had signed the treaty in council, while sixteen others had signed later in different places (the Senate had stipulated that all chiefs assent in council to the treaty), the United States Senate approved it on March 25, 1840, and authorized President Martin Van Buren to proclaim it, which he did on April 4 of the same year.[25] Yet, while ratification of the treaty occurred in 1840, it had been signed by the last of the thirty-two Senecas on January 15, 1838; Maris Pierce, still at Dartmouth, spent the next two years opposing its ratification.

There is little doubt that the Treaty of Buffalo Creek was negotiated with the Senecas under the influence of liquor, bribes, and threats. In short, the treaty was fraudulent, and many Senecas believed it to be neither just nor valid. Official white malfeasance was clearly evident.

In the weeks and months following the signing of the treaty, strong opposition to it developed, principally among the Senecas, other members of the Six Nations, the Quakers, and a few officials in Washington. Although Maris Pierce had been among signers of the treaty, this in no way indicated that he approved of or supported its provisions. His first inclination had been not to sign. Yet, doubtless like some other Seneca chiefs, he had done so

> in consequence of regarding the case of his people as hopeless, by reason of the bribery and intimidation practiced upon the chiefs, and because the only hope of being of any service to his nation seemed to lie in securing some new advantage in the treaty which he had the opportunity to do by signing. . . .[26]

There is clear evidence that intimidation had swayed a number of chiefs to sign the treaty. Ransom Hooker Gillett, the United States Indian Commissioner for New York, was asked by chiefs in council: "What will our Father, the President, do to us if we refuse to make the treaty?" Gillett, who represented the federal government at the treaty, is quoted as having replied: "He will punish you as a father punishes his disobedient child, unless you do as he desires; he will turn your face where he wishes you to go, before he stops punishing you."[27] Gillett went on to say that state law would be extended over the Senecas as punishment, that their privileges would be taken away, that they would lose their annuities, and that they would also lose their Indian agent. Those benefits would henceforth go to those Indians who consented to emigrate. Gillett further warned that any white person offering the Senecas advice or assistance in retaining their lands would be fined from one to two thousand dollars. Believing this, a number of chiefs felt that no further help was available, and that they might best submit to the government's wishes. Because of such threats, according to Big Kettle, "Some of the less firm in mind among our chiefs and people believed, and were intimidated."[28]

Perhaps more frequent than intimidation was the use of liquor to persuade Seneca chiefs to agree to the treaty. About three-quarters of a mile from the council house, company agents erected a tavern. There, chiefs and warriors met in secret negotiations amid much drunkenness. Other chiefs, opposing the treaty, were sometimes enticed there at midnight in an effort to change their views. When Gillett was condemned for allowing such practices, he replied that "in all the treaties he had ever read of, such things were universally practiced in the presence of the commissioner."[29]

Bribery was also widespread in negotiations leading to the treaty; at least ten Seneca chiefs swore affidavits to the effect that they had been bribed. Some had received amounts as large as 6,000 dollars. Others were paid 2,000 dollars, 1,000 dollars, or as little as 100 dollars, while eight chiefs received a total of 21,600 dollars to persuade still others to agree to the treaty. Ironically, the Ogden Land Company also arranged that these chiefs, richly rewarded, might retain for life their lands in western New York; only those who opposed the treaty would lose their lands and homes, and be forced to emigrate to the West.[30]

The nefarious nature of the negotiations which preceded the signing of the Treaty of Buffalo Creek deeply disturbed Pierce, who traveled between Dartmouth and western New York to keep informed of the trend of events. And some white officials, friendly to the Seneca cause, kept Pierce apprised of events in Washington and of attempts to amend the treaty. Samuel Prentiss, United States senator from Vermont, was one of these. Prentiss hoped that "no unjust means are used to deceive and mislead the Indians in a matter of so much interest to them."[31] Although Pierce had signed the treaty, lest Gillett's threats become a reality, he believed nevertheless that better terms might be obtained and that he should make known to whites the plight of the Seneca Nation. His nation and his home were threatened with removal and possible destruction. As a result, he undertook to acquaint whites, wherever possible, with the culture and achievements of the Six Nations, and to gain white sympathy for Indians.

The flexibility of the Dartmouth calendar provided Pierce with the needed time to accept speaking engagements. Probably the most notable speech Pierce made was to a large crowd at the Buffalo Baptist Church on August 28, 1838. He had returned to western New York before the beginning of his junior year, using the occasion to deliver an eloquent address on behalf of the American Indian, and the Seneca Nation in particular. It is the only speech Pierce made that appeared in print and survives to the present day.

On that August night in Buffalo, Pierce addressed the crowd as a spokesman for his people and as a leader in the Seneca Nation. He dealt at the outset with the question as to why the Indians had not been civilized and Christianized through the efforts of the whites. The white man, Pierce observed, had returned Indian generosity and hospitality with cupidity and hostility; whites desired only to seize the possessions of the Indians and to hunt them down like animals. Would not such treatment generate hatred, Pierce asked, and lead the Indian to resist future efforts at Christianizing and civilizing?

Far from being an animal, Pierce declaimed, the Indian had proved himself to be the physical and spiritual equal of the white man. Indians had amply displayed talents and skills in leadership. Cases in point included the lives and careers of Tecumseh, Red Jacket, and Osceola, with whom were numbered "a thousand others"; furthermore, because the Indian possessed a heightened moral sense or conscience, he was most capable of cultivating the highest precepts of white civilization and Christianity.[32] Was not the Cherokee Nation an outstanding example of this ability? They had turned from pagan worship to the God of the Bible, had established schools, had created an alphabet, and had cultivated the arts and letters in both English and Cherokee. Despite their advancement and their "civilization," they were to be driven from their homes.

Pierce then turned to the plight of his own people, who, as American Indians, were clearly capable of physical, intellectual, and moral refinement. Proof of this lay in the material progress made by the Seneca Nation in the recent past. There was great diligence and industry among his people, and the use of farming equipment had increased greatly. There were better and more numerous oxen, horses, wagons, and sleighs; and both men and women labored more in the fields than in years past.[33]

Buildings had also improved; barns and houses were better designed and constructed of finer materials. Laborers of all types had grown in numbers—mowers, reapers, blacksmiths, carpenters, shoemakers, and mechanics found ample work. Modes of living had also improved. The use of tables, chairs, bedsteads, and cooking utensils had increased, and regular meals had become customary. Treatment of the sick had also advanced, and skilled physicians were now relied upon. Seneca culture had become more refined; his people were now neatly dressed. His people were also better informed; many subscribed to papers in Washington, Philadelphia, and New York, as well as to the *Genesee Farmer.*[34]

Having described their material and spiritual progress, Pierce explained why the Senecas should oppose emigration from western New York to distant Missouri and Kansas:

> The right of possession of our lands is undisputed, so with us it is a question appealing directly *to our interest;* and how stands the matter in relation *to that?* Our lands are as fertile and as well situated for agricultural pursuits as any we shall get by a removal. The graves of our fathers and mothers and kin are here, and about them still cling our affections and memories. We are here situated in the midst of facilities for physical, intellectual, and moral improvement; we are in the midst of the enlightened; we see their ways and their works, and can thus profit by their example. We can avail ourselves of their implements and wares and merchandise, and once having learned the convenience of using them, we shall be led to deem them indispensable; we here are more in the way of instruction from teach-

> ers. . . . in the progress of our improvement, [we] may come to feel the want, and the usefulness of books and prints. . . . In this view of facts surely there is no inducement for removing.[35]

Pierce then considered the white arguments in support of Seneca removal: first and foremost, whites coveted Indian lands and claimed the right of preemption; second, they offered generous amounts of money which the Indians in their ignorance did not appreciate; and finally, the Indians would be better off removed from the vicinity of whites. They would find greater contentment in the neighborhood of fellow red men, "where the woods flock with game, and the streams abound with fish."[36]

Pierce then explained his reasons for rejecting the arguments. First, Pierce observed that the Senecas had no obligation to sell their lands to whites. If, however, they chose to do so, it would only be at a price equal to the value placed on the land by the Senecas themselves. The Senecas owed the whites no debt of gratitude in consequence of "their loving kindness or tender mercies."[37] Nor could the prices whites offered for land be considered generous. While the land speculators offered from one to two dollars per acre, they would then turn around and sell the same acreage for fifteen to fifty dollars per acre. Pierce believed the Senecas had perfect title to the land, and "could dispose of it at such prices as we may see fit to agree upon."[38] Although the land company had the preemptive right of purchase, they had no right to force the Senecas to accept their paltry offers. Finally, with regard to removal, Pierce clearly believed that there was no area to the west where his people could settle "with safety, free of molestation, and in perpetuity."[39] The whites' greed and white population pressures would eventually press the removed Senecas to move still farther west, and that could continue indefinitely. In addition, more warlike tribes to the west as well as white border settlers could harass his nation. From all these possibilities Pierce concluded that the Seneca Nation would be better off in their homeland and that to entertain removal was "stupid folly."[40]

Pierce ended his address with a moving appeal for sympathetic whites to oppose the demands of the land speculators, principally those from the Ogden Land Company. "Does justice, does humanity, does religion in their relations to us demand it? Does the interest and well-being of the whites require it? The plainest dictates of common sense and common honesty, answer *no*! I ask then in behalf of the New York Indians and myself, that our white brethren will not urge us to do that which justice, humanity, religion not only do not require but condemn. I ask then to let us live . . . where our fathers have lived. . . ."[41] Yet, as is often the case, those who needed to hear Pierce's appeal were not present that evening; no representative of the Ogden Land Company was in the audience at the Buffalo Baptist Church.

Soon after his Buffalo address, Pierce and fourteen other Seneca chiefs sent a letter to President Martin Van Buren expressing their opposition to the Buffalo Creek treaty and transmitting a formal decision made in open council "that we . . . being *wholly* and *unitedly* opposed and unwilling to emigrate, take this method and this opportunity of expressing our determination to that effect."[42] A few months later, the Seneca chiefs engaged Charles R. Gold as legal counsel to represent their interests in Washington. For a fee of one thousand dollars, Gold agreed to, "if possible, defeat the treaty now attempted to be forced upon the Seneca Nation by the Government of the United States, and that [my] aid and services shall not cease until it is finally determined that said Nation shall migrate or be permitted to live in peace and quietness upon said Reservation. . . ."[43] Still later, Pierce and three other Seneca chiefs presented "the views and desires" of the Seneca people to the Secretary of War, Joel Roberts Poinsett, in the hope that treaty terms might be modified or amended.[44] Yet it was by no means clear what effects such efforts might have. Pierce sought a wider audience.

During his last year at Dartmouth, Pierce tried his utmost to win white support for the cause of the Senecas. In March 1840, Pierce addressed a large, sympathetic, and enthusiastic audience in Parsipanny, New Jersey, where he explained to a church congregation the Six Nations Confederacy and described Indian manners and customs.[45] He also displayed native handicrafts, which included wampum, moccasins, wallets, and work bags for women. This he did in an effort to refute the frequent claim of contemporary white historians that Indian women were indolent. Indeed, on an earlier occasion, Pierce had argued with a college friend over women's rights, which he strongly upheld: "It is my sincere belief that the rights of women should be sacredly kept and freely exercised by them, but I do not agree with them acting in the same capacity with men."[46]

Early in May 1840, he delivered a lecture to the citizens of Woodstock, Vermont, on the ancient Iroquois Confederacy, in which he discussed the habits, customs, religion, and festivals of the League. Finally, not long before commencement, Pierce spoke to the Philomatheon Society at Meriden Academy on much the same subject. He hoped that it might help whites better to understand the wrongs committed against his people.[47]

As graduation time approached, a sense of sadness overcame Pierce as he observed the eighty members of the senior class preparing to leave for their homes.

> Where shall I go, he asked himself, where is my home, that I can call it my own? To the West? No—where I was born. Shall it be my native home and remain inviolate? I hope it was so, but alas, it is not so. Our people are in the state of a great dilemma—to go or stay—but must go, says the government of the U.S. Humanity speaks: they may stay. They ought to enjoy the home of their fathers.[48]

Pierce left in mid-August for Buffalo Creek Reservation. Once there, he and other Seneca chiefs attempted to deal with problems arising from incursions on Seneca lands by the Ogden Land Company; German settlers where also reluctant to remove themselves from claims that they had staked on Seneca lands. Whereas they had previously agreed to vacate, they now were claiming that they had legal title to their holdings from the Ogden Land Company; therefore, they refused to leave.[49] Uppermost in Pierce's mind was the Treaty of Buffalo Creek. Although he and other Seneca chiefs had opposed and had spoken against the treaty in the months following its signing, the treaty nevertheless had been ratified by the United States Senate and had been proclaimed by the president in the early months of 1840. It appeared that the Senecas had not only lost a battle, but the war itself.

In the months following Pierce's return to Buffalo Creek, reconsideration of the terms of the treaty was underway in Washington. Because Seneca resentment, largely mobilized by Pierce, had been so great against the treaty and because a few influential whites had joined the protests on behalf of the Senecas, the treaty was finally renegotiated in the spring of 1842.[50]

A preliminary draft of the amended treaty was read and explained to the chiefs and headmen of the Senecas in council on April 9, 1842. It proved to be far from satisfactory. The Senecas had anticipated having their reservations, taken by the treaty of 1838, returned to them. Article 1 of the amended treaty returned only Allegany and Cattaraugus; Articles 2 and 3 stipulated that the Ogden Land Company would retain both Buffalo Creek and Tonawanda Reservations, for which they would pay the Senecas 202,000 dollars.[51] Although the Seneca leaders agreed finally to accept its terms, they were not entirely satisfied with all conditions specified in the document and proposed further revisions. They wished to have the use of their improvements (on land ceded in 1838) for three more years, rather than for one; they hoped that the amount of land on each reservation (Buffalo Creek, Cattaraugus, Allegany, Tonawanda) would be apportioned according to the population before title to surplus land was quieted; and, as a special favor to two of their young chiefs, Maris Pierce and John Kennedy, they asked that each be granted fifty acres of land on the Buffalo Creek Reservation.[52] If, however, these requests would not be granted by the Ogden Land Company, the Senecas would accept the amended treaty so as not to have the 1838 agreement reinstated. As clearly wronged people, the Senecas were counseled by Pierce to appeal to the mercy of the government; then, if the proposed alterations could not be obtained, Pierce said, "we must submit to our fate."[53] The appeal went unheeded. Maris Pierce, who had acted as interpreter for the Senecas during the weeks of negotiations, joined seventy-seven other chiefs on May 20, 1842, in a formal signing of the treaty.

Maris Pierce never received his payment of fifty acres. Buffalo Creek Reservation was to be vacated by 1845; the Tonawanda band resisted for a time all efforts to remove them from their reservation, but finally, even they agreed to sell a portion of their remaining reservation lands. Their patrimony reduced by more than half, still the Senecas had survived. They were not removed to the West but instead retained a foothold in western New York. They endure to the present day, and Maris Pierce is the person most responsible for the Senecas remaining in New York.

At Dartmouth, Pierce had acquired an education which equipped him to deal in the world of the whites. And if his college education were not enough, for almost two years after his return to Buffalo Creek, he read law in the Buffalo offices of Tillinghast and Smith. This preparation proved invaluable to Pierce as an adviser to his people during the difficult negotiations of the amended Treaty of Buffalo Creek.

In November 1843, Pierce married Mary Jane Carroll, the daughter of a British army officer, in Utica, New York;[54] the newly married couple spent their first two years together at Buffalo Creek, and when this reserve was abandoned in 1845, they removed to Cattaraugus, where they remained for the rest of their lives. Pierce's later years were occupied with continued efforts not only to protect the rights of his people, but also to promote the general welfare of his nation. As an interpreter and secretary for the Seneca Nation, he dealt with such important matters as Indian emigration, timber sales, tribal factionalism, and relations with the Ogden Land Company. He also played a significant role in the Seneca political revolution of 1848, which introduced the elective system to the nation and its self-government. Maris Pierce remained an advocate of education for both Longhouse and Christianized Senecas. He preached sobriety and attempted to Christianize his people though he respected the rights of traditionalists. Throughout his life, he strove to create in whites a better understanding of his own people.

Maris Bryant Pierce proved to be an able interpreter of his culture to non-Indians. With a formal white education much like that of Joseph Brant and Ely S. Parker, his life is illustrative of an Indian leader whose roots were deeply planted in two complex cultures.[55] Like other Native Americans who shared similar experiences, Pierce chose to retain what he believed to be the best elements in both cultures. He exemplifies the Indian who spends a portion of his life working within mainstream society and government to protect his people's lands and interests; Pierce did this to the best of his ability, often under trying and disruptive circumstances.

From his earliest education with the Quakers to his years at Dartmouth, Pierce was exposed to influences which provided him with insight into white beliefs and attitudes. At Dartmouth he continued to take interest in Christianity; he regularly attended religious services, especially those conducted by the president of the college. On many of these occasions, he took careful notes on sermons delivered by various clergymen, commenting on their delivery or oratorical skills.[56] It is possible that here Pierce perfected the art of public speaking and further developed his talent in rhetoric. The Iroquois, like many other Indian groups, have traditionally held eloquence in high regard, and have honored their orators. And from his classical education Pierce saw in rhetoric an indispensable tool. Through its use, he would transfix and convince his white listeners of the truth of which he spoke.[57] In Seneca councils Pierce also used his art to good effect.

Pierce can also be considered a leader in the breadth of his views concerning the Native Americans and the problems they faced in white, nineteenth-century America. Pierce concerned himself not only with the fate of the Seneca Nation, but also with the fate of other nations in the Iroquois Confederacy and among fellow "Indians" throughout the country. He made common cause with the chiefs of the four Seneca reservations, involved himself in the concerns of the League, and more than once spoke as an interpreter of Indian culture and civilization to other Americans. On such occasions he continually referred to the "Aborigines of America" and "American Indians."

As a Christian, Pierce took a verse from the New Testament quite literally: "Strengthen the things that remain."[58] In the face of white onslaughts against both Seneca lands and culture, he learned to practice the art of survival. He adopted a practical attitude, what others later in the century would describe as pragmatic. If all of the Seneca lands could not be preserved, let part of them remain; to this end he was firmly dedicated. From the shreds of Seneca lands, which remained after the desires of whites had been satiated, springs today a Seneca cultural renaissance. Pierce, as a Seneca patriot, as a leader of his people, as a defender of their rights, and as a counselor of survival, would today find this rebirth a source of both satisfaction and exultation. His efforts over a century ago had not been in vain.

Notes

1. See Anthony F. C. Wallace, *The Death and Rebirth of the Seneca* (New York, 1969), pp. 194–96; see also Barbara Graymont, *The Iroquois in the American Revolution* (Syracuse, N.Y., 1972), passim.

2. Robert Morris to Thomas Morris, August 1, 1797, New York Historical Society, O'Reilly Collection, vol. 15.

3. Wallace, *Death and Rebirth*, p. 183.

4. Ibid.

5. Pierce was born in a village called "Old Town." The school was probably Tunessa, begun by three Quakers in 1806. It was located in South Valley near the Allegany Reservation.

6. *Buffalo Commercial Advertiser and Journal*, August 17, 1874, p. 3, col. 2; see also George T. Chapman, *Sketches of the Alumni of Dartmouth College* (Cambridge, Mass., 1867), p. 311.

7. John Tawse, *Report to the Society in Scotland for Propagating Christian Knowledge of a Visit to America* (Edinburgh, 1839), p. 27.

8. Ibid.

9. Frederick Chase, *A History of Dartmouth College and the Town of Hanover*, 2d ed. (Brattleboro, Vt., 1938), p. 8.

10. Ibid., p. 9.

11. Ibid., p. 8.

12. James Axtell, *The European and the Indian: Essays in the Ethnohistory of Colonial North America* (New York, 1971), p. 108; see also James Dow McCallum, ed., *The Letters of Eleazar Wheelock's Indians* (Hanover, N.H., 1932).

13. Leon Burr Richardson, *History of Dartmouth College*, vol. 2 (Hanover, N.H., 1932), p. 452

14. Oil Spring was located on Cuba Lake just north of the Allegany Reserva-

tion. The spring was a natural flow of petroleum. The Senecas use petroleum as a linament for rheumatic pains and ulcers.

15. "Book of Memorandum," February 29, 1840, Buffalo and Erie County Historical Society, Maris Pierce Papers (cited hereafter as BECHS, MPP).

16. Nathan Lord to Reverend John Codman, November 12, 1840, Dartmouth College Archives (cited hereafter as DCA); see also Richardson, *History of Dartmouth College*, vol. 1, p. 420

17. John Tawse to Reverend John Codman, October 24, 1840, DCA.

18. "Book of Memorandum," May 26, 1840, BECHS, MPP.

19. Ibid., May 6, 1840.

20. New York Assembly, document no. 51, *Special Committee to Investigate the Indian Problem of the State of New York* (Albany, N.Y., 1889), p. 23.

21. See Wallace, *Death and Rebirth*, pp. 323–24.

22. See Henry S. Manley, "Buying Buffalo from the Indians," *New York History* 28 (July 1947), pp. 313–29.

23. Treaty of Buffalo Creek, January 15, 1838, Articles 2 and 4, BECHS, MPP.

24. Ibid., Schedule C.

25. Ibid.; see also New York Assembly, document no. 51, pp. 24–28.

26. Maris Pierce's views, as paraphrased by Big Kettle, in Big Kettle, William Krouse, John Kennedy (Seneca chiefs) to Hon. Samuel Prentiss (United States Senator from Vermont), March 2, 1838, in Society of Friends (Hicksite), Joint Commission on Indian Affairs, *The Case of the Seneca Indians in the State of New York* (Philadelphia, 1840; reprint, Stanfordville, N.Y., 1979), pp. 112–13, 137.

27. Big Kettle and fifteen other chiefs to Hon. Samuel Prentiss, February 28, 1838, quoted in ibid., pp. 64, 117.

28. Ibid.; see also affidavits and depositions of various other chiefs, pp. 200–253.

29. Ibid., p. 117.

30. Ibid., pp. 24–25.

31. Samuel Prentiss to Maris Pierce, June 13 and 22, 1838, BECHS, MPP.

32. Maris B. Pierce, *Address on the Present Condition and Prospects of the Aboriginal Inhabitants of North America, with Particular Reference to the Seneca Nation* (Buffalo, N.Y., 1838), BECHS, MPP.

33. Ibid., p. 8.

34. Ibid., p. 10.

35. Ibid.

36. Ibid., p. 11.

37. Ibid.

38. Ibid.
39. Ibid., p. 12.
40. Ibid.
41. Ibid., p. 13.
42. Pierce and other chiefs to President Martin Van Buren, September 7, 1838, in Society of Friends (Hicksite), Joint Commission on Indian Affairs, *Case of the Seneca Indians*, p. 123.
43. Agreement between Charles R. Gold and Seneca chiefs, December 25, 1838, BECHS, MPP.
44. Pierce and other chiefs to Joel R. Poinsett (Secretary of War), January 24, 1839, ibid.
45. "Book of Memorandum," March 10, 1840, ibid.
46. June 14, 1840, ibid.
47. May 1, 1840; July 3, 1840, ibid.
48. July 19, 1840, ibid.
49. Seneca Council Proceedings of May 2 and May 4, 1844, ibid.; see also Arthur C. Parker, *The Life of General Ely S. Parker* (Buffalo, N.Y., 1919), pp. 70–92.
50. Wallace, *Death and Rebirth*, p. 324.
51. Amended Treaty of Buffalo Creek, May 20, 1842, BECHS, MPP.
52. Seneca chiefs and headmen to John C. Spencer (Secretary of War), April 10, 1842, BECHS, MPP.
53. Ibid.
54. Mrs. Maris B. Pierce to Elizabeth L. Comstock (Quaker clergywoman), n.d., Versailles, N.Y., ibid.; see also Chapman, *Sketches of the Alumni of Dartmouth College*, p. 311.
55. See R. David Edmunds, ed., *American Indian Leaders* (Lincoln, Nebr., 1980), pp. xi–xiv; William N. Armstrong, *Warrior in Two Camps: Ely S. Parker, Union General and Seneca Chief* (Syracuse, N.Y., 1978), p. ix.
56. See "Book of Memorandum," passim, BECHS, MPP.
57. See Lewis Henry Morgan, *League of the Ho-Da-No-Sau-Nee, or Iroquois* 2 vols. (New Haven, 1954), vol. 1, p. 102; vol. 2, pp. 104–5.
58. *Revelations* 3: 2.

Essay on Sources

Primary sources relating to Native Americans most often are those originating with whites; conversely, there is usually a paucity of sources—written manuscripts—coming from Native Americans themselves. Such is not the case with Maris B. Pierce, an educated Dartmouth graduate, who left a considerable collection of papers dating from his years at Dartmouth until his death in 1874.

The Maris B. Pierce papers, twelve folders in two cartons, are housed in the Buffalo and Erie County Historical Society in Buffalo, N.Y., and were donated to the Society by his widow in 1884. They contain council minutes, letters from Pierce to various Quakers and government officials as well as replies to Pierce by these individuals, as well as other correspondence from government officials concerning Seneca affairs. Pierce's account of his Dartmouth days is found in his "Book of Memorandum," a diary he kept covering the years 1838–40. While the Buffalo and Erie County Historical Society owns a copy of this on microfilm, the original is in the hands of the Pennsylvania Museum and Historical Commission, Harrisburg, Pennsylvania. Much material in the Pierce papers relates to matters concerning the Treaty of Buffalo Creek, proposals to remove the Senecas to western lands, Pierce's views on Seneca governmental reorganization, and his efforts to foster education and religious training among the Senecas at Cattaraugus Reserve. The Buffalo and Erie County Historical Society has a calendar of the Pierce papers, yet it is poorly devised and not in chronological order, which makes it difficult to use.

Dartmouth College Archives is a second source of manuscript material relating to Pierce, yet this consists of only a few letters from Presbyterian ministers to each other concerning Pierce's educational progress at Dartmouth, with an occasional reference to Pierce's early years, about which no substantial material exists.

Among printed primary sources, four exist which are of value. Maris B. Pierce,

Address on the Present Condition and Prospects of the Aboriginal Inhabitants of North America . . . (Buffalo, N.Y., 1838) presents his views on the Senecas' loss of lands in western New York and the proposed removal of the Seneca Nation to the trans-Mississippi West. This is an impassioned speech which Pierce gave in Buffalo in 1838, and is the only speech Pierce ever made which was printed in pamphlet form; copies are found in the Buffalo and Erie County Historical Society and in the Dartmouth College Archives. A second valuable source on Seneca affairs, particularly on the Treaty of Buffalo Creek, is Society of Friends (Hicksite), Joint Committee on Indian Affairs, *The Case of the Seneca Indians in the State of New York* (Philadelphia, 1840; reprint, Stanfordville, N.Y., 1979). Here are found many depositions made by Senecas to Quaker officials concerning the deceptions practiced on them prior to signing the Treaty of Buffalo Creek. In James Dow McCallum, ed., *The Letters of Eleazar Wheelock's Indians* (Hanover, N.H., 1932), one finds accounts by Indians of their educational progress in the early academies of eighteenth-century New England as well as white attitudes toward the education of Native Americans at that time. Finally, John Tawes, in his *Report to the Society in Scotland for Propagating Christian Knowledge of a Visit to America* (Edinburgh, 1839) provides a valuable description of Indian lands and settlements in western New York, particularly of the Buffalo Creek Reserve at the time the nefarious treaty by that name was being negotiated. He also discusses Pierce's progress at Dartmouth and quotes several college officials who found Pierce to be an outstanding student.

Among secondary sources, Anthony F. C. Wallace, *The Death and Rebirth of the Seneca* (New York, 1969) is probably the best work of its kind to date. He provides an excellent background on both Seneca history and culture, and deals with the period in the early nineteenth century when loss of Seneca lands became severe. Equally valuable is Barbara Graymont's *The Iroquios in the American Revolution* (Syracuse, N.Y., 1972), which is carefully researched and well written. She details the role played by the various Six Nations during the American Revolution and treats, among other things, the Seneca support of the British which engendered American colonial hatred in the years following the Revolution. An older work, New York Assembly, document no. 51, *Special Committee to Investigate the Indian Problem of the State of New York* (Albany, N.Y., 1889), is concerned largely with Mohawk and Oneida land losses and claims, yet devotes some space to Seneca land claims arising from treaties made in the nineteenth century.

Histories of Dartmouth College furnish one with descriptions of the school during Pierce's residence there, and among these, reference is made to Frederick Chase, *A History of Dartmouth College and the Town of Hanover*, 2d ed. (Brattleboro, Vt., 1928), and to Leon Burr Richardson, *History of Dartmouth College*, 2 vols. (Hanover, N.H., 1932). A briefer and more specialized work is that by George T. Chapman, *Sketches of the Alumni of Dartmouth College* (Cambridge, Mass., 1867) wherein one finds a brief biography of Maris Pierce.

Finally, among biographical works, three prove valuable as studies which may make it possible to determine what qualities of leadership these Native Americans had in common, which made them outstanding leaders among their people. R. David Edmunds, ed., *American Indian Leaders* (Lincoln, Neb., 1980), Arthur C. Parker, *The Life of General Ely S. Parker* (Buffalo, N.Y., 1919), and William N. Armstrong, *Warrior in Two Camps: Ely S. Parker, Union General and Seneca Chief* (Syracuse, N.Y., 1978) are among such studies, while James Axtell, *The European and the Indian: Essays in the Ethnohistory of Colonial North America* (New York, 1971) deals with the interaction of whites and Indians upon each other and how acculturation may have weakened some aspects of Native American character.

One journal article by Henry S. Manley, "Buying Buffalo from the Indians," *New York History* 28 (July 1947), is particularly useful in determining the chronology of Seneca land losses in the early nineteenth century and the methods used by the Ogden Land Company to deprive the Senecas of most of their land holdings in western New York. An obituary of Maris B. Pierce is found in the *Buffalo Commercial Advertiser and Journal* of August 17, 1874, which discusses at some length the outstanding contributions he made for the welfare of the Seneca Nation during his lifetime.

2

Nampeyo

Giving the Indian Artist a Name

Ronald McCoy

Nampeyo (1860–1942), a Hopi-Tewa potter in Arizona, may be rightfully regarded as a leader in Native American art. Her "rediscovery" of erstwhile Hopi techniques, and her training of others in her craft, helped to stimulate a revival in Hopi pottery. In a larger sense also, as Ronald McCoy explains in the following essay, Nampeyo helped to create an atmosphere in which Native Americans could be recognized as artists with names. That recognition in the United States has been belated, given the almost five centuries of Euroamerican contact with Indians. Today, Indian artists working in a variety of media have won national and international reputations for their works, and have sustained themselves in mainstream society through their art. If the spiraling prices fetched by certain artists' works are any indication, the popularity, indeed the speculative value, of American Indian art is increasing, which adds an interesting variable to the modern cultural equation. Do the compromises forced upon the Native American artist by art buyers from non-Indian cultures limit individual artistic expression? What makes a work distinctively "Indian?" Is it the artist's emphasis on the primitive, the simple, the "childlike" technique, or is it the manipulation of traditional Indian symbols and forms? Instead, is "Indian art" that art which is produced by North and South American Indians regardless of style or motif? The answer to the latter question is probably

no. Indian art, to be recognized as such in the larger society, must first be "Indian" in composition. But what of the larger contrbutions of Native Americans to the realm of art or at least the artful?

Art has traditionally competed for human time and energy with many other activities, from the mundane to the spiritual. Anthropologists and cultural historians have seen in native arts and crafts the development of social stratification and specialization in labor. This has been especially so in the studies of the elaborate cultures of Mesoamerica and their monumental edifices and other structures, which offer mute testimony to the skills in technology, architecture, painting, and sculpting. The Aztec, Olmec, and Mayan ruins with their decorations in bas-relief, mosaics, and geometric designs attest to the sophisticated technologies of only three distinctive cultures. Even among the least stratified and technologically complex societies in North America, products of the imagination dedicated to the most utilitarian ends often displayed great skill, as in the basketry of the Pomos of California or certain Shoshonean-speaking people of the Great Basin. For centuries, however, North American Indian "crafts"—whether Mayan or Paiute—were judged by criteria derived from Euroamerican culture.

Civilized Euroamericans usually found Indians wanting in a number of areas. The fact that Indians desired European trade goods demonstrated for some people that they stood in awe of European artifacts and skills. For a few decades after the American Revolution, however, when Americans self-consciously celebrated that which was good and pure and true in the bountiful environment of the New World improved upon by institutions transplanted and modified from the Old, American Indians became subjects for art and belles lettres. The romantic American artist looked into the primordial forest and discerned noble red men lurking among the trees. Yet even during the romantic period in the United States, the use of the Indian more often than not reflected the Euroamerican's disquietude with his own culture. Part of that disquietude persists in the present. Even today's sympathetic artists usually understand Native Americans only according to their own artistic needs and values.

When Nampeyo sifted through the sands around First Mesa in Arizona during the 1870s and 1880s, looking for potsherds, she found in them the inspiration for a celebration in clay of a culture older than memory; her success inspired others to search the past in their celebration of cultures vital to the present.

Late in the fall of 1875, photographer William Henry Jackson set up his camera on northeastern Arizona's First Mesa, a towering desert escarpment. Jackson, perhaps attracted by the broad, strangely knowing face or maybe by the curiously old quality gracing her eyes, selected his subject: a girl seated in the doorway of a flat-roofed stone house in Hopi-Tewa village.

This girl, about fifteen years old, wore a traditional black dress, trimmed near the hem with delicately embroidered red and green lines, with a dark *manta* draped over her shoulders. Strands of turquoise beads hung in loops around her neck, and pendants of that semiprecious stone dangled from each ear. Two large "butterfly" whorls of hair, one on either side of her head, indicated availability for marriage.

Jackson let light enter his camera, where it impregnated a glass plate with the girl's image. Unwittingly, he preserved what is probably the earliest likeness of Nampeyo, a master potter, to whom must go much of the credit for ushering in the phenomenon of the named American Indian artist.

Nampeyo's life, like those of so many early American Indian leaders, resembles a scene viewed through a lens far cruder than Jackson's. Although Nampeyo shifts maddeningly in and out of focus, most aspects of her life remain regrettably obscure; however, facets of her existence can be reconstructed.

Nampeyo was born around 1860 in First Mesa's Hopi-Tewa village, sometimes called Hano, which shares the easternmost tip of sprawling Black Mesa with two Hopi communities, Walpi and Sichomovi. She was the child of Kotsakao, a Tewa woman, and Kotsvema, a Hopi man from neighboring Walpi. In this matriarchal society, she automatically gained membership in Kotsakao's Corn Clan rather than in the Snake Clan claiming her father's allegiance. Nampeyo, Snake Woman, is her Tewa name; but she also carried a corresponding Hopi appellation, Tsu-mana, bestowed in recognition of Kotsvema's clan by her paternal grandmother at a naming ceremony twenty days after birth.[1]

As a child, Nampeyo observed her people planting and harvesting corn, beans, squash, gourds, and cotton in productive niches dotting the harsh land below the mesa. During masked ceremonials, which filled the calendar of religious ritual from winter's solstice until mid-summer, she received carved wooden representations of the Kachina spirits as gifts. Later, she learned about the artistic specialties of Hopi-Tewa and the Hopi villages: pottery from her own First Mesa, Second Mesa's coiled basketry, and wicker plaques made on Third Mesa. Nampeyo's father, other male relatives, and friends wove the clothes she wore. After her first menses custom dictated that she adopt the distinctive "butterfly" or "squash blossom" hairstyle that Jackson found her wearing in 1875, which one abandoned upon marriage.

Nampeyo's people exposed her to their history and lore, a subject in which she probably became reasonably well versed. The Tewas, Puebloans from New Mexico, settled at First Mesa after joining other tribes in seventeenth-century attempts at ridding themselves of Spanish domination. They probably arrived at First Mesa sometime between 1696 and 1701. Tewa traditions relate that their presence among the Hopis stemmed from an invitation extended by Walpi headmen. At first, they performed the unenviable task of guarding the precipitous trail leading up to the mesa's top. Later, after defeating Ute raiders, they earned the right to cultivate farmlands and to occupy a permanent village site.[2]

Beyond these things, Nampeyo learned the art of making pottery, a Southwestern Indian technology nearly two millennia-old, which apparently owes its existence to Mesoamerican influence. The Anasazi of Southwestern prehistory—builders of cities, progenitors of modern Puebloans—excelled at pottery manufacture, creating painted wares by around A.D. 600. Anasazi pottery varies in form, texture, color, and design by period and place; but it generally achieved an impressive sophistication and boldness in abstract decoration. Nampeyo's Hopi grandmother at Walpi acted as her mentor in mastering this craft, encouraging the girl's observation, and overseeing her efforts at imitation.[3]

As an apprentice potter, Nampeyo helped collect clay from ancient beds below First Mesa. On these expeditions she undoubtedly saw potsherds made at Sikyatki, a pueblo three miles northeast of the mesa, reduced to ruin two and a half centuries before her birth. What impact, if any, these yellow fragments—decorated with the curvilinear designs characteristic of Sikyatki wares—exerted upon the young girl remains unknown. Eventually, similar bits and pieces from the past proved critical in the development of Nampeyo's own art.

The method that Nampeyo employed for making pottery did not differ appreciably from that of the potters who lived at Sikyatki from the fourteenth through the early seventeenth century. Clay was pulverized by grinding it on a stone metate, moistened with water and tempered with sand, crushed rocks, or potsherds. The method of constructing wares remained the time-tested coil-and-scrape technique. When slipped with a wash to attain uniform color and texture, the ceramic was polished with a smooth pebble. Paint came from natural pigments and the only brush available remained that old standby, a chewed yucca leaf. Firing occurred in homemade kilns with wood or dung fuel, and during firing the potters spoke in whispers, fearing that loud talk might cause breakage.[4]

If the method of manufacturing pottery seemed static over the years, ceramic styles changed dramatically after the demise of Sikyatki and other ancient pueblos. Keres, Zuñi, Tewa, and Spanish influences impacted forcefully upon Hopi and Hopi-Tewa potters, so that by Nampeyo's time the swirls, curves, bands, and feathered motifs of former years had largely disappeared.[5] To Nampeyo fell the mission of forging the Sikyatki Revival, an artistic revolution which drew upon forms from the past, expanded upon them, and still influences the appearance of American Indian pottery throughout the Southwest.

Nampeyo as a child—helping her grandmother temper clay, making miniature pots, and sitting in on potting bees with older women—is a figure of reasonable historical reconstruction. We do not know conclusively that these events ever took place, but such incidents must have occurred for Nampeyo to have developed into what she became. Not until 1875 did Nampeyo emerge, albeit briefly, from obscurity.

In 1875, members of the Hayden Survey, also known as the U.S. Geological Survey, appeared at First Mesa. One of the men, obviously taken by Nampeyo, described her as beautiful and modest, short and plump, "but not unbecomingly so," and detected in her eyes "a voluptuous expression, which made them extremely fascinating."[6] William Henry Jackson, already widely acclaimed for his vistas of the Yellowstone region, took at least two photographs of Nampeyo, who served the visitors' meals at her brother's house. Nampeyo's brother, sometimes called Captain Tom, was a Hopi-Tewa headman, and the family enjoyed some prominence, with her mother serving as custodian of a sacred relic.[7]

Four years later, Nampeyo married a man named Kwivioya, but they apparently never lived together. Perhaps between the time of betrothal and the actual marriage—a process which can last several years among Hopis and Hopi-Tewas—the couple decided on abandoning the union. Then, around 1881, when she was about twenty-one, Nampeyo married Lesou, a native of Walpi. In accordance with the matrilocal dictates of First Mesa, she and her husband took up residence at Hopi-Tewa village. This marriage lasted until Lesou's death fifty-one years later.[8]

The obscurity so often surrounding Nampeyo prohibits a clear view of the next decade in her life, but it may be assumed that she passed her time engaged in those activities filling the lives of all Hopi-Tewa women. She made *piki,* corn bread resembling parchment, and gave birth to the five or more children she and Lesou raised.[9] She crafted pottery for use at home, as presents, and possibly for sale at the trading post that Thomas V. Keam received a license to establish in 1875 at Keams Canyon, twelve miles northeast of First Mesa.[10]

It is also likely that Nampeyo and Lesou collected potsherds, traces of the output of potters from abandoned settlements such as Kawaika-a, Awatovi, Jeddito, and, of course, Sikyatki.[11]

Nampeyo did not regard these sherds as templates for creating painted designs; they were, after all, only fragments. The function of the sherds, in connection with Nampeyo's art, lay in a different area: stimulation for the recreation and expansion of ancient design.[12] It is possible that the Sikyatki Revival may already have entered its initial stages during this period, if not before.[13] In any event, Nampeyo's time in the wilderness now neared its end. Indeed, photographer William Henry Jackson learned about 1890 that Nampeyo had emerged as the foremost potter among the Hopis and Hopi-Tewas.[14]

In 1891, Jesse W. Fewkes arrived at First Mesa.[15] Fewkes, a blue-eyed, sandy-haired, bearded 1875 Harvard honors graduate in natural science, succeeded anthropologist Frank Hamilton Cushing as director of the Hemenway archaeological expedition. By Fewkes's account, he and Nampeyo met early on in his First Mesa investigations.[16]

Beginning in 1895, three years after inspecting the site, Fewkes began excavations at Sikyatki. His crew consisted of fifteen Hopis and Hopi-Tewas, among them Nampeyo's husband Lesou.[17] During the course of the dig, Fewkes and his crew uncovered massive amounts of Sikyatki's colorful, exquisitely executed polychrome mortuary pottery. Later, Fewkes recalled that Nampeyo often visited his camp, borrowing pencils and paper for copying designs from these prehistoric wares.[18]

Walter Hough of the Smithsonian Institution, visiting Fewkes's base camp at Sikyatki in 1896, observed Nampeyo copying prehistoric designs for further study.[19] Hough, immensely impressed with her taste and skill, reported that Nampeyo's "pottery has attained the quality of form, surface, fire change, and decoration of the ancient ware which give it artistic standing."[20] Hough found Nampeyo's product "full of promise,"[21] and he purchased examples of her work for the U.S. National Museum's collections. Without hesitation, he described her as "the best potter at Hano,"[22] the Hopi-Tewa village where both groups' finest pottery was fashioned. Nampeyo, Hough explained, was something more than a potter; she was an artist-potter."[23]

But Nampeyo's work alarmed Fewkes. What precipitated this otherwise odd reaction was a matter well beyond Nampeyo's control: Fewkes's fear that uninformed buyers might regard her wares as genuinely prehistoric. Fewkes never hinted at any link between Nampeyo and attempts at passing her work off as the product of Sikyatki potters. Instead, he reserved his considerable wrath for "unscrupulous traders,"[24] who could purchase her pottery for a pittance and unload the pieces as items of prehistoric vintage, articles for which a large and lucrative market already existed. Nampeyo's output must have been enormous, even early on, because Fewkes reported: "Much of the pottery offered for sale by . . . dealers along the Santa Fe Railroad in Arizona and New Mexico is imitation prehistoric Hopi ware made by Nampeyo."[25]

The root of Fewkes's consternation lay in the Sikyatki Revival, the development in Hopi and Hopi-Tewa pottery manufacture which was founded upon the idea of recreating the dramatic effect of Sikyatki's painted wares. That Nampeyo occupied a position of leadership in the Sikyatki Revival is not disputed; equally clear is the fact that her position as a leader rested upon her expertise as a master potter.

When Hough visited First Mesa with Fewkes in 1896, he found that Nampeyo and Lesou owned a "house below the mesa [at Polacca], topped with a glowing red iron 'Government' roof"[26] but that she spent most of her time at her mother's home in Hopi-Tewa village. He described Nampeyo's clay-seeking journeys as truly "archaeological."[27] Finding the proper clays, Hough learned, was important for Nampeyo because these materials enabled her work to capture the fineness of surface quality attained by the Sikyatki potters she obviously admired. Fortunately, Hough described the clays used by Nampeyo. These were

> *hisat chuoka,* or ancient clay, white, unctious and fragrant, to which the ancient Sikyatki potters owed the perfection of their ware; the reddish clay, *siwu chuoka,* also from Sikyatki; the hard, iron-stained clay, *choku chuoka,* and white clay with which vessels are coated for finishing and decoration, coming from about twelve miles southeast of Walpi. In contrast with Nampeyo's four clays the Hopi women use only two, a gray body clay, *chakbutska,* and a white slip clay, *kutsatsuka.*[28]

After making a piece of pottery, Nampeyo often covered it with a slip which turned white upon firing, though she also used a yellow slip. The paints at Nampeyo's disposal were dark brown, made from ground stone mixed with tansy mustard, and a form of yellow ochre which burned red. Nampeyo ranked, by Hough's expert reckoning, as a quick worker and a rapid painter.[29]

Nampeyo created ceramic wares in a variety of forms, but her typical product was a shallow, widespreading water jar with a flat top and an open mouth. She painted decorations along the jar's shoulder, bordering top and bottom with a black band. She explained her technique of layout to anthropologist Ruth Bunzel, describing the ideal arrangement for the designs on such a water jar as "four designs around the top,—two and two. . . . These signs opposite each other should be alike."[30]

In any culture, an aesthetically pleasing, commercially successful creation is usually copied. Thus, while Nampeyo enjoyed no monopoly on making pottery that reflected a renascent Sikyatki style, she emerged as the most influential and best known of the potters engaged in the Sikyatki Revival.

Nampeyo encountered no problem in selling her wares. Her pieces were sold to the Keams Canyon post; to the Fred Harvey Company, which operated a chain of hotels and restaurants along the Santa Fe line; and to the store at Polacca, at the base of First Mesa, operated by her brother.[31] A water jar could be obtained from Nampeyo for anywhere from two to five dollars, with the latter price reserved for exceptionally large pieces; Nampeyo's twelve-inch bowls brought her seventy-five cents. If these prices seem low, consider that the work of other potters commanded much less.[32]

Significantly, one of Nampeyo's pots was not just another pot; it was, as Hough foresaw, an artistic ceramic by Nampeyo. She attained recognition as an artist, in her time, not only among her own people but among Euroamericans as well. Nampeyo's work held special worth because it was the product of her labor and genius.

In 1898, George A. Dorsey, curator of anthropology at Chicago's Field Museum of Natural History, and the Reverend H. R. Voth, a Mennonite missionary intimately acquainted with the Hopi country, arranged for the appearance of Nampeyo and Lesou at an exhibition of her craft in the Chicago Coliseum. Six years later and again in 1907, the Fred Harvey Company, acting with the encouragement of Don Lorenzo Hubbell, pioneering trader among the Navajos at Ganado, hired her to display and manufacture her wares at the company's Grand Canyon lodge. In 1910 she returned to Chicago for another exhibition of pottery making.[33] Such public exposure inspired curiosity and brought both publicity and patrons, one of which seems to have adversely affected Nampeyo.

In 1920, William Henry Jackson, the man who had photographed Nampeyo in connection with his work for the Hayden Survey nearly half a century earlier, asked a friend to deliver a copy of Nampeyo's portrait to her on First Mesa. This friend was Southwestern archaeologist Neil M. Judd who, in complying with Jackson's request, discovered that Nampeyo had gone blind.[34]

Nampeyo continued molding pottery, but she was obviously incapable of painting the bold and intricate lively designs which had earned her so much recognition. Now, her daughters and Lesou painted, as she had done for her own grandmother.[35] Occasionally, a piece was signed with a daughter's name followed by the renowned cachet of Nampeyo, a practice not in vogue before the 1920s and one in which Nampeyo herself probably never engaged.[36]

"When I first began to paint," Nampeyo once recalled, "I used to go to the ancient village [of Sikyatki] and pick up pieces of pottery and copy the designs. That is how I learned to paint. But now I just close my eyes and see the designs and I paint them."[37] One can only speculate what life was like for Nampeyo in a world of darkness. The daughters who helped her with the pottery when she became blind now turned into full-time potters themselves, and they were becoming established in their art when Lesou died in 1932.

Time began grinding down for Nampeyo, too; and on July 20, 1942, at about six o'clock in the evening, probably aged eighty-two, she died at First Mesa.[38]

A certain amount of controversy surrounds discussion of Nampeyo's role in the Sikyatki Revival and the subsequent birth of modern Hopi and Hopi-Tewa pottery.

Lesou also probably deserves credit for helping to stimulate the emergence of the style which became so closely associated with his wife. This, if only because his job with Fewkes provided Nampeyo with ready access to a corpus of prehistoric pottery that went far beyond the sherds which she had previously collected.

Some authorities argue that Fewkes should garner much of the glory.[39] "The origin of this transformation [the Sikyatki Revival] was due partly" to himself,[40] Fewkes wrote, claiming that after Nampeyo inspected his excavations in 1895 "all the pottery manufactured by her was decorated with modified Sikyatki symbols."[41]

But Nampeyo collected sherds long before Fewkes had even heard of First Mesa, and evidence of the Sikyatki Revival's origin points to a date preceding that ruin's excavation. True, Fewkes's activities at Sikyatki afforded Nampeyo an opportunity for broadening her study of ancient wares. But Fewkes does not seem to have encouraged her work, quite the contrary; and even he viewed her pottery as a modification, not duplication, of the Sikyatki style. In fact, it appears unlikely that Fewkes's position in the Sikyatki Revival was anywhere near as pivotal as has sometimes been claimed.[42] Indeed, one can hardly be faulted for suspecting that the Fewkes-taught-Nampeyo argument might owe more than a little to the familiar refrain that few, if any, American Indians are capable of coming up with an original idea of their own.

What probably happened is that Nampeyo took advantage of Fewkes's excavations and made a fuller study of Sikyatki wares, with which she was already familiar. Then she incorporated the old designs into her work, which even at that time operated under the impetus of inspiration derived, at least in part, from observations of sherds at Sikyatki and other sites.

But Nampeyo did not merely copy Sikyatki wares; she amplified upon the style. Bunzel, reporting that "the copying of Sikyatki pieces is by no means as slavish as is claimed,"[43] noticed that she never once saw a Hopi or Hopi-Tewa potter, including Nampeyo, copying motifs directly from a sherd onto a modern ceramic piece. Nampeyo took from the past, went beyond imitation, and provided fruition for a new style which may well have been in an embryonic stage around the time of her birth.[44]

However, there was a good deal more to the Sikyatki Revival than the study and extension of design. Hough noticed that Nampeyo's "aged father and mother are final authority on the interpretation of ancient symbolic or cult representations in art."[45] This suggests, at least, not only a revival of an art form but a continuation of symbolic forms based upon existing esoteric knowledge. In a sense, then, those who participated in the Sikyatki Revival, like Nampeyo, not only produced pleasing ceramics but also tried to dig deeper into their own heritage.

Today, pottery attributed to Nampeyo, avidly sought by private collectors and museum curators, commands astronomical prices at auctions. Of course, Nampeyo's is not the only name in Southwestern Indian pottery or in Indian art generally. But she blazed the way by which Euroamerican patrons perceive what Walter Hough understood late in the nineteenth century: a pot may be just a pot, but pottery done by an artist is artistic pottery.

Ruth Bunzel believed two geniuses reigned in the field of modern Puebloan ceramics. One of these was Julian Martinez of San Ildefonso, influenced early this century by Hopi and Hopi-Tewa designs, who, with his wife Maria, developed a highly polished black ware. The other genius was Nampeyo, whose "unerring discrimination and lively perception . . . vitalized what would otherwise have been so much dead wood" and "recreated the Sikyatki sense of form" through work that could only be characterized as a "revolution."[46]

American Indian artists have moved in various directions since Nampeyo began picking up potsherds from the ground below First Mesa and seeing on them designs capable of revitalization, dormant motifs still imbued with sparkling liveliness. Some American Indian artists, such as R.C. Gorman, Charles Loloma, Earl Biss, and Oscar Howe, embarked upon paths their ancestors might not recognize but which are appreciated by many American Indians and Euroamericans alike. Others, like Preston Monongye, Randy Lee White, the Lelooskas, and Helen Hardin harken to older ways and, like Nampeyo, add something of their own essence to the finished work. A good example of this trend is found in the dramatic paintings of Dan Namingha, Nampeyo's great-great-grandson, and the work of her many other descendants who live in the demanding world of art.[47]

Still, it is exceedingly difficult to imagine any of these artists single-handedly breaking into the realm of saleable art without Nampeyo's example. She helped create a climate in which American Indians could be recognized as artists with names, not just as roadside curio salespeople.

Our perception of modern American Indian art as art owes much to the belated recognition of American Indian artists as gifted individuals possessing singular talents and styles of expression. This crucial development received a vital infusion of stimulation early in the twentieth century, and its genesis may be traced largely to the work of Nampeyo, who brought both recognition and revolution to modern Puebloan pottery.

Nampeyo was not the first American Indian who knocked at the door of our aesthetic perception, but before her life was over she had left that door ajar to allow others entry.

Notes

1. Edmund Nequatewa, "Nampeyo, Famous Hopi Potter," *Plateau* 15, no. 3 (January 1943), p. 40.

2. Erik K. Reed, "The Origins of Hano Pueblo," *El Palacio* 15, no. 4 (April 1943), pp. 73–76; Michael B. Stanislawski, "Hopi-Tewa," in William C. Sturtevant, gen. ed., *Handbook of North American Indians,* vol. 9, *Southwest* ed. Alfonso Ortiz (Washington, D.C., 1979), p. 600.

3. Nequatewa, "Nampeyo," p. 4.

4. Alfred E. Dittert, Jr., and Fred Plog, *Generations in Clay* (Flagstaff, Ariz., 1980), pp. 9, 73–75, 104; Walter Hough, *The Hopi Indians* (Cedar Rapids, Iowa, 1915), pp. 80–81.

5. Ruth L. Bunzel, *The Pueblo Potter* (New York, 1969), p. 80; Edwin L. Wade, "The Thomas Keam Collection of Hopi Pottery," *American Indian Art Magazine* 5, no. 3 (Summer 1980), pp. 54–61.

6. E. A. Barber, quoted in Harry C. James, *Pages from Hopi History* (Tucson, 1974), p. 198.

7. J. Walter Fewkes, "The Group of Tusayan Ceremonials Called Katchinas," *Fifteenth Annual Report of the Bureau of American Ethnology* (Washington, D.C., 1897), p. 277; Theodore R. Frisbie, "The Influence of J. Walter Fewkes on Nampeyo: Fact or Fancy?" in *The Changing Ways of Southwestern Indians,* ed. Albert H. Schroeder (Glorieta, N.M., 1973), p. 234. Captain Tom, also called Tom Polcacca, owned a store at the base of First Mesa, and a town bearing his name sprang up around this enterprise. Stanislawski, "Hopi-Tewa," p. 588, fig. 1.

8. Nequatewa, "Nampeyo," p. 40.

9. Ibid., p. 40.

10. Frisbie, "Influence of J. Walter Fewkes," p. 232.

11. Robert Ashton, "Nampeyo and Lesou," *American Indian Art Magazine* 1, no. 3 (Summer 1976), p. 30; John E. Collins, "Nampevo, Hopi Potter" (Fullerton,

Calif., 1974), p. 8; Dittert and Plog, *Generations in Clay,* p. 31; Frisbie, "Influence of J. Walter Fewkes," p. 234.

12. Bunzel, *Pueblo Potter,* pp. 55–56, 88; Mary-Russell F. Colton and Harold S. Colton, "An Appreciation of the Art of Nampeyo and her Influence on Hopi Pottery," *Plateau* 15, no. 3 (January 1944), p. 44.

13. Ashton, "Nampeyo and Lesou," p. 30.

14. Clarence S. Jackson, *Picture Maker of the Old West* (New York, 1947), p. 296. See also Collins, "Nampeyo," p. 9.

15. For Fewkes, see Walter Hough, "Jesse Walter Fewkes," *American Anthropologist,* n.s., 33, no. 1 (January-March 1931), pp. 92–97.

16. Fewkes, "Group of Tusayan Ceremonials," p. 277.

17. Frisbie, "Influence of J. Walter Fewkes," p. 232.

18. Fewkes, *Designs on Prehistoric Hopi Pottery* (New York, 1973), pp. 116, 177. This work is an unabridged reprint of Fewkes's two excellent works on Sikyatki pottery, originally published in the seventeenth and thirty-third annual reports of the Bureau of American Ethnology (Washington, D.C., 1898 and 1919).

19. Walter Hough, "A Revival of the Ancient Hopi Pottery Art," *American Anthropologist,* n.s., 19, no. 2 (April-June 1917), p. 322.

20. Ibid., p. 323.

21. Ibid., p. 322.

22. Hough, *Hopi Indians,* p. 20.

23. Ibid., p. 76.

24. Fewkes, *Designs,* p. 116.

25. Ibid., p. 177.

26. Hough, *Hopi Indians,* p. 75.

27. Ibid., p. 76.

28. Ibid., p. 77.

29. Ibid., p. 80.

30. Bunzel, *Pueblo Potter,* pp. 37, 41.

31. Ibid., p. 5; J. J. Brody, "Pueblo Fine Arts," in *Handbook of North American Indians,* vol. 9, *Southwest,* pp. 604–5; Fewkes, *Designs,* p. 177; Nequatewa, "Nampeyo," p. 40.

32. Bunzel, *Pueblo Potter,* p. 5.

33. Collins, "Nampeyo," pp. 19–20; James, *Pages,* p. 199; Nequatewa, "Nampeyo," p. 42.

34. Neil M. Judd, *Men Met Along the Trail* (Norman, Okla., 1968), pp. 104–5.

35. Collins, "Nampeyo," p. 20.

36. Ashton, "Nampeyo and Lesou," p. 33.

37. Bunzel, *Pueblo Potter,* p. 56.

38. Nequatewa, "Nampeyo," p. 42.

39. J. J. Brody, *Indian Painters and White Patrons* (Albuquerque, 1971), p. 67; Dorothy Dunn, *American Indian Painting of the Southwest and Plains Area* (Albuquerque, 1968), p. 99; Ruth Underhill, "Pueblo Crafts" (Washington, D.C., 1944), p. 99.

40. Fewkes, *Designs*, p. 177.

41. Ibid., p. 116.

42. Frisbie, "Influence of J. Walter Fewkes," pp. 231–244.

43. Bunzel, *Pueblo Potter*, p. 56.

44. Wade, "Thomas Keam Collection," p. 60.

45. Hough, *Hopi Indians*, p. 76.

46. Bunzel, *Pueblo Potter*, p. 88.

47. Guy Monthan and Doris Monthan, "Dextra Quotskuyva Nampeyo," *American Indian Art Magazine* 2, no. 4 (Autumn 1977), p. 158.

Essay on Sources

Nampeyo's was a nonliterate world and she wrote neither about her art nor her life. Uninvolved in political affairs, not sought as a spellbinding speaker on the lecture circuit, hers was a life lived for the most part in obscurity. Naturally, these factors pose problems for researchers.

The best source currently available on details of Nampeyo's life remains a three-page article—in *Plateau* 15, no. 3 (January 1943)—written by Edmund Nequatewa in 1943, shortly after Nampeyo's death. Nequatewa, in putting together "Nampeyo, Famous Hopi *[sic]* Potter," relied upon the memories of her family and friends. This makes the piece an invaluable starting point in any study of Nampeyo and her work. Although not always cited in subsequent appreciations of Nampeyo, Nequatewa is obviously the source most often consulted at the beginning of the investigative journey.

Walter Hough's prescient observations about Nampeyo's artistry and his reportage of her pottery-making techniques constitute another source of great interest. Hough's views are cogently presented in *The Hopi Indians* (Cedar Rapids, Iowa, 1915) and, in abbreviated form, in "A Revival of the Ancient Hopi Pottery Art," *American Anthropologist,* n.s., 19, no. 2 (April-June 1917). The ethnocentric views expressed by Hough in *The Hopi Indians,* which were a part of his time, make this a somewhat dated volume. Nevertheless, his eyewitness account of watching Nampeyo constructing pottery and his discussion of the types of clays and paints she employed retain considerable interest and value.

Ruth L. Bunzel visited Nampeyo, analyzed her style in depth, and recognized a revolutionary development in Puebloan ceramics when she saw one. Bunzel published her highly informative conclusions in *The Pueblo Potter* (New York, 1969).

Jesse W. Fewkes's reports on Sikyatki ceramics were issued by the Smithsonian Institution's Bureau of American Ethnology in 1898 and 1919. Both reports are available in a one-volume paperback edition, *Designs on Prehistoric Hopi Pottery*

(New York, 1973). Fewkes's work in this area is useful for comparing the Sikyatki wares with Nampeyo's work.

As noted in the preceding article, controversy still attends Fewkes's supposed role in the Sikyatki Revival. Theodore R. Frisbie dealt adroitly with this thorny subject in "The Influence of J. Walter Fewkes on Nampeyo: Fact or Fancy?" in *The Changing Ways of Southwestern Indians*, ed. Albert H. Schroeder (Glorieta, N.M., 1973). This remains the fullest treatment to date of a disputed and significant point.

3

Dr. Susan LaFlesche Picotte

The Reformed and the Reformer

Valerie Sherer Mathes

Susan LaFlesche Picotte (1865–1915) achieved renown as the first Indian woman doctor of medicine. She was the youngest daughter of Joseph LaFlesche (Estamaza or "Iron Eyes"), the half-French and last recognized chief of the Omaha tribe, and his mixed-blood wife, Mary Gale. Although she had been raised to revere her Indian heritage, her aspirations were influenced by her father, who embraced assimilation. Her father had abandoned the traditional Omaha earth lodge years before Susan's birth, living instead in a two-story frame house in a settlement known to the Omaha traditionalists as the home of "The Make Believe White Men." Like her elder sister and brother, Susette and Francis, Susan learned early to conform to the world of the dominant culture. Susette La-Flesche became famous as "Bright Eyes," the Indian "princess" who spoke on behalf of Indian policy reform, touring the East in the company of her equally famous husband, minister, and journalist Thomas Henry Tibbles. Under the tutelage of Alice Cunningham Fletcher, Francis became the first Indian anthropologist employed by the Smithsonian Institution's Bureau of American Ethnology.

Because of the spectacular success of the LaFlesche children, and that of an extraordinary group of acculturated mixed-bloods like Charles A. Eastman, Arthur C. Parker, and Gertrude Bonnin, Indian policy reformers could point with pride and satisfaction to the transformation that was possible in a single lifetime. If this were true, what might other American Indians achieve? Susan LaFlesche Picotte talked, dressed, and behaved like other women of the middle

class, but her achievements were offered as eternal lessons to other American Indians. Regardless of her ethnicity, her accomplishments were exceptional. Few women of her generation—and still fewer Indian women—became medical doctors.

Although she never lived in the traditional Omaha culture, as did other members of her tribe during her lifetime, Susan LaFlesche Picotte never abandoned her identification with her people; if anything, she assumed even greater responsibilities as both a representative of her people and of her "race"—pressures which must have been at times quite burdensome. If she had a blind spot—one shared by numerous other Indian reformers of her generation—it was her unswerving faith in the process of assimilation. Her life, after all, was testimony to its efficacy. Like her friend and supporter, Alice Fletcher, Susan recognized the tribal tie as an obstacle to "progress," as she defined it; the individual homestead and education in the white man's schools was the only way for her people and other Indians to succeed in white America. The solution to the "Indian problem," however, proved more complex and elusive than reformers like Susan had imagined.

Few Indians in nineteenth-century America had the opportunity to become practicing physicians. Only the careers of Charles Eastman, a Sioux practitioner, and Dr. Carlos Montezuma, a Yavapai from Arizona, are well known. Yet equally remarkable was Susan LaFlesche, an Omaha woman who earned a medical degree in an era when few of her white sisters could aspire to the same goal.[1] Susan grew up during the Indian reform period of the late nineteenth century and was deeply influenced by the assimilationist policies of the humanitarians. Consequently, once she received her degree, she went on to become a reformer in her own right.

The chain of events that brought Susan to national prominence began in 1867 when Congress, responding to the dilemma of continuing warfare on the frontier, sent an investigating committee led by Senator James B. Doolittle to the western tribes. In its much publicized report, the Doolittle Commission noted with alarm the decreasing native population and declared that "in a large majority of cases Indian wars are to be traced to the aggressions of lawless white men, always to be found upon the frontier."[2]

Congress, partly as a result of the Doolittle investigation, created a commission composed of civilians and military leaders to meet with the hostile tribes for the purpose of isolating and eliminating the causes of warfare. The Peace Commission was empowered to negotiate peace treaties and to select suitable reservations as permanent homes for the tribes. The government promised to provide schools, domesticated animals, farming and other equipment, and instruction in agriculture and the mechanical arts.[3]

Eastern reformers, who were generally unfamiliar with Indians, agreed with the commission's findings and held the army responsible for past bloodshed. From the reformers' romantic viewpoint, the Indians, if given a chance, would settle down peacefully as imitation white farmers. As a result of their lobbying, the reformers persuaded President Ulysses S. Grant and his Commissioner of Indian Affairs, Ely Samuel Parker, a Seneca Indian, to implement a "Peace Policy."[4] This involved forcing the Indians to accept reservations and then "civilizing" them according to the suggestions of the Peace Commission. The army was restrained from punitive campaigns while the Peace Policy was implemented, although many did not expect it to succeed.

Grant originally wanted to use army officers as Indian agents, but Congress objected to any action that would deprive it of an important source of patronage. In a move to even the score, Grant skillfully agreed to accept civilian agents recommended by the nation's religious leaders. Congress, put on the spot, could not refuse without admitting its own corruption.

The implementation of this reform, called the "Quaker Policy," had a profound effect on Susan LaFlesche, who grew up on the reservation in Nebraska.[5] In 1869, the Hicksite Friends, one of the two branches of the Society of Friends, were assigned the Northern Superintendency, which included the Omaha Agency. Samuel Janney, appointed superintendent, believed the Indians must abandon the hunt and replace their tribal chieftain. He was also convinced that they should abolish their communal lifestyle and become independent, landowning farmers.[6] Janney's ideas coincided with the goals of nineteenth-century reformers. Susan was four years old when the first Quaker agent arrived in June 1869.[7] The Quakers implemented their program of education and civilization for the next dozen years, making an indelible impression on young Susan and charting the course of her life.

Susan's success in the white world was attributable in part to the attitudes of her father, Joseph LaFlesche, the last Omaha chief. Joseph was the son of a French fur trader and his Indian wife. Concerned over the children's future, he refused to have his daughters tattooed and his sons' ears pierced. "I was always sure that my sons and daughters would live to see the time when they would have to mingle with the white people," he said, "and I determined that they should not have any mark upon them that might be detrimental in their future surroundings."[8] Born about 1818, Joseph had witnessed many changes which convinced him that accommodation to the ways of the whites was essential. The Omahas had once lived in the region watered by the Ohio and Wabash rivers but had migrated to eastern Nebraska. Following the passage of the 1830 Indian Removal Act by Congress, the tribe had ceded claims to its eastern lands in 1830 and 1836. In an 1854 treaty, the Omahas gave up rights to hunting grounds west of the Missouri River, retaining only a tract of three hundred thousand acres. In return, they received annuities, a gristmill, a blacksmith shop, and protection from hostile tribes when necessary.

One treaty provision gave the Board of Foreign Missions of the Presbyterian Church four quarter sections of land to continue their missionary work among the tribe.[9] In 1846, the Presbyterians established their first permanent mission among the Omahas at Bellevue; when the Indians ceded their lands and moved to a new reservation, the missionaries promptly followed them and in 1857 built a three-story building of natural stone that served as housing and as a boarding school for the tribe's children.[10]

According to Mrs. M. C. Wade, a Presbyterian missionary, Joseph LaFlesche embraced Christianity early. In 1889, when writing his obituary, Mrs. Wade declared: "He turned not to the right hand or to the left from the Word of God as far as he knew its teaching, and the regret of his life was that he could not read it." She concluded that "his soul seemed hungry for more than he could reach here, and it is good to know that he is satisfied with the fullness of the Savior's presence now to be like Him."[11]

In addition to becoming a Christian, Joseph also adopted the white man's housing. In the late 1850s, he hired white carpenters to construct a two-story frame house, with the lower floor serving as a trading store. As a result, Susan and her younger siblings were not born in the traditional Omaha earth lodge. Joseph also established a town site as well as roads throughout the reservation. He fenced one hundred acres and divided the land into smaller fields for each man in the village to farm.[12] Joseph was therefore well on the way to becoming an independent farmer: the ideal citizen and the backbone of American democracy, according to Jeffersonian philosophy.

Joseph also secured education for his children. Fortunately for Susan, the Presbyterian missionaries, like most missionaries, felt responsible for educating Indian girls as well as boys. In 1857, Omaha missionary I. R. Rolph wrote to the Board of Foreign Missions, "It makes my courage wan to think of educating boys here and inspiring them with a relish for the habits of the white man, if they have only the prospect before them of taking up in the end with a partner for life whose ambition would be only for hunters *[sic]* fare and satisfied with the habits of the wigwam."[13]

In general, nineteenth-century reformers believed in instructing women in the arts of housekeeping. They were convinced that to educate the men of the tribe and then allow them to return to an "uncivilized" home defeated the purpose of education. Educating women was therefore essential, for as wives and mothers they would serve as examples to their children. Because it was often impractical to send all Indian girls to school in the East, the government established in 1892 the position of field matron to educate Indian women at home. These matrons, hired by the Indian office, were to teach Indian women the care of the home, preparation and serving of food, sewing, laundry, care of domestic animals, care of the sick, and proper observance of the Sabbath.[14]

This strong interest in the household was in keeping with mid-nineteenth century American philosophy. American women were believed to possess their own separate "sphere," that of domesticity, which was centered totally within the home. Home was a sanctuary where the weary husband could return from his day's work to find a refuge, and where children were nurtured. Women were expected to sustain traditional moral values, to guard democracy, and to instill the work ethic in their children.[15] "The exemplary home was a paradigm of serenity and harmony, a dramatic contrast to its tempestuous surroundings. . . . The insistence that women's sphere be limited to the home became a prevailing dogma of nineteenth-century faith," according to a modern-day scholar in women's history.[16]

One of the proponents of this "women's sphere" was Catharine Beecher, eldest daughter of Lyman Beecher and sister of Henry Ward Beecher and Harriet Beecher Stowe. Catharine glorified domesticity in her "Treatise on Domestic Economy," published originally in 1841 and reprinted nearly every year from 1841 to 1856. Together with her larger compendium, *The American Woman's Home,* published in 1868, Catharine Beecher's writings influenced the society's conception of the role of women. She, according to Kathryn Sklar, "defined the parlor as a cultural podium and described the home not as . . . isolating women from political and social influence, but as the base from which their influence on the rest of the culture was launched."[17] Catharine Beecher's philosophy endured for nearly half a century, and Susan echoed it. Learning that she would have financial assistance to attend medical college in order to help her people, Susan wrote in June 1886, "I hope to go into their homes and help the women in their housekeeping, teach them a few practical points about cooking and nursing, and especially about cleanliness." She testified personally to the value of Beecher's philosophy: "I feel that as a physician I can do a great deal more than as a mere teacher, for the *home* is the foundation of all things for the Indians, and my work I hope will be chiefly in the homes of my people."[18]

Based on the teaching of household skills, the education of Indian women was largely a vocational approach. Fortunately, Susan also received academic training. Her education began at the Omaha Agency, initially under Presbyterian missionaries[19] and later with Quaker teachers who taught her geography, history, grammar, arithmetic, and spelling.[20] In September 1879, Susan and her sister Marguerite entered the Elizabeth Institute for Young Ladies in Elizabeth, New Jersey.[21] Unfortunately, little is known about the two and a half years Susan spent at the Elizabeth Institute. In 1882, she and Marguerite returned to the reservation; Susan spent the next two years working at the mission school teaching a class of small children.[22] In 1884, again accompanied by Marguerite, Susan entered Hampton Normal and Agricultural Institute in Hampton, Virginia. Hampton Institute was established in 1868 by Gen. Samuel C. Armstrong to educate Negro freedmen. However, the first Indian students entered Hampton in 1878, when Lt. Richard Henry Pratt, a young army officer, arrived with about twenty male Indian students who were former prisoners at Fort Marion, Florida. Thus began a long and successful experiment in educating Indians in Virginia.[23] Pratt and Armstrong believed that girls should be added to the program, and soon both sexes were being "trained." But Pratt, uncomfortable in educating Indians along with blacks, established an Indian school at Carlisle Barracks, Pennsylvania, in 1879.

From 1884 until 1886, Susan and Marguerite, dressed in uniforms, attended classes in Hampton's disciplined atmosphere. More emphasis was placed on domestic chores than on academic learning; however, since both sisters could read and write English fluently, they were placed in the normal course of study and proceeded at their own academic pace. The remainder of their day was probably devoted to housekeeping skills, for by 1883 Hampton had sewing, housekeeping, and laundry departments. Female students were expected to care for their own clothing, to clean their rooms, and to sweep and dust corridors and halls as well as other parts of Winona Lodge, which served as their dormitory.[24] There were, however, lighter moments, and both girls participated in the social side of school life. Susan particularly enjoyed her music lessons and was willing to pay extra to learn to play the piano.[25]

Susan graduated from Hampton on May 20, 1886, as salutatorian. After presenting her address, entitled "My Childhood and Womanhood," she was awarded the Demorest prize for the highest score of any student in her junior year. Her abilities were recognized by many, including Armstrong, principal and founder of Hampton, who described her as "a young woman of unusual ability, integrity, [and] fixedness of purpose. . . ."[26] On another occasion, he described her as a "level-headed, earnest, capable, Christian woman . . . clear-headed, and independent; naturally, a deep, but not a sentimental woman."[27] Alice Cunningham Fletcher, an ethnologist and fellow of Harvard's Peabody Museum, attended the commencement ceremonies at Hampton and was particularly impressed with Susan. Fletcher noted that her dress was simple but neat, and her face was "lovely." She "looked well, spoke clearly and every one was delighted with her. I am so glad that she is to go forward in her grand career. She is I think the first Indian girl to advance so far."[28]

Fletcher was in part responsible for Susan's medical education. The ethnologist had first become acquainted with the LaFlesche family in 1881, during a four-month stay with the tribe. She worked closely with Susan's brother, Francis, and many years later *The Omaha Tribe* was published under their joint authorship. From July to October 1883, Fletcher was bedridden with an attack of inflammatory rheumatism, and Susan carefully tended to her. The following year Fletcher attended her first Lake Mohonk Conference of Friends of the Indian, where authorities from the government and reformers gathered annually to discuss Indian policy. There, she met Sara Thomson Kinney, president of the Connecticut Indian Association and her husband, J. C. Kinney, editor of the Hartford *Courant.*[29] They probably discussed Susan, for when it came time for her to go to medical college, Fletcher and the Kinneys combined their efforts to locate a college and to obtain financing for her.

"Federal schools," Robert Trennert has written, "did not train Indian women for the conditions they faced upon returning home."[30] Industrial education for Indian women was, therefore, essentially a failure. Had Susan's education ended with her graduation from Hampton, and had it been strictly vocational, she would have been among the many who were still unprepared to fit into Anglo-American society. At Hampton, however, both Dr. Martha M. Waldron, the school physician, and General Armstrong had encouraged her to study academic subjects, and both considered her capable of attaining a medical degree.

It was probably Doctor Waldron, a graduate of the Woman's Medical College of Pennsylvania, who was responsible for the selection of her alma mater. On March 20, 1886, she wrote on Susan's behalf to Alfred Jones, secretary of the executive committee of the college, asking for a scholarship. Jones replied that money was out of the question for 1886; if Susan wished to apply, all applications must be in her own handwriting. She must also include testimonials as to her health, character, and educational qualifications.[31] Susan quickly complied. Mrs. Kinney sent her a train ticket to Philadelphia and asked her family to see that she was on her way east by the first of October, in order to arrive in time for the start of classes on the seventh.[32]

Most of Susan's expenses for the college were financed by the Connecticut Indian Association of which Mrs. Kinney was president.[33] The organization, founded in 1881,[34] was an auxiliary of the Women's National Indian Association. Its aims included "aid [to] Indians, in civilization, industrial training, self support, education, citizenship, and Christianization."[35] Susan's medical training was appropriate to their program. In May 1886, at the suggestion of President Kinney, the Connecticut association had agreed to underwrite the entire expense of Susan's education for the next three years. Aware that the government regularly paid 167 dollars a year for Indian students at boarding schools like Hampton and Carlisle, Kinney requested a similar grant for Susan's expenses from Commissioner of Indian Affairs John D. C. Atkins. Following an exchange of letters, including a personal recommendation from General Armstrong, the commissioner agreed to Kinney's proposal. The government provided 167 dollars a year, and the Connecticut Indian Association assumed responsibility for the remainder of her educational expenses.[36]

Once the agreement had been completed, Mrs. Kinney appealed to the people of Connecticut for donations. In an association pamphlet, she wrote that the education of Susan "should appeal very powerfully to the benevolent, and particularly to the hearts of women." "In undertaking it," she continued, "we feel that we shall be doing real missionary work, and that in helping one woman, we shall, through her Christian influence, reach, help, and elevate her people." She described Susan as gentle, refined, and unselfish, noting that "in her sweet, quiet way, we feel she would minister not only to the physical needs of those for whom she cared, but for all their deeper wants would strive to lead them to the Great Healer."[37]

Upon learning of her financial assistance, a delighted Susan wrote Mrs. Kinney on June 16 that "it has always been a desire of mine to study medicine ever since I was a small girl for even then I saw the needs of my people for a good physician."[38] Weary and suffering from motion sickness since leaving Omaha, Susan detrained in Philadelphia during the first week of October. No doubt apprehensive about her new venture, she was welcomed by Mrs. Seth Talcott, chairman of the business committee of the Connecticut Indian Association, and by Dr. Elizabeth Bundy, a professor at the college.[39] She was immediately placed in suitable YWCA housing and provided with supplies and the necessary clothing.

For three years Susan wrote lively and interesting letters home. They tell of the people she met, the classes she took, the fear she had of taking examinations, and the multitude of sights she encountered. Learning the routes of the streetcars, Susan visited the sights of Philadelphia, an opportunity afforded to few nineteenth-century Indian women. She frequented the Philadelphia Academy of Arts and commented on the paintings of Benjamin West; she attended numerous musical performances and enjoyed literary and theatrical events, including "The Mikado" and a performance by Lily Langtry in "Wife's Peril." She accompanied her brother Francis to the Philadelphia Mummer's Parade and commented wryly that the masqueraders disguised as Indians looked "pretty well for Indians."[40]

Having been raised in the country, Susan tried to get out of the confines of the city at every opportunity. She liked to walk through Fairmount Park, collecting pinecones, and travel to Virginia to visit her sister Marguerite at Hampton. She visited the Indian boys at the Educational Home in West Philadelphia and the Indian children at Philadelphia's Lincoln Institute.[41]

Other letters prescribe medical advice to various family members. When her mother developed a sore on her hand, Susan sent a packet of carbolated vaseline and castile soap. She was constantly advising her sister, Rosalie, to get plenty of exercise, fresh air, and sleep. To Ed, Rosalie's husband, Susan prescribed less quinine and more restful meals.[42] Thus, in her own small way, she began to reform her family's health before she even graduated from medical college.

These letters also reflect the process of acculturation that Susan was personally experiencing. At Hampton her daily contact had been only with other Indian girls, but at the medical college she associated only with white students. Obviously, some of the whites' cultural traits rubbed off on the young Omaha woman. She was accepted by them completely, participated in all social gatherings, lived with a white roommate, and was chosen as corresponding secretary of the Young Woman's Christian Association.[43] She even dressed like them, wearing her hair piled on top of her head because they asked her to wear it that way.[44]

But Susan had come to the college to study medicine, and that she did with pleasure. In her first year she attended lectures in chemistry, anatomy, physiology, histology, materia medica, general therapeutics, and obstetrics.[45] In addition, she attended daily clinics at the Woman's Hospital; took weekly examinations in chemistry, anatomy, and physiology; and dissected cadavers. Her letters reveal her continued interest in her studies. "We dissect from 8–10 PM. I don't mind it at all in any way whatever," she wrote to Rosalie. Then she jokingly added that she was going to wield the knife but "not the scalping knife. . . ."[46] In describing a dissection, she wrote that it was "interesting to get all the arteries and their branches—everything has a name from the little tiny hole to the bones. It is splendid."[47] At first, she dreaded taking examinations, and in March 1887, she asked Rosalie to pray for her. A week later, she wrote that she had passed her chemistry examination and described her anatomy examination as "lovely." "I had made a . . . point to study certain bones and we were asked to describe those very bones and one or two others," she said, "so I got on swimmingly."[48]

In the spring of 1888, Susan passed her chemistry, anatomy, and physiology examinations. She described them as "delightful" except for the suspense in waiting to be notified of final grades. As second-year students, Susan and her classmates had to wait until almost midnight before they received their letters. A calmness came over her as she opened hers. When it was clear she had passed, she was "glad, so glad." Commencement for the graduates was held on March 15, and a reception followed. Susan wrote of those assembled: "They are very enjoyable—One sees there, the Medical brotherhood, some grown gray in the service, some in the full tide of their work. . . ." She added that the "prospectives, looking forward with eagerness to the time when they too shall have the honored M.D. after their names," stood in the background.[49] Susan was probably looking forward to the next year, when she would be similarly honored.

Although Susan did not have a boyfriend while she attended the Medical College, she had met at Hampton a young Sioux, Thomas Ikinicapi, whom she fondly called "TI." Apparently, she had made some promise to the Connecticut Indian Association that she would not marry during her college years, but she was nevertheless extremely fond of TI and spoke often of him in her letters. She visited Hampton frequently and spent as much time with him as she could. "He was," Susan once remarked, "*without exception* the handsomest Indian I ever saw."[50]

While attending the college, holidays must have been a lonely time for her. Fortunately, she spent her first Christmas with Marguerite at Hampton. She spent the first summer teaching at Hampton, but she returned home the following summer because her parents were both ailing.[51] Writing to Mrs. Kinney, she remarked, "I had all kinds of work to do—I can tell you one thing and that is a Western woman has to know how do [*sic*] everything that a man does besides her own work, for she had to be ready for any emergency that may occur when men are not around."[52] Susan did most of the household and field work that summer; she harnessed horses, ricked hay, measured land for a fence, cooked, sewed, and managed to squeeze in some nursing. The Omahas suffered a severe measles epidemic that summer, and Susan did her best to treat the sick. She soon realized that her people had much to learn about health conditions. "If one wants to accomplish much work they must go out every day," she wrote to Mrs. Kinney. "So much can be done, by going to see them and while you are there tell them how to tidy up or show them *how*, which is still better." She concluded, "They have so much to learn not only about cleanliness but about business, land, money, & horses. . . ."[53] When she returned to the reservation with her medical degree in hand, Susan would devote the remainder of her life to teaching the Omahas about hygiene and cleanliness.

Susan graduated at the head of her class of thirty-six women on March 14, 1889.[54] Dr. James B. Walker, in praising her in his commencement address, noted that "she will stand among her people as the first woman physician. Surely we may record with joy such courage, constance and ability."[55] As a result of a competitive examination, Susan was selected as one of six graduates to serve as an assistant to the resident physician in the Woman's Hospital in Philadelphia.[56] Before beginning her internship on May 1, Susan took a brief vacation, spending several days with members of the Connecticut Indian Association, whom she called her Connecticut "mothers." She was kept busy speaking before branches in Farmington, Guilford, New Britain, Norwich, Waterbury, and Winsted.[57]

In June 1889, Susan wrote to the Commissioner of Indian Affairs, applying for the position of government physician to the Omaha Agency Indian School. In the letter, she gave her educational background and ended by saying, "I feel that I have an advantage in knowing the language and customs of my people, and as a physician can do a great deal to help them."[58] On August 5, 1889, she accepted the position when it was offered.[59] In December, Omaha Agent Robert Ashley requested that Susan be allowed to treat the adults of the tribe as well as the children. Commissioner Thomas Jefferson Morgan agreed.[60] Susan was soon in charge of the health care of the 1,244 Omahas.

The young Omaha woman served as physician to her tribe until October 20, 1893, when she resigned because of both her and her mother's health.[61] During those four years, Susan made Herculean efforts to serve her people. The Omaha Reservation, thirty by forty-five miles in size, had unpaved roads; tribal members were scattered. Until she purchased a team and buggy, Susan walked to visit any patient living within a mile of her office; if she needed to travel a greater distance, she hired a team. She often set out about 8:00 A.M., making calls for six miles in one direction before returning to her office for lunch. Then she set out again on afternoon rounds, sometimes returning as late as 10:00 P.M. She seldom mentioned her physical exhaustion. She treated diseases ranging from influenza, dysentery, and cholera to an epidemic of conjunctivitis, an eye ailment spread by unsanitary conditions. During her first winter, there were two epidemics of influenza; and in September 1891, she saw over 130 patients. By December, the influenza "raged with more violence than during the two preceding years. Some families were rendered helpless by it, sometimes all the family but one or two being down with it. . . . Almost every day during the month I was out making visits," Susan continued. "Several days the thermometer was 15 to 20 degrees below zero, and I had to drive myself."[62] Between October 1891, and the spring of 1892, Susan saw more than six hundred patients.

Not all her activities, however, were devoted to medicine. Susan took time to help her sister Marguerite, the principal teacher at the government school, in continuing their father's work in advocating the assimilation of the Omaha people. The sisters served as advisers to their tribe. They encouraged couples to marry by license and with church sanction, and they advocated that tribal members perform Christian services for the dead. Susan spoke before various Christian groups and also served as interpreter for church services when necessary. In 1891, the Women's National Indian Association asked her to serve as medical missionary to her tribe. Because they had sponsored her medical school education, Susan accepted the appointment. She wrote annual reports and, whenever possible, spoke before various auxiliaries. In return, the women collected boxes of clothing, gifts, supplies, and money for Susan's activities. Some branches donated books and other reading matter to her small library. In bad weather, older Omahas could be found spending a pleasant hour in Susan's office perusing magazines or visiting with the young doctor.[63]

During the fall of 1892, Susan continued her arduous round of house calls as well as attending to walk-in patients and the school children. Soon, however, the long buggy rides over rough reservations roads in inclement weather began to take their toll on the frail young doctor, whose health had never been robust. In college she had complained of numbness and breathing difficulties, but decided that it must be psychological.[64] By early January 1893, Susan was bedridden. As Rosalie wrote to Francis, "Susie has been sick for several weeks, her ears have been troubling her very much, she says she has pain in her head and the back of her neck constantly."[65] These symptoms were but a harbinger of more troubles to come. For the remainder of her short life, Susan was afflicted with an ailment which eventually caused deafness and ultimately death.[66]

By the summer of 1894, however, her health had improved sufficiently for her to surprise her family and friends by marrying Henry Picotte, a Sioux from the Yankton Agency and brother of Marguerite's late husband, Charles.[67] Now thirty years old and with her promise to the Connecticut Indian Association fulfilled, Susan probably decided it was time to end her status as an "old maid." Within a year, however, she was again seriously ill. She "had been very sick," Rosalie wrote to Francis. "I had given up all hopes of her when she commenced to improve."[68]

She slowly regained her strength, and the young couple moved into a house across from the Presbyterian Church in the town of Bancroft. Two boys were soon born to Susan, but she continued to practice medicine among both Indians and whites and quickly won the respect of the local doctors. But, in 1897, her health declined again, and her family feared for her life. White and Indian neighbors rallied to her side, bringing food, flowers, fruit, and good cheer. She later wrote to a friend at Hampton that "when I got well enough to go out, I received so many congratulations from all, I felt so encouraged to try to do right and live a better life. When I felt a little depressed," she continued, "I would think there was not much use in trying to help people, that they did not seem to appreciate it but this summer taught me a lesson I hope I'll never forget."[69]

Once more Susan threw all her energies into helping both Indians and whites. She became one of the organizers of the Thurston County Medical Association, served several times on the health board of the town of Walthill, and became a member of the State Medical Society. As chairman of the State Health Committee of the Nebraska Federation of Women's Clubs for three years, she became involved politically in the effort to get health-related bills through the Nebraska legislature. She also took the lead in bringing about several specific health reforms, such as the campaigns against tuberculosis, the house fly, and the common drinking cup. She also was instrumental in getting a hospital built in Walthill.[70] Her most determined health-related reform was her crusade against "demon rum."

Susan apparently acquired her prohibitionist tendencies from her father, who as a young man had witnessed the senseless murder of an innocent Indian by a drunken Indian. He vowed, when he assumed a position of authority, to break the drinking habits of the Omahas.[71] In 1856, three years after he assumed the position of chief, he organized a police force which administered corporal punishment to any member of the tribe found drunk. Until his death in 1888 very little liquor was to be found on the reservation.[72] In the year before his death, the Omahas became citizens as a result of the General Allotment or Dawes Act and were therefore eligible to vote. Joseph cast his first ballot in January 1887, proudly leading a company of his people to the polls.[73] To Susan, however, voting and citizenship marked the beginning of alcohol abuse on the reservation. Local politicians with whiskey to dispense came to solicit the Omahas' vote, explaining to them that since they had the same rights as white men they could drink all they wanted.[74]

Susan's prohibitionist feelings had been reinforced in college by lectures from leading temperance crusaders, such as Harriet Whitehall Smith and Francis Willard.[75] In 1891, she also became a temperance speaker, lecturing on "the spread of intemperance among her people."[76]

During her four years as government physician, Susan was able to work night and day among her people in perfect safety. But soon the influx of liquor on the reservation changed that, and within two decades the church stood empty and farms were abandoned or neglected. The Omahas, described by Susan as "a fine specimen of manhood," had degenerated physically because of the excessive use of alcohol. "The Indian child . . . is a weak puny specimen of humanity,"[77] continued Susan, and therefore an easy prey to tuberculosis.

Susan recounted horror stories of numerous street brawls resulting in deaths, while women pawned their clothing and men spent their rent money to obtain liquor, causing entire families to suffer as a consequence. Even "little children were seen reeling on the streets of the town,"[78] she wrote. In her 1893 report as medical missionary, she pointed out that whiskey was as plentiful as water. "If a drunken Indian smashes a buggy and assaults a woman and child by beating them and nothing is done," she asked, "what can prevent him from doing it again?"[79] There was a saloon on the reservation that the Indians said was "like a fountain, and the liquor wells from it as if from a spring."[80] She recounted some bizarre deaths caused by liquor. In 1894, for example, "Harry Edwards fell from a buggy, was not missed by his drunken companions and in the morning was found frozen to death."[81] In the same year, another Omaha was dragged to death by a runaway horse because he was too drunk to save himself. Some died from exposure and pneumonia, while others committed murder and were sent to the penitentiary. Then, in the late 1890s, Congress passed the Meiklejohn law, sponsored by George Meiklejohn, which prohibited the sale of liquor to Indians. For several years the situation was reversed because a commissioner was assigned to implement the law. By 1900, after the official had been removed to save money, the alcoholic rate was again on the increase. In January, Susan implored the Bureau of Indian Affairs to replace the liquor commissioner. "Of what use will be the money saved from the abolishment of the Commissioner if our people are to be demoralized, mentally, morally and physically?" she asked.[82]

Francis, in a letter to Susan's nephew, agreed that since the Omahas could get liquor easily, they were working less. "The illicit traffic of liquor among the Indians and the indiscriminate leasing of their lands have done them more harm than anything that happened to them in their history," he wrote. "Even now we hear of some desperate deed committed through their drunkenness."[83]

In 1902 a law was passed that allowed the Omahas to sell their heirship land. Susan noted that one Indian had sold his entire holdings in 1904 for only six thousand dollars and then invited his friends to a gathering, treated them all to liquor, distributed money to each one, and bought himself three buggies. The total proceeds from the sale of his land were spent within one year.[84]

A change for the better took place around 1906, according to Susan, partly because the Indians had become disgusted with themselves and partly because of agent John M. Commons. Commons held up their annuity monies and would not give them their rents from leasing their lands until they behaved. He also took a personal interest in them, visited their homes, and showed them how to plant small gardens. Even church attendance was on the rise.[85] "Mr. Commons," Susan wrote, "has been tireless and constant in his fight against bootlegging on this Reservation. . . . Very few agents or superintendents sent here have interested themselves enough to accomplish any thing in this way."[86]

In November 1906, Susan and Marguerite's second husband, Walter Diddock, bought house lots in the newly established town of Walthill, which had been carved out of Indian land by the railroad. Largely owing to Susan's urging, the Secretary of the Interior ruled that by a deed restriction no liquor could be sold in towns that had once been a part of the Omaha Reservation.[87] Agent Commons, in his 1907 report, noted that no liquor could be sold in Walthill, "and persons found drunk there are promptly dealt with in the proper manner. . . . I think there are indications of a better condition amongst these people."[88]

Through Susan's efforts a small improvement had been made in her tribe's abuse of liquor. Unfortunately, this small victory had not been achieved at home. After years of hard drinking, her husband Henry died in 1905, leaving her as the sole support of an invalid mother and two small boys. Following his death, the Presbyterian Board of Home Missions appointed her missionary to the Omaha tribe and provided her with housing as well as a small stipend.

One of Susan's most important political battles for her people was fought during one of her most serious illnesses. In the spring of 1909 she was close to death from a severe case of neurasthenia.[89] A trained nurse remained with her for almost six weeks, with specialists and the local doctor visiting her as often as three times a day.[90] By June her health was sufficiently improved to allow her to begin a series of communications with government officials. In the same month, she protested the transfer of Superintendent Commons.[91] Several days later, she protested to Commissioner R. G. Valentine that outside pressure had been exerted by certain liquor and land interests, whom she named, to get "Commons out of the way so they can do as they please with the Indians."[92]

It seems that certain men had organized a syndicate to buy land at the end of the trust period, and Susan felt that the presence of Agent Commons was necessary to protect her people from land fraud. "If you remove him," she wrote to Valentine, "you will take away a man whose wide knowledge and experience of white people and Indians and conditions here, together with faithful and conscientious service, has made him valuable to the Department and to the Omahas."[93] Unfortunately, Commons did not remain.

The land problems that Susan referred to were the result of the passage in 1882 of the Omaha Allotment Act. One of the nineteenth-century reformers' most cherished goals was allotment of land in severalty to American Indians. This was made possible by the passage in 1887 of the General Allotment Law, or the Dawes Act, which followed six years of debates in Congress.[94] Five years earlier Congress had passed the Omaha Allotment Act, for which Alice Cunningham Fletcher actively lobbied. Both the Omaha treaties of 1854 and 1865 provided for allotting 160 acres to each family and less to individuals. When Fletcher arrived at the Omaha Reservation in 1881, many of the people had little faith in the certificates issued under the 1865 treaty. She circulated a petition requesting "a clear and full title to the land" for each petitioner.[95] This petition, signed by only 53 of the 1,121 members, was presented to the United States Senate by John R. Morgan of Alabama. Fletcher succeeded in obtaining support of the Nebraska delegation because her proposal included a provision for the sale of part of the land in the uninhabited western end of the reservation. The Omaha Severalty Act became law on August 7, 1882, and Fletcher was appointed to carry out the allotment of land, a task that she continued until June 1884. Unanticipated problems later arose over the disposal of tribal funds, the legal rights of allottees (they were not yet citizens), and the leasing of lands—problems that Susan had to deal with.[96]

Under the 1882 Omaha Act individual holdings were only eighty acres. The unallotted land was sold. The government had, however, included a twenty-five year trust period during which time the allotted land was inalienable.[97] The last allotment papers had been delivered in 1885; thus, the trust period would end in 1910. The government arbitrarily extended the trust period for an additional ten years because it considered Indians, in general, to be uneducated and in need of protection. This was, of course, not true of the Omahas, who had a higher literacy rate than many tribes. Susan rose to the defense of her people, describing them as "independent and self-reliant . . . [and] as competent as the same number of white people."[98]

This decision to extend the trust period caused extreme hardship for the Omahas. To make matters worse, the government had consolidated the Winnebago and Omaha agencies, which meant longer travel for tribal members intent on carrying out agency business. Susan remarked that the two tribes were quite different and that the Interior Department would find it had made a "mistake if it thinks it can govern both tribes alike." She continued proudly, "You can never push an Omaha down or pass a thing over his head; he will light on his feet facing you."[99]

In addition to the consolidation of the agencies, the government replaced A. G. Pollock, the new Omaha superintendent. Susan observed that the Omahas were, for the first time in their history, unanimous on one thing—their desire to keep Pollock. "They have expressed their perfect confidence in him," she wrote; "they told him they had found the man they were looking for, and they wished him to lead them out of their troubles."[100]

Protests arose from whites and Indians alike over increased government regulations. "Every business action of the individual is supervised and hedged about with red tape and paternal restrictions," wrote the editor of the *Walthill Times*.[101] What the Omahas wanted was the right, like other citizens, to lease their lands and to draw upon their money. The tribe had a trust fund from reservation sales amounting to about 250 dollars for each member. Before a tribal member could get his money, however, he had to have two witnesses attest to his competence. About half of the tribe was able, in this manner, to get their money, but the others had to go before a competency commission. This took time and caused suffering. The sick often came to Susan to beg her to write letters for them about their money. "I have watched them die without it," she wrote in a newspaper article.[102] To Commissioner Valentine in July 1909, she complained about the rules and the resultant delays, and related a story of a woman suffering from tuberculosis. She requested her money, but six weeks passed while the agent and Indian Office corresponded, and in the meantime the poor woman died.[103] As Susan had predicted, the entire tribe rebelled and turned to her to free them from these strangling regulations.[104]

Susan was the unanimous choice to serve as one of the delegates to argue the case before the Secretary of the Interior and the United States Attorney General. She originally declined because of poor health, but people threatened to place her bodily on the train. "The Omahas depend on me so, and I just have to take care of myself till this fight is over," she wrote to a friend at Hampton.[105]

Despite weakness caused by neurasthenia, which prevented her from digesting her food, she appeared before the Secretary of the Interior on February 7, 1910.[106] She protested the red tape that made it difficult for her people to get their own money as well as the problems in traveling to the new combined agency. Because of Susan's expertise the delegation was successful, and most of the Omahas were subsequently considered competent to rent or lease their lands and to receive their monies.[107]

For the remainder of her life, despite the heavy demands of her medical practice and her declining health, she struggled against "demon rum." The degenerative ear disease which she had endured for years made her increasingly deaf, and the pain extended well down into her back. But she continued to serve as teacher, preacher, field worker, and physician at the agency's Blackbird Hills Presbyterian Church, where she held church services, read the Bible in the Omaha tongue, interpreted hymns, and held simple Christian burials over the dead.[108]

In 1914, a year before her death, she wrote Commissioner Cato Sells concerning the problem of liquor traffic among her people. Two weeks earlier an old man had been murdered. The accused, who later committed suicide, had been drinking "lemon extract," but nothing had been done about the crime.[109] Although probably not with as much vigor as she had tackled alcoholism, Susan began to study tuberculosis more closely, giving lectures at the Indian church as well as to the local townspeople. When Walthill observed National Tuberculosis Day, local doctors were invited to give lectures on the subject, and their talks were later published in the local paper.[110] While writing to Commissioner Sells, Susan suggested that children attending government schools be examined monthly for the disease. She told of an eighteen-year-old girl who had contracted the disease at boarding school and had infected both her mother and grandmother; all three had died.[111]

Since communicable diseases could easily be passed through the common drinking cup, Susan began a campaign to eradicate its use. Her article on the evils of the cup was published in the Walthill newspaper, and her health committee actively crusaded against its use and succeeded in obtaining state legislation to abolish it. Disposable cups were soon to be found in local stores, and sanitary drinking fountains were built in the schools. Soon, disposable ice cream dishes and spoons were also available at the local drugstore.[112]

Her campaign against the common house fly was unique. In designing a poster with flies all around its border engaging in various occupations such as eating the dead, emerging from a garbage can, playing in a consumptive's spittoon, and carrying typhoid, Susan hoped to convince her people that flies meant filth and filth meant disease. Calling flies "the most dangerous insects known to man," she informed the citizens about what flies did and then proceeded to show how to get rid of them. She encouraged the use of screens on doors and windows and the use of poisons, including chloride of lime, sprinkled over privy vaults and garbage boxes, and formaldehyde used in a shallow dish or on flypaper. Fly traps were soon being sold in local hardware stores. She also suggested to Commissioner Sells that lectures on flies be given at government Indian schools and that the children should conduct a fly campaign. Finally, she sent a copy of the poster to the commissioner.[113]

Susan's death on September 18, 1915, must have shattered the small community of Walthill, which had come to depend so heavily on her medical advice as well as on her counsel. On September 24, the *Walthill Times* added an extra page to carry her eulogies. On September 19, after a simple funeral service in her home, Susan was buried beside her husband in the Bancroft Cemetery. As one longtime friend wrote:

> Hardly an Omaha Indian is living who has not been treated and helped by her, and hundreds of white people and Indians owe their lives to her treatment, care and nursing. . . . We are confronted here with a character rising to greatness, and to great deeds out of conditions which seldom produce more than mediocre men and women, achieving great and beneficial ends over obstacles almost insurmountable.[114]

Susan's life spanned the decades of Indian reform that emphasized the forced assimilation of the Indians. Susan had benefited from some of these ideals and had been assimilated. She had, in turn, used her training and skills to help others. She became a reformer in her own right. She successfully fought alcoholism, secured her people's rights to their lands and money, and worked with missionaries to bring Christian principles to the reservation. She did not criticize the Omaha traditions, as many reformers did, but instead recalled numerous stories and legends, thereby preserving the traditions for generations.[115] Susan walked with dignity and grace in a world that encompassed the reservation and the city, and attained a position in the field of medicine which few contemporary white women reached. She was a remarkable nineteenth-century woman by any standards. The fact that she overcame certain handicaps of being born on a reservation makes her achievements all the more remarkable.

Notes

1. See Valerie Sherer Mathes, "Susan LaFlesche Picotte: Nebraska's Indian Physician, 1865–1915, *Nebraska History 63* (1982), pp. 502–30; Norma Kidd Green, "Four Sisters: Daughters of Joseph LaFlesche," *Nebraska History*, 45 (1964), pp. 165–76; Norma Kidd Green, *Iron Eye's Family: The Children of Joseph LaFlesche* (Lincoln, Nebr., 1969), pp. 122–62; and Laurence M. Hauptman, "Medicine Woman Susan LaFlesche, 1865–1915," *New York State Journal of Medicine* 78 (1978), pp. 1783–88.

2. *Documents of United States Indian Policy*, ed. Francis Paul Prucha (Lincoln, Nebr., 1975), p. 103; the complete report can be found on pp. 102–5. See also Francis Paul Prucha, *American Indian Policy in Crisis: Christian Reformers and the Indian 1865–1900* (Norman, Okla., 1976), pp. 12–16; Henry E. Fritz, *The Movement for Indian Assimilation 1860–1890* (Westport, Conn., 1981), pp. 29–33; and Robert Winston Mardock, *The Reformers and the American Indian* (Columbia, Mo., 1971), pp. 20–24.

3. For detailed information on the Peace Commission, see Prucha, *American Indian Policy in Crisis*, pp. 16–29; Fritz, *The Movement for Indian Assimilation*, pp. 62–71; and Mardock, *The Reformers and the American Indian*, pp. 25–46.

4. For a discussion of the Peace Policy, see Robert M. Utley, "The Celebrated Peace Policy of General Grant," *North Dakota History* 20 (1953), pp. 121–42; Prucha, *American Indian Policy in Crisis*, pp. 70–71; Fritz, *The Movement for Indian Assimilation*, pp. 72–86; Mardock, *The Reformers and the American Indian*, pp. 47–228; and Donald E. Worcester, "The Friends of the Indians and the Peace Policy," in *Forked Tongues and Broken Treaties*, ed. Donald E. Worcester (Caldwell, Idaho, 1975), pp. 254–91.

5. For a discussion of the Quaker Policy, see Clyde A. Milner, *With Good Intentions: Quaker Work among the Pawnees, Otos, and Omahas in the 1870s* (Lincoln, Nebr., 1982), pp. 1–26.

6. Ibid., pp. 15–16. For a complete discussion of the Omahas under the Quakers, see pp. 153–85.

7. There is some confusion over the date of Susan's birth. The tombstone at the Bancroft, Nebraska cemetery reads June 17, 1865, but according to a questionnaire she completed in November 1888, she was born in Oakland, Nebraska, in June 1866. Hampton Institute Archives, Hampton, Va.

8. Alice C. Fletcher and Francis LaFlesche, *The Omaha Tribe*, vol. 2 (Lincoln, Nebr., 1972), p. 634.

9. Ibid., p. 622. For a complete text of the 1854 treaty, see *Indian Treaties, 1788–1883*, ed. Charles J. Kappler (New York, 1972), pp. 611–14.

10. Milner, *With Good Intentions*, p. 169; Fletcher-LaFlesche, *The Omaha Tribe*, vol. 2, pp. 626–27.

11. Michael Christopher Coleman, "Presbyterian Missionaries and Their Attitudes to the American Indian, 1837–1893" (Ph.D. diss., University of Pennsylvania, 1977), p. 179.

12. Fletcher and LaFlesche, *The Omaha Tribe*, vol. 2, p. 633; Milner, *With Good Intentions*, p. 156. On his farming ability, see Alice C. Fletcher to Sara T. Kinney, January 21, 1887, Sara Thomson Kinney Collection, Connecticut State Library, Hartford.

13. Coleman, "Presbyterian Missionaries and Their Attitudes," p. 130.

14. *Annual Report of the Commissioner of Indian Affairs, 1892* (Washington, D.C., 1892), p. 101.

15. See Nancy F. Cott, *The Bonds of Womanhood: "Woman's Sphere" in New England, 1780–1835* (New Haven, Conn., 1977), pp. 61–71, 199–201. See also Barbara Leslie Epstein, *The Politics of Domesticity: Women, Evangelism, and Temperance in Nineteenth Century America* (Middletown, Conn., 1981); and Barbara Welter, *Dimity Convictions: The American Woman in the Nineteenth Century* (Athens, Ohio, 1976), pp. 21–41.

16. Barbara J. Berg, *The Remembered Gate: Origins of American Feminism—The Woman and the City, 1800–1860* (New York, 1978), pp. 66–67.

17. Kathryn Kisk Sklar, *Catharine Beecher: A Study in American Domesticity* (New Haven, Conn., 1973), p. 137.

18. *Lend-A-Hand* (1886), See also *Southern Workman* (July, 1886), p. 83. Hampton Institute Archives.

19. *Southern Workman* (July, 1886), p. 82.

20. Douglas Street, "LaFlesche Sisters Write to *St. Nicolas Magazine*," *Nebraska History* 62 (1981), p. 522. Susan's letter on her academic training is published here in full. In 1869, when Quaker agents arrived, the Presbyterian boarding school was closed for ten years while agents experimented with day schools. In

1879, the Quaker Day School closed and the Presbyterians reopened their boarding school.

21. Reformers often saw education as a crucial tool of assimilation, and many believed that boarding schools off the reservation would be more profitable since students were totally removed from home environments—thus making it easier to obliterate their cultural heritage. For a discussion on Indian education, see Francis Paul Prucha, ed., *Americanizing the American Indians* (Cambridge, Mass., 1973), pp. 191–292. See also Wilbert H. Ahern, "Assimilationist Racism: The Case of the Friends of the Indian," *The Journal of Ethnic Studies* 4 (1976), pp. 24–28.

22. Questionnaire, November 18, 1888, Hampton Institute Archives.

23. For information on Hampton, see *The Hampton Normal and Agricultural Institute and Its Work for the Education of the Indian* (ca. 1892–1893), Hampton Institute Archives; and Mary Frances Armstrong and Helen W. Ludlow, *Hampton and Its Students* (New York, 1874).

24. For a discussion of Indian girls' education, see Robert Trennert, "Educating Indian Girls at Nonreservation Boarding Schools, 1878–1920," *The Western Historical Quarterly* 13 (1982), pp. 271–90; see also Green, *Iron Eye's Family*, p. 126, and Hauptman, "Medicine Woman," p. 1784.

25. Susan LaFlesche to Miss Richards, August 7, 1885, Hampton Institute Archives.

26. Samuel Armstrong to the Commissioner of Indian Affairs (hereafter cited as CIA), August 20, 1886, Records of the Bureau of Indian Affairs, Record Group 75, Letters Received from Susan LaFlesche, 1886–1893, File 22530, National Archives, Washington, D.C. (hereafter cited as RG 75, BIA, NA).

27. Armstrong's letter dated June 1886, to Mrs. Kinney, was enclosed with her letter to CIA, September 6, 1886, RG 75, BIA, File 23847, NA.

28. Alice C. Fletcher to Rosalie Farley, May 21, 1886, LaFlesche Family Papers, Nebraska State Historical Society, Lincoln (hereafter cited as LFP, NSHS). See also Mathes, "Susan LaFlesche Picotte," p. 504.

29. For a detailed study of Fletcher's Indian work, see Rebecca Hancock Welch, "Alice Cunningham Fletcher, Anthropologist and Indian Rights Reformer" (Ph.D. diss., George Washington University, 1980); Frederick E. Hoxie, "Beyond Savagery: The Campaign to Assimilate the American Indians, 1880–1920" (Ph.D. diss., Brandeis University, 1977), pp. 83–89; and Amelia Stone Quinton, "Care of the Indian," in *Woman's Work in America*, ed. Annie Nathan Meyer (New York, 1891), pp. 375–77. For a detailed discussion of the Lake Mohonk Conference, see Larry E. Burgess, "The Lake Mohonk Conference on the Indian 1883–1916" (Ph.D. diss., Claremont Graduate School, 1972), pp. 32–39.

30. Trennert, "Educating Indian Girls," p. 289.

31. Alfred Jones to Martha Waldron, March 26, 1886, Fletcher-LaFlesche MSS, National Anthropological Archives, Smithsonian Institution, Washington, D.C. (xerox copy supplied by the Archives and Special Collections on Women in Medicine, The Medical College of Pennsylvania and Hospital, Philadelphia). See also Mathes, "Susan LaFlesche Picotte," p. 505.

32. Francis LaFlesche to Ed Farley, September 27, 1886, LFP, NSHS. See also Sara T. Kinney to CIA, September 16, 1886, RG 75, BIA, File 24837, NA.

33. Sara T. Kinney to Ed Farley, October 10, 1886 and Alice C. Fletcher to Rosalie Farley, May 2, 1886, LFP, NSHS; *Lend-A-Hand* (1886), Hampton Institute Archives; Sara T. Kinney to Miss Richards, May 14, 1886, Hampton Institute Archives; and Sara T. Kinney to CIA, September 6, 1886, RG 75, BIA, File 23847, NA.

34. For a detailed discussion of the Women's National Indian Association, see Helen M. Wanken, "Women's Sphere and Indian Reform: The Women's National Indian Association, 1879–1901" (Ph.D. diss., Marquette University, 1981), pp. 65–70.

35. Ellen Terry Johnson, *Historical Sketch of the Connecticut Indian Association, from 1881 to 1888* (Hartford, Conn., 1888), p. 3.

36. Sara T. Kinney to CIA, September 6, 1886, RG 75, BIA, File 23847, NA. On September 10, the Connecticut Indian Association contracted with the government for Susan's support. See Sara T. Kinney to CIA, September 10, 1886, RG 75, BIA, File 24280, NA. On September 15, 1886, the government agreed to pay $167 per year if the Connecticut Indian Association agreed to "clothe, feed, lodge, and care for, and educate . . . from October 1, 1886 to June 30, 1887 . . . Susan LaFlesche." Four vouchers for $41.75 were issued in 1886–1887. On July 1, 1887, the agreement was again entered into; however, the amount was reduced to $125 per year; finally, on October 10, 1888, a third agreement was entered into again for $125. Vouchers for the last two years were issued. These agreements and vouchers are in the Sara Thomson Kinney Collection, Connecticut State Library. See also Johnson, *Historical Sketch*, pp. 13, 23; and Mathes, "Susan LaFlesche Picotte," pp. 505–6, 511.

37. A copy of the pamphlet was enclosed with Mrs. Kinney's letter to CIA. Sara T. Kinney to CIA, September 6, 1886, RG 75, BIA, File 23847, NA.

38. *Lend-A-Hand* (1886), Hampton Institute Archives.

39. Sara T. Kinney to Rosalie Farley, n.d., LFP, NSHS. Johnson, *Historical Sketch*, p. 13.

40. LaFlesche to Farley, December 1, 1886; April 4, 1887; January 4, 1888; November 17, 1886; January 19, 1887, LPF, NSHS.

41. LaFlesche to Farley, March 9, 1887; January 12, and February 12, 1887; January 19 and 26, 1887; and October 24, 1886, LFP, NSHS.

42. LaFlesche to Farley, October 29, 1886, November 17, 1886; February 2, 1887; probably January 1–4, 1888; and March 2, 1887, LFP, NSHS.

43. Kinney to CIA, June 29, 1887, RG 75, BIA, File 16996, NA.

44. LaFlesche to Farley, January 12, 1887, LFP, NSHS.

45. Kinney to CIA, June 29, 1887, RG 75, BIA, File 16996, NA. *Thirty-Eighth Annual Announcement of the Woman's Medical College of Pennsylvania* (Philadelphia, 1887), p. 5.

46. LaFlesche to Farley, November 5, 1886, LFP, NSHS.

47. LaFlesche to Farley, November 17, 1886, LFP, NSHS.

48. LaFlesche to Farley, March 2, 1887, and March 9, 1887, LFP, NSHS.

49. LaFlesche to Kinney, April 2, 1888, Sara Thomson Kinney Collection, Connecticut State Library.

50. LaFlesche to Farley, October 24, 1886, LFP, NSHS; Mathes, "Susan LaFlesche Picotte," pp. 517–18.

51. LaFlesche to Farley, March 2, 1887, LFP, NSHS.

52. LaFlesche to Kinney, November 19, 1888, Sara Thomson Kinney Collection, Connecticut State Library.

53. Ibid.

54. *Fortieth Annual Announcement of the Women's Medical College of Pennsylvania* (Philadelphia, 1889), p. 1; Susan LaFlesche Picotte Alumna File, Medical College of Pennsylvania.

55. "The First Woman Physician Among her People," *The Medical Missionary Record* 4 (1889), p. 126, Medical College of Pennsylvania.

56. LaFlesche to CIA, n.d., RG 75, BIA, File 15736, NA.

57. Wanken, "Women's Sphere," p. 71.

58. LaFlesche to CIA, June 13, 1889, RG 75, BIA, File 15736, NA.

59. LaFlesche to CIA, August 5, 1889, RG 75, BIA, File 21752, NA.

60. Robert H. Ashley to CIA, December 10, 1889, RG 75, BIA, File 35955, NA.

61. Reports Changes in School Employees, RG 75, BIA, File 40940, NA; *Talks and Thoughts* (December 1893), Hampton Institute Archives. Susan LaFlesche, "Report of Physician for Omahas," *Annual Report of the Commissioner of Indian Affairs, 1893*, (Washington, D.C., 1893), p. 197. *Southern Workman* (February 1894). Theodore Finks, ed., "The First Indian Woman Physician," *Home Mission Monthly* 38, 4 (February 1924), pp. 86–87. "The First Indian Woman Physician," *Bulletin of Council of Women for Home Missions* (adapted from *Home Mission Monthly* (1932), p. 447.

62. "Present Medical and Hospital Work: Sketches of Delightful Work," The Women's National Indian Association (January 1893), pp. 46–47, Hampton Institute Archives. For a detailed discussion of her medical activity see Susan LaFlesche, "My Work as Physician Among my People," *Southern Workman* (August 1892), Hampton Institute Archives. "Report of Susan LaFlesche, M.D. Medical Missionary of the Women's National Indian Association among the Omaha Indians," Women's National Indian Association (October 24, 1891), pp. 4–8, in Sophia Smith Collection, Smith College, Northampton, Mass.

63. Mathes, "Susan LaFlesche Picotte," p. 512.

64. LaFlesche to Farley, ca. 1887, LFP, NSHS.

65. Farley to Francis LaFlesche, January 1, 1893, LFP, NSHS.

66. This probably was osteomyelitis, an infection of the bone which occurs much less frequently today because of the use of antibiotics.

67. *Southern Workman* (August 1894), Hampton Institute Archives.

68. Farley to Francis LaFlesche, July 29, 1895, LFP, NSHS.

69. LaFlesche to Miss Richards, December 9, 1897, Hampton Institute Archives.

70. Mathes, "Susan LaFlesche Picotte," pp. 524–25. With donations from the Home Mission Board of the Presbyterian church and the Society of Friends, as well as other donations, a hospital was built and opened in January 1913. See also "Pioneer Medical Woman: Dr. Susan LaFlesche Picotte," *Medical Woman's Journal* 37 (1930), p. 20.

71. Fletcher and LaFlesche, *Omaha Tribe,* vol. 2, pp. 618–19.

72. "Testimony of Susan LaFlesche Picotte, investigating the death of Henry Wagner," May 22, 1914, LFP, NSHS.

73. Fletcher to Kinney, January 21, 1887, Sara Thomson Kinney Collection, Connecticut State Library.

74. Susan LaFlesche Picotte, "The Varied Work of an Indian Missionary," *Home Mission Monthly* 22 (1908), n.p. (courtesy of the Presbyterian Historical Society, Philadelphia). See also "Testimony of Susan LaFlesche Picotte, investigating the death of Henry Wagner," May 22, 1914, LFP, NSHS.

75. LaFlesche to Farley, January 19, 1887, LFP, NSHS.

76. *Annual Report of the Women's National Indian Association,* (December 1892), p. 21.

77. "Testimony of Susan LaFlesche Picotte, investigating the death of Henry Wagner," May 22, 1914, LFP, NSHS.

78. LaFlesche to CIA, January 27, 1900, Hampton Institute Archives.

79. *Talks and Thoughts* (July 1893), Hampton Institute Archives.

80. Ibid.

81. "Testimony of Susan LaFlesche Picotte, investigating the death of Henry Wagner," May 22, 1914, LFP, NSHS.

82. LaFlesche to CIA, January 27, 1900, Hampton Institute Archives. See also "Another Appeal," *The Indian's Friend* (Philadelphia, March 1900), p. 8.

83. Francis LaFlesche to Caryl Farley, February 3, 1901, LFP, NSHS.

84. "Testimony of Susan LaFlesche Picotte, investigating the death of Henry Wagner," May 22, 1914, LFP, NSHS.

85. Ibid.

86. LaFlesche to CIA, July 2, 1909, Hampton Institute Archives.

87. Ibid.

88. John M. Comons, "Report of Superintendent in Charge of Omaha Agency, August 7, 1907," *Annual Report of the Commissioner of Indian Affairs, 1907* (Washington, D.C., 1907), pp. 1–2.

89. A functional nervous disorder first named and described in 1869, it was regarded primarily as a woman's disease. Lower-class women suffering from the symptoms were often diagnosed as insane and institutionalized. However, the typical neurasthenic was a woman of good standing in society—"just the kind of woman one likes to meet with—sensible, not over sensitive or emotional, exhibiting a proper amount of illness. . . . and a willingness to perform their share of work quietly and to the best of their ability." Lorna Duffin, "The Conspicuous Consumptive: Woman as an Invalid," *The Nineteenth Century Woman: Her Cultural and Physical World,* ed. Sara DeLamont and Lorna Duffin (New York, 1978), pp. 37–39.

90. LaFlesche to Clara M. Folsom, February 15, 1910; and LaFlesche to Miss Andrus, June 24, 1909, both in Hampton Institute Archives.

91. Telegram, LaFlesche to Robert C. Ogden, June 27, 1909, Hampton Institute Archives.

92. LaFlesche to CIA, July 2, 1909, Hampton Institute Archives.

93. LaFlesche to CIA, July 13, 1909, Hampton Institute Archives.

94. For a discussion of various reformers' views on allotment, see Prucha, *Americanizing the American Indian,* pp. 7–145; see also Wilcomb E. Washburn, *The Assault on Indian Tribalism: The General Allotment Law (Dawes Act) of 1887* (Philadelphia, 1975); D. S. Otis, *The Dawes Act and the Allotment of Indian Lands,* ed. Francis Paul Prucha (Norman, Okla., 1973); and Hoxie, "Beyond Savagery," pp. 188–205.

95. Text of the petition can be found in Fletcher and LaFlesche, *The Omaha Tribe,* vol. 2, p. 636. Welch, "Alice Cunningham Fletcher," pp. 51–63; Hoxie, "Beyond Savagery," pp. 85–86.

96. Hoxie, "Beyond Savagery," pp. 85–89.

97. Milner, *With Good Intentions*, pp. 183–84.

98. Susan LaFlesche Picotte, "Dr. Picotte Discusses the New Policy," *Walthill Times*, December 28, 1909 (written originally for the *Omaha Bee*).

99. Ibid.

100. Ibid.

101. Green, *Iron Eye's Family*, pp. 155–57.

102. LaFlesche Picotte, "Dr. Picotte Discusses the New Policy."

103. LaFlesche to CIA, July 13, 1909, Hampton Institute Archives.

104. LaFlesche to Clara M. Folsom, February 15, 1910, Hampton Institute Archives.

105. Ibid., and postcard stamped January 27, 1910.

106. Ibid.

107. Green, *Iron Eye's Family*, p. 157.

108. Susan LaFlesche Picotte, "The Varied Work of an Indian Missionary," *Home Mission Monthly* 22 (1908). *New Era* (November 1908); *Indian Leader* (January 22, 1909); *Southern Workman* (February 1909), *Arrow* (September 24, 1909), all in Hampton Institute Archives.

109. LaFlesche to CIA, April 29, 1914, LFP, NSHS.

110. Susan LaFlesche Picotte, Chairman, "Report of the Health Committee of the State Federation of Women's Clubs," ca. 1913–1914, LFP, NSHS.

111. LaFlesche to CIA, April 29, 1914, LFP, NSHS.

112. Susan LaFlesche Picotte, Chairman, "Report of the Health Committee of the State Federation of Women's Clubs," ca. 1913–1914, LFP, NSHS.

113. "War Declared on the Fly: From Breeding Place to Feeding Place," poster; Susan LaFlesche Picotte, Chairman, "Report of the Health Committee of the State Federation of Women's Clubs," ca. 1913–1914; and LaFlesche to CIA, April 29, 1914, LFP, NSHS.

114. Harry L. Keefe, "The Mystery of Her Genius," *Walthill Times*, September 24, 1915.

115. Susan LaFlesche Picotte, "Primitive Farming Among the Omaha Indians"; "A Fish Story (A Winnebago Legend)"; "The Dance of the Turkey"; "How Wahunthinshiga Won the Races"; "How the Silver Fox Taught the Coyote to Fish"; "When and How Fire came to be First Used"; and "Folk Lore Tales of the American Indians," et al., found in LPF, NSHS. See also "The Origin of the Corn: Dr. Susan LaFlesche Picotte Relates Some Interesting Legends," *Walthill Times*, March 8, 1912; "The Home Life of the Indian," *The Indian's Friend* (Philadelphia, June 1892), p. 39.

Essay on Sources

Few scholars of Indian history have yet discovered the delightful history of Susan LaFlesche Picotte; therefore no book-length biography has been written. A chapter devoted to a brief description of her life can be found in Norma Kidd Green's *Iron Eye's Family: The Children of Joseph LaFlesche* (Lincoln, Nebr., 1969). However, several scholarly articles have been written about her: Norma Kidd Green, "Four Sisters: Daughters of Joseph LaFlesche," *Nebraska History* 45 (1964); Laurence M. Hauptman, "Medicine Woman Susan LaFlesche, 1865–1915," *New York State Journal of Medicine* 78 (1978); and Valerie Sherer Mathes, "Susan LaFlesche Picotte: Nebraska's Indian Physician, 1865–1915," *Nebraska History* 63 (1982).

Serious scholars interested in Susan must consult these three manuscript collections: LaFlesche Family Papers, Nebraska State Historical Society, Lincoln; Letters Received from Susan LaFlesche, 1886–1893, RG 75, Bureau of Indian Affairs, located in the National Archives and Records Service, Washington, D.C.; and the Collis P. Huntington Memorial Library Archives, Hampton Institute, Hampton, Virginia. For materials on Susan's connection with the Connecticut Indian Association, the reader may consult the Sara Thomson Kinney Collection, Connecticut State Library, Hartford. Minor additional letters can be found in the Presbyterian Historical Society and the Archives and Special Collections on Women in Medicine, the Medical College of Pennsylvania and Hospital, both located in Philadelphia. Finally, because of her appointment as medical missionary to the Women's National Indian Association, some of Susan's reports were published in the organization's monthly periodical, *The Indian's Friend*, and in their annual reports and promotional leaflets.

4

Henry Chee Dodge

From the Long Walk to Self-Determination

David M. Brugge

The lifetime of Chee Dodge (1857–1947) spanned the years of war, exile, repatriation, and the emergence of tribal government among the Navajos; years when Navajo society was transformed from semi-sedentary bands and local family groups into the largest tribe living on the largest reservation in the United States.

From their arrival in the Southwest sometime after A.D. *1300, Navajos, the People or* Diné, *have responded and adapted to a variety of influences, incorporating agriculture and artistic techniques, certain religious beliefs, and a matrilineal clan system from the Pueblo cultures. After the arrival of Europeans on the far northern frontier of New Spain in the late sixteenth century, the Navajos thrived as horsemen and later as herders of sheep. They also earned a reputation as warriors. In time, peace reigned between Navajos and Spaniards, only to lapse as Hispanic New Mexicans attempted to encroach upon Navajo country. The Mexican period, 1821–1846, continued the process of alternating war and peace. But it was the arrival of the "New Men," as the Navajos called the Anglo-Americans, at the time of the Mexican-American war, that caused the greatest changes in the life of the* Diné.

Anglo-Americans initially followed much the same tradition in dealing with the Navajos as the Spaniards and Mexicans, and with much the same result.

Eventually, military forts were built in Navajo country and soldiers were sent to bring the People to heel because of their frequent raiding of New Mexican settlements. American peacemakers had erred, as had their predecessors, in their belief that there existed a responsible, centralized authority that could speak for the tribe like a king or an emperor. War and peace headmen with whom the Anglo-Americans negotiated possessed no coercive power, nor could they speak individually or collectively for the Navajos until a consensus had been achieved throughout the tribe. Treaties were further weakened by the linguistic barrier that existed between the Diné *and the New Men. No Navajo in the mid-nineteenth century could speak English; no Anglo-American could speak Navajo. Negotiations were conducted in three languages, as each phrase was translated from English to Spanish to Navajo and back again. Inevitably, misunderstandings ripened into open conflict.*

The outbreak of the American Civil War only delayed the military campaign to chastise the Navajos. In September 1862, Brig. Gen. James H. Carleton became military commander in New Mexico. Carleton determined to remove the Navajos. He decided that the Navajos and the Mescalero Apaches were to be settled on the Bosque Redondo in eastern New Mexico. Col. Christopher "Kit" Carson led the campaign against the tribes. Carson and his troops marched throughout Navajo country and laid waste the settlements over a wide area. The military campaign and a particularly harsh winter combined to devastate the tribe.

In December 1864, 8,354 Navajos were settled around Fort Sumner at the Bosque Redondo. There followed almost four years of disease, starvation, and death. It was not until June 1868, with the government realizing that Carleton's program of forced assimilation had proved to be a disaster, that a new treaty was signed between the Navajos and federal peace commissioners. By the terms of the treaty the Navajos accepted a reservation of 3.5 million acres—an area considerably smaller than their original homeland. The Long Walk and the years of exile are still remembered with bitterness in the oral traditions of the tribe.

Chee Dodge survived the Bosque Redondo. On the 1868 treaty reservation he grew to adulthood. Dodge, of mixed parentage, became the first Navajo speaker of English, the first tribal interpreter, and, more than a half-century later, the first chairman of the Navajo tribal council. He was present at the creation of the Navajo Nation.

Henry Chee Dodge, better known as Chee Dodge and remembered in Navajo by variants of the name *Hastiin Adiits'a'ii*—"Man who Interprets" or more literally, "Man who Understands (Languages)"—was born to a Navajo mother of the *Ma'iideshgizhnii* or Coyote Pass Clan. The identity of his father and the date of his birth are less well established. Most sources indicate that his father was a captive of Spanish or Mexican descent named Juan Cocinas, Aneas, or Cosinisas.[1] There is documentary evidence that strongly suggests that his father was actually Henry L. Dodge, Navajo agent from 1853 until his death in November 1856. Should this be true, Henry C. Dodge could not have been born any later than 1857. Augustus C. Dodge, a brother of the late Navajo agent, wrote in 1875 that he had learned that he had a nephew then eighteen years old living at Fort Defiance, who was the son of a Navajo woman and of his brother. It was reported that the youth was fluent in English, Spanish and Navajo—a description that would fit few people living at that time better than Henry C. Dodge. Dodge himself, in an affidavit sworn to in 1888, claimed to be the son of a Navajo woman and a white army officer, to have been born at Fort Defiance, and to be about thirty years of age.[2]

As further support of this evidence, it can be asserted that the photographs which exist of Dodge show a man who appears more probably of northern European ancestry than of Mediterranean background. It is necessary to point out, however, that European physical characteristics do not closely coincide with national boundaries. Unfortunately, there apparently are no pictures extant of either of the two men who have been suggested to be his biological father.

Navajo tradition does indicate that as a boy during the Carson campaign of 1863–64 Dodge was separated from his relatives following the presumed death of his mother at the hands of the Hopis. Juan Cocinas, his father or stepfather, had been killed when Dodge was only a year old. Dodge was passed from one family to another, perhaps a victim of his obvious half-white origin, until he was finally adopted by an old man and his granddaughter. If he were six or seven years old at this time, rather than merely four as has been asserted, he would have been old enough to have contributed in small ways to the work that this remnant of a family needed in order to survive. He accompanied them on the Long Walk to exile at Fort Sumner on the Pecos River, and four years later he was with them as they and the other Navajos held at the fort were allowed to return to their homes.[3]

Back at Fort Defiance he was reunited with his aunt who was married to a white man, Perry H. Williams, who worked as a trader or as a clerk at the agency, perhaps both at different times.

Regardless of the actual identity of his father, it was Agent W. F. M. Arny's belief that he was a son of Henry L. Dodge, and this belief made it possible for him to attend school. During this period, he lived with Arny's family and attended the Fort Defiance Indian School where he learned to read and write. Arny also assigned him to learn weaving, anticipating that he would replace the weaving instructor when she left.[4] In actuality, he was first appointed agency interpreter under Arny.[5] Although Dodge received only a few months of formal schooling, he learned quickly and seemed to have had a natural aptitude for languages. This skill brought him employment, first with his aunt's husband in the store and agency, later with freighters transporting goods to the fort from Santa Fe, and still later with the army at Fort Wingate where he worked for Dr. Washington Matthews, the pioneer ethnographer of the Navajos.[6]

As official interpreter for the Navajo Agency at Fort Defiance, Dodge became involved in some of the more dramatic and important events in Navajo affairs of the period. His linguistic ability, natural intelligence, and courage brought him rapid advancement. In 1882, he accompanied the agency farmer on a mission to contact the headman Hoskeninni *(Hashkeneini)* of the Monument Valley area and to investigate the killing of two white prospectors in that region. In 1883, he was at the side of Agent Dennis Riordan on a daring trip up Canyon de Chelly to arrest a man named Klah *(Tł'aai,* "Left-handed") who was accused of killing Peter Tracy, an Anglo settler on the San Juan River. Riordan's high praise of Dodge, in a situation that an army detachment had refused to enter, helped to establish his reputation. When a Navajo police force was organized the following year, Dodge was placed in charge, and this was perhaps the appointment that led to his replacement of Manuelito as "head chief."[7]

In 1884, two more white prospectors were killed in the far northwestern part of Navajo country. Dodge served as the agency interpreter for the investigation of the case. In May, he translated a lengthy report by Pete, a Navajo scout who made the initial inquiries. In July, Dodge served as interpreter for Agent John Bowman in the questioning of "Tug-yazzie"

(Dagha Yazhi, "Little Mustache"). In the following month, he was sent with troops from Fort Wingate on an unsuccessful march to attempt the arrest of Hoskeninni's son.[8]

He also had more pleasant assignments. In the same year, he accompanied a delegation of Navajos on a trip to Washington, D.C.[9]

These events, unfortunately, tell us little about him as a person. Obviously, while still a young man he had the opportunity to know and learn from the tribe's leaders in a way provided to no other person of his generation. He also was able to observe from the vantage point of an insider all the details of intercultural interaction on the highest levels. He undoubtedly had identity problems. It can be assumed that most whites viewed him as a "half-breed" and that his acceptance in Anglo society was limited in many ways. It is probable that many Navajos had reservations about his reliability; but as a very skilled interpreter he was in a position of such potential power that few would want to offend him. An event in 1888 presented a chance for him to demonstrate his loyalty to his mother's people.

As a result of Hopi complaints against the Navajos, Col. E. A. Carr, commanding officer at Fort Wingate, was ordered to send troops to remove the Navajos from the region around the Hopi villages to the Navajo Reservation. Dodge served as Carr's interpreter, and he advised Carr that removal of these Navajos from their homes so late in the season (mid-November) would cause great suffering, and that he did not believe that the Hopis actually wanted their Navajo neighbors evicted from their homes. As a result of Dodge's efforts, the army merely required that a few families who had taken over springs close to the Hopi villages move to other locations.[10]

It seems highly likely that the conflicts which arose from his work as interpreter increased with time. He had been saving much of his salary and by 1890 was able to invest in a partnership with Stephen H. Aldrich in a trading post at Round Rock in the Chinle Valley. Aldrich had other business interests, and Dodge took the job as manager of the new store with Charles Hubbell, brother of the famous John Lorenzo Hubbell who traded at Ganado, as his clerk.[11]

It was about this same time that Dodge married his first wife, *Asdzą́ą́' Tsi'naajinii,* and began to develop a farm near Crystal. He also invested some of his money in livestock, some of which he bought at Cuba, New Mexico.[12]

Dodge either continued as a government employee or developed sufficient confidence in Charles Hubbell's ability that by 1892 he was once again working for the agency. Whatever the case, he was acting as a federal worker when he assisted Agent Dana L. Shipley in that year by obtaining the promises of several parents in the Round Rock area to send children to the government school at Fort Defiance. In October, he accompanied Shipley and several other agency employees on a trip to the northern part of the reservation to collect the children. The small group split into three parties. Dodge and Shipley, along with three agency policemen, one of whom was a brother-in-law of Dodge, went to Round Rock, while others went variously to Canyon de Chelly and the Carrizo Mountains. A prominent leader in the Carrizo region, Black Horse, concerned because of reports of mistreatment of students at the Fort Defiance School, gathered a number of followers and proceeded to Round Rock to confront the agent. They found him in the trading post, and after some arguing, they grabbed him, dragged him from the building, and beat him severely. Dodge and Hubbell led the three policemen, and they were able to rescue Shipley. They brought him back into the post and barricaded the doors and windows. A messenger, Dodge's brother-in-law, was then sent to obtain the help of a detachment of troops that was nearby. He was given Dodge's horse because it was the fastest one available. With this horse he was able to outrun three of Black Horse's men and to return with the troops the next day. Dodge interpreted during a tense meeting between the military and the Black Horse faction. His skillful handling of this situation—including his adroit use of kinship terms, addressing Black Horse as "older brother," and providing food from his store to feed the crowd once an agreement had been reached—contributed significantly to the success of the army in arranging a truce and in escorting the agency personnel back to Fort Defiance without further violence.[13]

Dodge and Aldrich continued as partners at Round Rock, for the disturbance had not adversely affected their business. In December 1893, their license to trade there was renewed by Agent Edwin H. Plummer. In the following year, Dodge wanted to establish his own post at Fort

Defiance, but the plan did not work out. Through 1903, he and Aldrich continued as partners in the Round Rock store.[14]

The lack of frequent mention of Dodge in the agency records during the years from 1892 to 1905 suggests that he was primarily concerned with his own affairs: his business, his ranch, and his family. His first wife did not attend to family matters during Dodge's absences, and he finally learned that she was gambling away much of their wealth. He soon divorced her, apparently in the informal Navajo manner. Following this, he married the two daughters of his adoptive "big sister" from the days at Fort Sumner. While his ranching on the reservation and the fact that his first wife was Navajo had tended to emphasize his identity as Navajo rather than white, his marriage to plural wives confirmed this choice, regardless of whether this was his intention. For his new wives, however, he built a white man's style of home, designed by a German architect in Flagstaff. He was clearly able to make use of both cultural traditions in his decisions.[15]

Dodge's knowledge of the ways of the whites brought him prestige beyond what his wealth alone might have provided. He was beginning to be recognized as a headman. Navajos came to him for assistance in settling disputes, and whites also sought his aid. In 1898, he was among the men who helped the Franciscan fathers establish their mission at Saint Michaels.[16] During these years his family was growing. A son, Tom, was born in 1899 to his younger wife; and two years later, a second son, Ben, was born to the other wife, Nanabah. A daughter, Mary, was born in 1903.[17]

There is considerable confusion surrounding the identities of Dodge's wives and children. There are two entries for Dodge in the Saint Michaels Mission census, and these do not coincide. The most complete entry fills two cards and lists eight wives and six children; Tom, Ben, Antoinette, Annie, Josephine, and Veronica. This, by no means, is indicative of promiscuous behavior. Five of these women were members of the *Tse njikini* Clan, and four of them were actual sisters, with the other woman being at least a clan sister. One other woman, a member of the *Ta'neeszahnii* Clan, appears to be a cousin of the four sisters. Only his first wife and the mother of Josephine, the last-born child noted, have no obvious relationship to the others.[18] Rather than invoke the white man's standards, it is worth considering Dodge's marital career in terms of Navajo culture.

First, Dodge apparently actually married all of these women. There is no hint of illegitimacy in such data as exist. Second, and most significant, is the interrelationship of most of these wives. Dodge was not only a wealthy man by Navajo standards, but a dutiful son-in-law who was willing to include a wife's sisters, and perhaps even classificatory sisters, in his household. It is likely that most of these marriages were initiated by the family of the women rather than by Dodge.

In 1905, several Navajos at Chinle assaulted Agent Reuben Perry while he was attempting to arrest a man accused of rape. Shortly after Perry's return to Fort Defiance, a Nightway ceremony held near Saint Michaels was attended by a large number of Navajos. Navajo leaders from many places spoke to the crowd, and among them were Black Horse and Dodge, who both strongly supported the agent.[19] Dodge used the image of the horse to describe the Navajos' situation; like the horse, they also were ruled by alien authority. He then invoked a very real threat of further restrictions, should they not obey their master, the agent.[20] The horse as representative of conditions has long been a favorite motif in Navajo usage.[21] Use of powerful imagery and strong arguments were essential, for the coercive nature of Euroamerican authority was largely foreign to Navajo custom.[22] Dodge's skill in describing the workings of Anglo-American society in terms familiar to Navajos undoubtedly further enhanced his reputation among his mother's people. However, it should be noted that by this time he was no longer viewed by the agents in the Anglo role of trader; now he was cast in the Navajo role of headman or "chief."

Dodge's influence in the tribe grew rapidly during this period and spread far beyond his own community. In March 1907, when U.S. Indian Inspector James McLaughlin attempted to persuade the Shiprock Navajos that they should lease land for mineral development, they refused to act on the matter for two reasons: first, it was the wrong time of the year to make such decisions; and second, Besh-le-ki *(Beesh Łigaii,* "Silver"), Chee Dodge, Charley Mitchell, and Black Horse were not present. This would seem to indicate that Dodge was one of the four most prominent men in the tribe at that time. Following a great deal of pressure by McLaughlin and by William T. Shelton, the superintendent for the northern Navajo area, the people agreed to appoint an eleven-man committee to deal with the request. Dodge was to be a member of the committee. The final outcome, if any, of the committee's dealings is not known.[23]

His business endeavors continued to prosper. In 1911, his partnership with Aldrich at Round Rock was reported to have purchased 6,510 dollars worth of blankets and 582 dollars worth of silver jewelry.[24] Two years previously, his house at Crystal was described as "well furnished— but— too far beyond the means of most Navajos" to be a model of what they should do.[25] During the early years of this century, Dodge was also considered to be a Catholic by the Franciscan fathers, who assisted him with his paperwork and allowed him to maintain an apartment at the Saint Michaels Mission. He also sent his four children to Catholic schools. He had a reputation, however, for being a heavy drinker.[26] The strains of trying to adapt in one way or another to the expectations of two very different societies, one Native American and the other of European origin, were probably already strong.

There were still crises in Anglo-Navajo affairs that required the skills Dodge had employed since his youth. In the fall of 1913, one crisis occurred which must have brought with it questions that perturbed his most private thoughts.

In September, Shelton, the strong-willed superintendent at Shiprock, sent his police to arrest Little Singer *(Hataalii Yazhi)*, who was reported to have three wives. Little Singer was not at home, so the police arrested his wives and placed them in the Shiprock jail. When Little Singer returned home and found his wives missing, he went to Shiprock with his father *Bizhoshii* and nine companions; there, they overpowered one of the policemen and liberated the women from jail. *Bizhoshii* then led all of them to the top of Beautiful Mountain, where they defied Shelton's demand for their surrender. With Charley Mitchell, Black Horse, and Peshlakai *(Beesh Łigaii)*, Dodge participated in the lengthy negotiations that eventually involved not only Shelton but Superintendent Peter Paquette from Fort Defiance, the Franciscans at Saint Michaels, representatives from the Washington office of the Indian service, a United States marshal, and Gen. Hugh L. Scott with four troops of cavalry. Not until the end of November did the small band surrender; peacefully, it must be noted. None were sentenced to more than thirty days in jail, an outcome that Shelton accepted with poor grace.[27] That such a furor could result from a respected religious leader having more than one wife must have caused Dodge discomfiture over the white man's handling of Navajo culture and social differences.

Even so, Dodge's business interests continued to prosper. He was reported to be one of only five Navajos who owned an automobile in 1915. It was a Buick touring car, and he employed one of his sons as chauffeur to travel to meetings.[28]

Obviously, his identity as a Navajo was firmly established by this time. His involvement in tribal affairs was not at all superficial. Together with Charley Mitchell and "Old Man Silversmith" (probably *Beesh Łigaii),* he decided on the rules for the inheritance of medicine bundles when a singer died without bequeathing his religious property to another.[29] Such examples of internal tribal affairs are not well documented, however.

On the other hand, many of his activities as an intermediary between Navajos and whites are well known. He frequently wrote to governmental authorities to express his views. In 1918, for example, he wrote to Commissioner of Indian Affairs Cato Sells to urge consistency in the administration of the Navajo Reservation, suggesting that one man should be in charge.[30] Perhaps the conflicts between the five superintendents, such as the clash between Shelton and Paquette during the *Bizhoshii* incident, convinced Dodge that a more unified approach was needed.

A continuing problem in which he took an extended interest was the plight of the Navajos off the reservation. In 1915, both Dodge and Father Anselm Weber wrote to Washington to protest the apparent collusion between white ranchers and the Santa Fe land office in blocking approval of Navajo allotment applications. Early in 1917, Dodge led a delegation of eastern Navajos to Washington to present a petition asking for aid. The Secretary of the Interior ordered a report and the Commissioner of Indian Affairs recommended an expansion of the reservation, but the ranchers were more powerful politically. Again in 1920, following a visit by Etsitty Nez (*Atsidii Neez,* "Tall Smith"), a local leader in the eastern region, Dodge wrote two more letters to Commissioner Sells describing the problems of these Navajos and asking for an extension of the reservation boundaries. Superintendent Samuel F. Stacher at Crownpoint made efforts to trade lands in such a way as to create blocks under Navajo control. This naturally required that some Navajos relinquish their claims to lands, which were to be left then to the white ranchers. Dodge attempted to support the interests of all the Navajos, and soon he and Stacher were at odds over the issue. By the end of 1921 each man was writing intemperate words to or about the other.[31]

Dodge also became involved in another controversy. In 1920, he served as interpreter for a meeting between the Shiprock Navajos and oil companies wanting leases on the reservation. This led to charges that he had been bribed by the companies.[32] A more significant result of the oil leasing question, however, was the establishment in 1922 of a three-man council to do business on behalf of the tribe as a whole. The members of this first tribal council were Dodge, Charley Mitchell, and Dugal Chee Bekiss (*Daghaa' Łichii' Bik'is*, "Red Mustache's Brother"). This council signed three leases for a total of 4,800 acres, but all were canceled seven months later when the lessees failed to find oil.[33]

The chronic rivalry between the northern Navajos, with their agency at Shiprock, and the rest of the tribe, especially those in the south under the agency at Fort Defiance, was to be a major factor in tribal politics for the remainder of Dodge's career. Early in 1923, Superintendent Evan W. Estep, at Shiprock, was spreading rumors that Dodge had been bribed by subsidiaries of Standard Oil. Paquette defended Dodge's reputation, especially to the new special commissioner, Herbert J. Hagerman, whose primary duties related to dealing with the Navajos as a single, unified tribal entity. Estep was fired by the Commissioner of Indian Affairs, but Hagerman thought that he should be reinstated. After a series of conferences with Dodge, Hagerman believed that he had been able to persuade the Navajo headman of the value of simultaneously approving oil leases and avoiding disputes.[34]

In the meantime, the first elected tribal council was formed. It held its first meeting on July 7 at Toadlena and chose Dodge as chairman. A delegate from Shiprock, Jacob Morgan, quickly clashed with Dodge. Morgan was well educated, a Christian convert, and a strong supporter of assimilation. The immediate issue was the firing of Estep. A resolution was passed authorizing Hagerman to sign leases on behalf of the tribe but only after promises were made to get more land for the Navajos.[35]

While Dodge retained the conviction impressed on him as a youth that only the federal government was to be trusted in dealings with the whites, he was no mere pawn of officialdom. In 1925, he helped oppose a government effort to obtain an extension of an oil lease and led a campaign to obtain for the tribe a right to decide what should be done with the funds obtained from leases. He even suggested that federal unreasonableness in the boarding school program might be a deliberate attempt to goad the Navajos into violence so that the government might take over the handling of the oil business from the tribe.[36]

In 1926 it took a personal visit from Commissioner of Indian Affairs Charles H. Burke to convince Dodge that he should support leasing.[37] Dodge does not appear to have been opposed to leasing in principle so much as he was determined that the tribe should have a say in spending the lease money. His concern for the eastern Navajos, who lived off the reservation in New Mexico, was one of the factors involved in his thinking. During a visit to Washington in 1927, he recommended that some one million dollars be used to purchase land in New Mexico. At a council meeting later in the year, he and Morgan were again on opposite sides. While Morgan had no objection to the tribe spending its own money, he wanted it used for water development on the reservation and to assist young educated Navajos. A compromise that cut the amount to be used for land from 50 percent to 25 percent of the royalties so outraged Dodge that he suggested that the council be disbanded.[38] Dodge's loyalty to the people living off the reservation was strong and was manifested in other ways as well. In 1930, for instance, he was active in protesting the dismissal of an allotting agent whose services were needed to help many eastern Navajos retain rights to their lands.[39] His support was still important to the success of government programs in Navajo country. Superintendent John G. Hunter enlisted Dodge's backing to organize the community meeting system of chapters in the Southern Navajo Agency.[40]

The Great Depression exacerbated the ill feeling between Dodge and Morgan and between their respective supporters. Dodge has been quoted as saying that the Navajos had put their "servant children" in school and kept the best children at home, a mistake for which they were now suffering.[41] That he had in mind Morgan and his Returned Students Association, which was founded in 1932, seems very likely.[42] On the other hand, Morgan attacked the Dodge faction for allegedly claiming that the depression was the fault of "the young, educated men on the Tribal Council."[43] Dr. C. S. Salisbury has asserted that the two leaders nearly came to blows over his request for a tribal contribution of five hundred dollars to purchase an ambulance for the hospital at the Presbyterian Mission at Ganado.[44]

In July 1932 a series of events took place that offer some insights into the way Dodge was dealing with the pressures of his position. He was still, at more than seventy years of age, caught between the cultures of his parents—cultures so divergent in their world view that they were not easily reconciled. Dodge still looked more like a white man than a Navajo, and he often visited white friends in Gallup. He had long indulged in alcohol, both at the homes of these friends and at his own place at Crystal. According to reports, in 1932 in Gallup he became drunk, apparently with friends who felt little responsibility for his welfare under those circumstances. He wandered toward the north side of town, and in the dark he fell into the arroyo of the Rio Puerco, where he became trapped in quicksand. His cries for help were heard by a Hispanic man who rescued him and took care of him for the night. During the night there was a flash flood down the arroyo that would have drowned Dodge had he not been rescued.

This story was related to Frank Mitchell and Curley Hair at Saint Michaels Mission in July, probably shortly after the event. The next day they, together with John Foley and Son of the Late Little Blacksmith, drove to Crystal. They found Dodge at his sweathouse with two other men. The visitors participated in the sweat baths and gave an account of their trip. Dodge and Son of the Late Little Blacksmith appear to have been related in a way which encourages joking in Navajo culture; they engaged in mutual teasing in a fashion that few whites would be able to appreciate.

They questioned Dodge about the incident in Gallup, and he readily admitted that the story was true as they had heard it. He promised that they would never again hear anything of that sort about him; and they never did. They spent the night at Dodge's home. No wife was living with him, but he had employees who prepared rooms for them. They sat up well into the night while Dodge told them stories about past events, early traditions, and how the Navajos had lived long ago.[45]

In 1933, Thomas Dodge, an attorney in Santa Fe, was elected to the tribal council, replacing his father. The Returned Students Association supported half of the candidates elected to the council that year. Morgan and Thomas Dodge had long been friends, and they seemed able to keep up this relationship even when they found themselves in opposition politically. The times seemed ripe for achieving some accord between the two factions, and the election of Dodge as chairman of the new council should have been a happy omen. Even the presence of former council members did not seem too disruptive.[46]

The prospect of harmony in tribal politics was an illusion, however. Franklin D. Roosevelt had been elected president, and he had appointed John Collier to head the Bureau of Indian Affairs. Dramatic changes were imminent; and one change, stock reduction, would soon rend the basic fabric of Navajo life. An autumn meeting of the council was held at Tuba City, where Collier proposed the first round of his program to alleviate the erosion which, according to the range management experts, Navajo livestock was causing. The government planned to buy ewes for one dollar to one dollar and fifty cents per head. Chee Dodge remarked from the sidelines that for that price the Navajos would cull their herds, retaining their most productive stock, and that the lamb crop would be as big as ever. The council split eight to four in their vote, and Dodge's prediction was, as might be expected, correct.[47]

In the spring of 1934, at a council meeting at Fort Defiance, Collier introduced plans for a second reduction to be funded by the tribe. Chee Dodge found the new approach acceptable and urged its approval. Morgan spoke up to protect small owners, those who had fewer than one hundred sheep. At the same meeting, Collier made his initial proposal of reorganization of the tribal government under the Wheeler-Howard Act.[48]

By April all semblance of accord had disappeared. At a council meeting held at Crownpoint in that month, Morgan launched a "furious attack" on the Wheeler-Howard proposal while Dodge defended it. Another split vote of seven for and five abstentions provided as strong an endorsement as the government was able to obtain.[49] Tribal reorganization required a tribal election, however, and the supporters and opponents soon began their respective campaigns.

By the beginning of 1935 Chee Dodge had had second thoughts regarding the reorganization proposal. What brought on his change of mind is not known. The agency claimed that he was merely being contrary and was becoming childish in his old age; however, the urgent need felt for his support in the matter indicates that he was still highly influential in Navajo politics, so much so that the government brought him to Washington to discuss the matter, but to no avail.[50]

In May, a new superintendent was able to win over Chee Dodge, apparently in part because he appointed Thomas Dodge to a position as his assistant. The coup did not have the intended effect, however. An abrupt reversal of this sort raised questions, and Morgan's supporters exploited the circumstances by spreading the rumor that Chee had accepted a government bribe of fifty thousand dollars.[51] The election was a defeat for Collier. The votes that decided the issue were cast in the northern and eastern jurisdictions, where Morgan had the strongest following.[52] The decisive issue was probably not the terms of the Wheeler-Howard Act but Navajo response to stock reduction, which was rapidly becoming a disaster.

By 1936 a year and a half had passed without a session of the tribal council. Chee Dodge became increasingly critical of the administration. In June, he publicly confronted Collier, accusing him of instituting a reduction program that was causing "hunger and epidemics" among the Navajos. In July, Dodge and Morgan joined forces to denounce the Collier regime at a meeting in Ganado from which federal officials were barred. Opposition to federal authority and an alliance with Morgan were apparently more than Dodge could sustain for long. Collier, in a meeting in Albuquerque, was able to win Dodge back to his side.[53]

The divisions within the tribe were factors in the poorly organized and ineffectual testimony that various Navajos, including Chee Dodge and Jacob Morgan, gave before Congress in 1936 in support of a boundary bill that would have returned a good deal of the lost land on the east to the tribe. Dodge attempted to avoid controversy by a discursive account of the history of the claim, but his approach was far too Navajo in tone to sway a white audience. Too many of the other Navajo witnesses took advantage of the occasion to attack Collier because of stock reduction. In doing so, they undermined before Congress the man who was promoting the return of their land; they had not realized what the practical effect of their words would be. Collier was forced to admit that his reduction program had resulted in grave injustice to many Navajos, and the real purpose of the testimony was lost in the process.[54]

At an age when most politicians would have retired, perhaps to assume the role of elder statesman, Dodge was being drawn into an escalating power struggle that would call for exertions of substantial proportions. In November 1936, the council established an executive committee comprised of Jim Shirley, Marcus Kanuho, Nalnishi *(Naalnishi*, "Worker"), George Bancroft, Fred Nelson, Allen Neskahi, Chee Dodge, and Dashne Clah Cheschillege *(Tłaai Chiishch'ilí'igii*, "The Curly-haired Left-hander"). Henry Taliman, a Navajo veteran of World War I, headed the committee. Father Berard Haile went along as an aide of sorts, for he was secretary among his other duties. The committee met in the scattered communities throughout Navajo country to obtain the election of 70 men to make up a constitutional assembly. It was a difficult chore undertaken in an unusually harsh winter. Storms and breakdowns slowed their progress. Most of December, all of January, and the greater part of February were required to compile a list of 250 local leaders from whom the 70 would be selected. Differences between the older, traditional leaders and the younger, educated men lurked just beneath the surface. Dodge, who had been the first member of the tribe to speak English, favored the traditionalists, and even Taliman hesitated to challenge him. In March the committee convened and sifted the names. A clear majority of the assembly would be older men, but the new generation of leaders was not excluded entirely. Even Morgan was included.[55]

Dodge was not a member of the constitutional assembly, but he did address the initial session, urging the delegates to conform to the government's wishes. The proceedings very nearly broke down entirely in succeeding sessions, however, as Morgan and his adherents vigorously opposed the idea of a constitution. Ultimately, Thomas Dodge drafted a constitution which was approved by the assembly but rejected by Secretary of the Interior Harold Ickes.[56]

In the summer of 1937 the stock reduction issue was so critical that there was danger of open rebellion. When Thomas Dodge, Howard Gorman, and E. R. Fryer, then Navajo general superintendent, were asked to speak at a meeting at Teec-Nos-Pos, in an area that strongly supported Morgan, Chee Dodge led a delegation of armed followers who stayed in the background but made the crowd aware of their presence. Although the Morgan faction gave incendiary speeches, the presence of Chee Dodge's group and a dramatic omen, a snake crawling from below the wagon on which the speakers stood, apparently defused any planned violence.[57] Despite this fiasco, Morgan was elected tribal chairman in the fall.[58]

Morgan failed to live up to expectations once he became chairman, but he is remembered today by many Navajos for his courage in opposing the government. Chee Dodge carried the next two elections; he died on January 7, 1947, before he could take office following the second of these elections.[59]

Dodge's life bridged the passage of the Navajos from an independent tribal people to an enclave within the territory of a world power; from a traditional culture to participation, even if reluctant at times, in an increasingly complex world. Two events late in his life show something of his own efforts to reconcile the divergent outlooks of the world in which he lived.

Sometime during the 1930s Dodge championed the selection of Frank Mitchell as tribal judge. In advising Mitchell in the matter, Dodge told him that witchcraft did not work and could not harm him, so that Mitchell need have no fear when making decisions on the bench.[60] It was Dodge, however, who saw to it that the Fort Defiance Hospital was dedicated with the services of Pete Price, a Navajo Blessingway singer. This was the first public building to be so blessed and set a precedent that has become customary in Navajo country today.[61]

Notes

1. Virginia Hoffman, *Navajo Biographies,* vol. 1 (Phoenix, 1974), p. 189; Frank McNitt, ed., *Navaho Expedition: Journal of a Military Reconaissance from Santa Fe, New Mexico to the Navaho Country Made in 1849 by Lieutenant James H. Simpson* (Norman, Okla., 1964), p. 182 n. 20. I wish to thank Mr. and Mrs. Michael J. Andrews for assistance with data in the census files of Saint Michaels Mission and Lauren Rimbert for typing the final manuscript. The orthography of Navajo names has been standardized with Robert W. Young and William Morgan, *The Navajo Language, A Grammar and Colloquial Dictionary* (Albuquerque, 1980). Young has also graciously provided advice on terms that presented special problems. John Kessell provided a copy of his manuscript report on the Navajo Tribal Council in the 1920s.

2. Frank McNitt, *Navajo Wars: Military Campaigns, Slave Raids and Reprisals* (Albuquerque, 1972) pp. 295–96 n. 13.

3. Hoffman, *Navajo Biographies,* pp. 181–89.

4. Arny to Commissioner of Indian Affairs (hereafter cited as CIA), March 4, 1875, Records of the Bureau of Indian Affairs, RG 75, New Mexico Superintendency, 3031, A–194/75, National Archives (hereafter cited as NA), Washington, D.C.

5. Dodge, Affidavit, March 10, 1880, RG75, Letters Received (hereafter cited as LR), 8271–1888, Incl. 38, NA.

6. Hoffman, *Navajo Biographies,* pp. 187–89; Donald L. Parman, *The Navajos and the New Deal* (New Haven, Conn., 1976), pp. 17–18.

7. Ibid., p. 18, Frank McNitt, *The Indian Traders* (Norman, Okla., 1962), p. 179; Mary Shepardson, *Navajo Ways in Government: A Study in Political Process* (Menasha, Wis., 1963), p. 83; D. M. Riordan to CIA, September 15, 1883, RG 75, LR, 17513–1883, NA.

8. McNitt, *Indian Traders,* pp. 182, 184; J. Lee Correll, "Navajo Frontiers

in Utah and Troublous Times in Monument Valley," *Utah Historical Quarterly* 39 (Spring 1971), pp. 152–60.

9. Hoffman, *Navajo Biographies*, p. 191.

10. United States District Court for the District of Arizona, *Healing vs. Jones, No. Civil 597, Prescott, Opinion of the Court, Appendix to Opinion—Chronological Account of Hopi-Navajo Controversy, Findings of Fact and Conclusions of Law and Judgement* (San Francisco, 1962), pp. 124–25.

11. Hoffman, *Navajo Biographies*, pp. 191–92; McNitt, *Indian Traders, p. 279.*

12. Hoffman, Navajo Biographies, p. 192.

13. Left-Handed Mexican Clansman, Howard Gorman, and the Nephew of Former Big Man, *The Trouble at Round Rock* (Haskell, Kansas, 1952); Hoffman, *Navajo Biographies*, pp. 192–94; McNitt, *The Indian Traders*, pp. 279–81; Frank Mitchell, *Navajo Blessingway Singer, The Autobiography of Frank Mitchell, 1881–1967* (Tucson, 1978), pp. 50–54.

14. Ibid., p. 69 n. 1.

15. Hoffman, *Navajo Biographies*, pp. 194–96.

16. Mitchell, *Navajo Blessingway Singer*, pp. 107, 246.

17. Hoffman, *Navajo Biographies*, p. 198.

18. Franciscan Friars, Census cards on file at Saint Michaels Mission, Saint Michaels, Arizona, n.d.

19. MicNitt, *Indian Traders*, p. 288.

20. Aubrey W. Williams, Jr., *Navajo Political Process* (Washington, D.C., 1970), p. 14.

21. David M. Brugge, "Motivation and Function in Navajo Rock Art," *American Indian Rock Art* 4(May 1976), p.146.

22. Williams, *Navajo Political Process*, pp. 6–7; Shepardson, *Navajo Ways in Government*, pp. 47–48.

23. John D. Kessell, *The Navajo Tribal Council in the 1920s*, Navajo Tribe vs. United States of America, dkt. nos. 69, 229, and 353), (Albuquerque, 1981), pp. 3–4.

24. McNitt, *Indian Traders*, p. 257 n. 18.

25. David M. Brugge, *A History of the Chaco Navajos* (Washington, D.C., 1980), p. 230.

26. Parman, *Navajos and the New Deal*, p. 19.

27. McNitt, *Indian Traders*, pp. 348–58.

28. Mitchell, *Navajo Blessingway Singer*, p. 117 n. 28; Parman, *Navajos and the New Deal*, p. 18.

29. Mitchell, *Navajo Blessingway Singer*, pp. 271–72.

30. Lawrence C. Kelly, *The Navajo Indians and Federal Indian Policy, 1900–1935* (Tucson, 1968), p. 66.

31. Brugge, *History*, pp. 49, 79, 295, 299–300, 314–16, 321.

32. Parman, *Navajos and the New Deal*, p. 17.

33. Kessell, *Navajo Tribal Council*, p. 13 n. 6; Peter Iverson, *The Navajo Nation* (Westport, Conn., 1981), p. 20; Robert W. Young, *The Navajo Yearbook, Report No. VIII* (Window Rock, Ariz., 1961), p. 375.

34. Kelly, *Navajo Indians*, pp. 67–68.

35. Ibid., pp. 69–70; Iverson, *Navajo Nation*, pp. 21–22; Donald L. Parman, "J. C. Morgan: Navajo Apostle of Assimilation," *Prologue* 4 (Summer 1972), pp. 83–98.

36. Kelly, *Navajo Indians*, p. 177; Kessell, *Navajo Tribal Council*, pp. 23, 30.

37. Ibid., pp. 34–35.

38. Kelly, *Navajo Indians*, pp. 120–21; Parman, *Navajos and the New Deal*, pp. 21–22.

39. Brugge, *History*, p. 372.

40. Williams, *Navajo Political Process*, pp. 35–36.

41. Mitchell, *Navajo Blessingway Singer*, p. 56.

42. Parman, *Navajos and the New Deal*, p. 87.

43. Brugge, *History*, p. 376.

44. Parman, *Navajos and the New Deal*, p. 87 n. 11.

45. Mitchell, *Navajo Blessingway Singer*, pp. 250–56.

46. Parman, Navajos and the New Deal, pp. 39–40.

47. Ibid., p. 46; David F. Aberle, *The Peyote Religion Among the Navaho* (Chicago, 1982), p. 56.

48. Parman, *Navajos and the New Deal*, p. 54.

49. Ibid., p. 56.

50. Ibid., p. 73.

51. Ibid., p. 75.

52. Iverson, *Navajo Nation*, p. 34.

53. Parman, *Navajos and the New Deal*, pp. 121–23.

54. Ibid., pp. 150–51.

55. Ibid., pp. 92 n. 25, 161–66; Iverson, *Navajo Nation*, p. 36.

56. Parman, *Navajos and the New Deal*, pp. 92–93; Iverson, *Navajo Nation*, pp. 36–37.

57. Parman, *Navajos and the New Deal*, pp. 179–83.

58. Ibid., p. 191.

59. Iverson, *Navajo Nation*, p. 51.

60. Mitchell, *Navajo Blessingway Singer*, pp. 262–64.

61. Ibid., pp. 221, 238 n. 9.

Essay on Sources

In this essay I have relied largely on secondary sources for an interpretation of the life of an important figure in Navajo history. In part, this is a result of personal circumstances during the period of writing, and partly it is due to the fact that I am not a historian and have felt comfortable as an anthropologist in applying some anthropological concepts to materials already made available by competent researchers in the historical tradition, while also combining these data with some of the rich oral history extant in ethnographic sources. An in-depth, full-length biography is long overdue, and it would be possible today to integrate both Navajo and white views by judicious use of the two kinds of collections.

The archival collections are well known to most historians and include the National Archives; federal records centers in Colorado, California, and possibly Texas; the archives of the Franciscan missionaries of the Province of Cincinnati; the Hubbell Papers at the University of Arizona; the Day Papers at Northern Arizona University; the archival collections of the Navajo Nation; and newspaper stories, both from papers published in reservation bordertowns such as Gallup and Farmington (with the latter particularly useful for data on Dodge's arch-rival, Jacob Morgan) and some from more distant cities such as Albuquerque and Phoenix. In addition, the papers of the major political figures in New Mexico and Arizona, including Herbert J. Hagerman and Carl Hayden, and the records of congressional hearings on Indian affairs, will be important sources.

Oral history has been recorded from a relatively early period, but most that relates to Dodge's career is of relatively recent origin and is included in collections such as the Doris Duke collections at the University of Utah and the University of New Mexico; the oral history collections at Hubbell Trading Post National Historic Site, Rough Rock Demonstration School, Navajo Community College, and Window Rock in collections held by the Navajo Nation. Published traditional accounts are of variable quality, but those which present careful direct translation of the informant's words, such as the account by Left-Handed Mexican Clansman and Frank Mitchell's autobiography, are especially valuable. Those accounts which are heavily edited often contain information not available elsewhere, but they must be used with more caution.

One final note for those tempted to undertake studies of Dodge's life. A good understanding of Navajo values during his lifetime is essential for any fair assessment of his accomplishments and failures. It is important to realize that Navajo values are no more unchanging than are those of other societies. While Dodge was influential in the development of the values of modern Navajo society, he was not a proponent of radical change, nor could he have effected such change had he desired to do so.

5
Charles Curtis
The Politics of Allotment

William E. Unrau

Humanitarian reformers of the post–Civil War decades envisioned the Five Civilized Tribes of the Indian Territory as potential exemplars of assimilation. The Cherokees, Choctaws, Chickasaws, Creeks, and Seminoles had progressed far along the road to assimilation. With redoubled efforts by the reformers the tribes could be brought into American life, and the efficacy of lands in severalty, of education, and of Christianity could be demonstrated to the rest of America's native race. Humanitarians were also matched in their enthusiasm for the disappearance of the territory by other Americans who looked covetously at the lands reserved in perpetuity for Indians. Citizens in Texas, Kansas, and Arkansas saw the rich lands being only marginally used by the Indians. Their desire to destroy the Indian Territory and the independence of its inhabitants increased. The Five Civilized Tribes, however, continually rejected legislative proposals for the liquidation of their homeland. Treaties written with the government during the years of Indian Removal reinforced tribal resistance. These treaties stipulated that the tribes would be forever free from white interference. Indian treaties, however, were made to be broken.

The Civil War had disrupted life in the Indian Territory. The Five Civilized Tribes, under pressure, signed treaties with the Confederacy and aided the war effort. At the end of the war, despite the fact that there had been large pro-Union factions among the Cherokees, Seminoles, and Creeks, the United States acquired through forced sale vast tracts of land. The Five Civilized Tribes retained the

eastern half of the territory, while the remainder of the land was to be used as homes for western tribes who were to be resettled on reservations as part of the government's program of concentration.

Efforts to bring an end to tribal control in the Indian Territory and to establish regular territorial government were reflected in the numerous bills introduced in Congress during the 1870s. The Five Civilized Tribes continued to thwart legislative action by reliance on their treaties. In the 1880s, however, the spirit of Indian policy reform quickened as Congress, supported increasingly by the humanitarians, moved toward a solution to the "Indian Problem." Newer and more persuasive arguments were found for ending tribal governments and dividing Indian lands.

Although the Five Civilized Tribes were originally exempted from the Dawes Act, reformers and their political allies persisted in their efforts and eventually succeeded in dismantling the Indian Territory. In March 1889, President Benjamin Harrison appointed a commission which had been authorized by Congress to negotiate further land cessions. Later, courts were established in other parts of the territory, and finally, through the Curtis Act of June 28, 1898, tribal laws and tribal courts were abolished. All persons in the Indian Territory, regardless of race, came under United States authority. The Curtis Act further authorized the Dawes Commission—established by Congress in March, 1893, to negotiate for the extinguishment of tribal title to the lands of the Five Civilized Tribes—to proceed with the allotment of lands in severalty once the tribal rolls were completed. Beginning in 1898 and continuing until 1907, the commission entered 101,506 persons on the rolls. Despite continuing opposition, allotment proceeded and the tribes inevitably succumbed; Indian Territory disappeared.

Charles Curtis (1860–1936) is remembered for his authorship of the bill which destroyed the Indian Territory, but mostly he is known for his single, four-year term as vice-president of the United States during Herbert Hoover's administration. Curtis, an Indian of mixed heritage, claimed affiliation with both the Kaw and Osage tribes. Rather than proving to be a liability, Curtis's "Indianness" became a political asset; he used his heritage to advantage. He saw in his great-great-grandfather Nompawara ("White Plume"), a Kaw chief, a quality of greatness that he described as "progressive": Nompawara had cooperated with federal authorities. Curtis also saw "greatness" as a potential for all Indians if only the impediments to their progress in civilization were removed. Curtis, "The Injun" as his opponents derisively called him, did much to remove those impediments. Unlike other prominent Indian leaders of his generation, he would never be de-

scribed as a reformer. He shared none of their sentimentality for an Indian heritage. Although he was an Indian only by remote ancestry, his willingness to use his identity to advantage was certainly not unique. His willingness to speak as an "Indian" on behalf of other Indians was shared by many of his acculturated, mixed-blood contemporaries. But Charles Curtis was a man with an eye on the main chance.

The following essay examines in detail for the first time the disputed genealogy of Charles Curtis and his rather atypical perceptions of what it meant to be an Indian.

In February 1936, on the occasion of the death of Charles Curtis, *Time* magazine stated that the deceased man was one of the few men who truly had enjoyed being vice-president of the United States. But service as vice-president in the Hoover administration was undistinguished for the friendly, backslapping, ultraconservative Republican whose first loves were poker and horse racing; and although "Our Charley" still held a warm spot in the heart of his countrymen, his only chance for a niche in history lay in the fact that he was the half-brother of Dolly Curtis Gann—whose naughty encounters with Alice Roosevelt Longworth were the high point of Washington society in the late 1920s and early 1930s—and that he was the first man of Indian blood to be elected to the second highest office in the land.[1]

In the words of one wag, the trinity for Curtis meant "the Republican Party, the high protective tariff, and the Grand Army of the Republic." As Kansas congressman from the old Fourth District from 1892 to 1907 and as senator from 1907 to 1928 (he was briefly out of office from 1913 to 1915), Curtis supported the gold standard, high tariffs, prohibition, restrictive immigration, deportation of aliens, and generous veterans' benefits; opposed the League of Nations; and took the view that depressions were natural occurrences that inevitably would be followed by periods of greater prosperity. On the other hand, perhaps due to the influence of women in his public and private careers, he was a champion of female suffrage, and he supported government assistance to farmers, particularly if those farmers resided in his native Kansas.[2]

Above all else, Curtis was a consummate politican. Never one to take a strong stand or to speak out in public on controversial issues, he preferred to work behind the scenes, to exploit the dynamics of party organization, and through personal relations with his colleagues, to get things done "without a fuss."[3] Certainly his role as Republican whip under Henry Cabot Lodge, and as Republican floor leader after Lodge's death in 1924, attest to these characteristics. His close touch with his constituents was a source of particular comment by his contemporaries. William Allen White, who first met Curtis in 1891, described the Curtis strategy just prior to a speaking engagement at a small hamlet near Emporia, Kansas, in 1896:

> [A] mile or two before we got to Plymouth, he pulled out a little book on which were the names of the Republicans of Pike Township . . . and like a pious worshipper out of a prayer book he began mumbling their names to impress them on his memory. It was a curious rite, I thought, and I giggled. But it was dead serious to Curtis. He has a little book like that for every township in Kansas, and carried the county's Republican poll list when he went into a county. In that way he survived politically for forty years. No matter what the issue was, it did not concern him. He knew that if he could call a man's name in a crowd, shake hands with him and ask him about his wife and children, whose names were also in the little book, he had that man's vote.[4]

Such activity was all the more effective because of the rapidity with which Curtis answered his mail. The fact that he was often addressed on a first-name basis apparently reflected at least a modicum of personal acquaintance with his correspondents. It was reported on one occasion that Curtis and his staff answered nearly fourteen hundred letters within twenty-four hours of their arrival in Washington.[5]

Yet there was another side to what came to be known as the "Curtis luck" in politics—a side that has been ignored or at least greatly underestimated by students of Curtis. This has to do with his role as an Indian leader, particularly in the shaping and implementation of federal allotment policy at the turn of the century. Early in his career his political enemies bestowed upon him the appellations of "the Injun" or "the Noble Red Man of the Forest," but often to the advantage of Curtis rather than his detractors. As a novice congressman, Curtis enjoyed more than usual attention when Speaker of the House Thomas B. ("Czar") Reed took a liking to him, called him "the Indian," and listened to his often practical advice on ways to overcome committee obstruction to difficult congressional issues. These references to his Indianness did not go unnoticed by Curtis, who learned to exploit his Kaw (or Kansa) tribal genealogy with great effectiveness. In February 1902, for example, he proudly paraded Chief Wahshungah and other members of a Kaw delegation in full native garb before President Theodore Roosevelt. And in the 1928 campaign, Curtis's generally boring speeches were made more palatable by the emotional appeal of flag-waving, hand-shaking, blaring band music, and especially the performance of a dancing Indian "princess."[6]

Viewing Charles Curtis as an important Indian leader requires first of all an understanding of his genetic and legal affiliation with the Kaw tribe, dating back to his birth in North Topeka, Kansas, on January 25, 1860. In an unfinished autobiographical statement prepared in his later years Curtis's reminiscence was more that of a heroic white pioneer than that of a proud Indian:

> We, the sons and daughters of the pioneers are proud of the work of our fathers and mothers. They came to Kansas to help free it and to reclaim what was known, when they came west, as a desert. They have transformed the plains into a garden spot of the world and have, in Kansas, created one of the greatest states in the Union.[7]

In the same autobiography, however, Curtis presented an important clue regarding his perception of Indian greatness, when he described his great-great-grandfather White Plume (or Nompawara) as "one of the ablest and most *progressive* [emphasis added] Indians of his day [and] a warm friend of Lewis and Clark . . . in their work among the Indians of that section of the country."[8]

In calling his great-great-grandfather "progressive," Curtis was recalling White Plume's cooperation with federal land agents and the patrimony he had provided his heirs by the Kaw treaty of 1825. By this treaty the tribe relinquished claims to nearly twenty million acres of land in western Missouri and future Kansas in return for a two million-acre tract west of future Topeka. Also included in the agreement was an article that granted fee-simple 640-acre sections to each of the twenty-three half-bloods of the Kaw Nation, one of whom was Julie Gonvil Pappan, Curtis's maternal grandmother.[9] It was a divisive agreement in the extreme, one that permanently divided the tribe along blood and cultural lines, and established the long-range setting for final tribal dissolution in 1902.

Considerable disagreement has prevailed regarding the Curtis genealogy. The popular press on occasion described Charles as a one-quarter Kaw, or as a combination of one-eighth Kaw and one-eighth Osage. In 1903 an Indian Territory newspaper, published near the recently allotted Kaw Reservation, was certain of Curtis's one-quarter Kaw blood quantum. The official tribal census compiled by the Pawnee Agency in October 1929 listed Curtis as one-eighth Kaw, but as late as 1940 the same agency had changed it to one-quarter. And in the 1930s, until corrected by Curtis himself, one scholar took the position that the former vice-president was a half-blood.[10]

The available documents confirm the fact that Curtis was a blood descendant of White Plume, son of the distinguished Osage leader, Pawhuska. Sometime prior to 1825, White Plume was officially adopted by the Kaw tribe, allegedly for acts of bravery but more likely because of his marriage to a Kaw woman. Unlike the majority of his new brethren, and certainly contrary to leaders of the three full-blood factions, White Plume came under the influence of Father Joseph Anthony Lutz of the St. Louis Catholic Doicese. Lutz, whose missionary efforts among the Kaws were inconsequential generally, prevailed on White Plume to abandon his traditional ways and to have one of his full-blood nieces join with Louis Gonvil (Gonville?) in a "legitimate, Christian marriage." Julie, a daughter born to this union, married Louis Pappan, a fur trade laborer from the St. Louis area who had sought employment near the mouth of the Kansas River. During the early stages of white migration over a branch of the Oregon Trail through northeastern Kansas, Louis and his brother Joseph, who had married Julie's sister Josette, established a thriving ferry service across the Kansas River, opposite future Topeka, on the "Kaw Mile Three" allotment Josette had been granted in 1825. Louis Pappan also saw to it that his daughter Ellen (sometimes listed as Helen) entered a Catholic convent in St. Louis. In the late territorial period Ellen returned to Kansas, where in 1859 she married Oren A. Curtis, a restless full-blood white who had traveled from his native Eugene, Indiana, through twenty-nine different states. Apparently interested in a more stable livelihood, Curtis assisted his father-in-law in the ferry business and looked with apprehension on the fertile bottomland that his wife might one day inherit. On January 25, 1860, on "Kaw Mile Four" (as the allotment just east of Josette Gonville Pappan's "Kaw Mile Three" was called) in present North Topeka, Charles Curtis was born. He was an eighth-blood Kaw.[11]

The year 1863 was an important one in the future Indian leader's development. As a result of her experience in St. Louis, Ellen Pappan Curtis saw to it that her infant son received Catholic baptism in the St. Mary's Immaculate Conception Church on the nearby Potawatomi Reservation. She also instructed young Charles in the French language and gave every indication that he should grow up well removed from the Kaw Reservation some sixty miles west of Topeka. But her untimely death in 1863 altered the situation radically. That same year her widowed husband married and then divorced Ratchel Hatch. Oren Curtis was by nature an unsettled person, and perhaps deeming it necessary to remove himself from the setting of his recent bereavement and domestic difficulties, he obtained an officer's appointment in the Fifteenth Kansas Cavalry for service against the Confederacy in Missouri. Thus, at the age of three Charles was placed in the care of his paternal grandmother, Permelia Hubbard Curtis, who with her husband William and their large family had followed her son to Kansas in 1860. While her husband engaged in real estate development on the Kaw half-blood lands, Permelia ruled her family with a stern will—so stern that she regarded "being both a Methodist and Republican as essential for anyone expected to go to heaven." Such was the environment that young Charles experienced until 1866, when he was abruptly placed in the care of Julia Pappan, his maternal grandmother on the Kaw Reservation near Council Grove.[12]

Precisely why Permelia Curtis temporarily relinquished custody over Charles is difficult to determine. The Civil War was over; the reservation near Council Grove was then dominated by full-bloods alien to their mixed-blood relatives in Topeka, St. Louis, and elsewhere. Certainly the area was deficient in Methodists and Republicans. The most reasonable explanation is that in 1866 there was serious talk of a Kaw removal treaty, one that might settle tribal land affairs in Kansas once and for all. Given the possibility of a generous financial settlement, it was desirable for the young eighth-blood to reside on the reservation to guarantee that he would be listed on the official tribal roll. On the other hand, it is possible that Mrs. Curtis may have felt an obligation to share her grandson and to allow him to experience the more relaxed atmosphere of reservation life. Whatever the case, the fact is that young Charles enjoyed his Council Grove experience until the Southern Cheyenne "raid" of 1868.[13]

Certainly one of the more confused incidents in early Kansas history, the "raid" appears to have been the principal factor in Curtis's return to Topeka and the early molding of his attitudes regarding tribal acculturation. From the time of the tribe's confinement to the Council Grove reservation in 1846, relations with the Southern Cheyennes and Arapahos deteriorated as a consequence of the dwindling buffalo supply on the high plains to the west. The situation was aggravated by the Sand Creek Massacre in eastern Colorado Territory in 1864. The construction of the Kansas branch of the Union Pacific Railroad and the continuing encroachment of white squatters on Indian land did nothing to improve the situation. In the winter of 1866 the Cheyennes stole forty-two Kaw horses, and in the following fall the Arapahos seized an additional thirty-four. Following the murder of a Kaw herder at a buffalo camp near Fort Zarah in December 1867, the Kaws attacked a major Cheyenne encampment, killing fourteen while losing one of their own. As the Cheyennes retreated north and west to obtain reinforcements, the Kaws fled back to Council Grove in freezing weather and a state of starvation. En route, sixty Kaws died and more horses were lost. At Council Grove the survivors learned of rumors that the Cheyennes were planning to attack their reservation the following spring. For young boys such as Curtis, it was indeed a time of excitement and fearful awareness of grave differences between semi-sedentary reservation Indians and the less "civilized" nomads of the Plains.[14]

On June 3, 1868, approximately one hundred Cheyennes appeared at the agency headquarters south of Council Grove. A few scattered shots were fired, considerable shouting and charging with horses took place, but no one was injured. The incident lasted less than four hours and gained for the Cheyennes some sugar and coffee from white residents of Council Grove, a small amount of plunder from outlying white farms, and some cattle from several Texas drovers who were operating illegally in that vicinity. Later, at Fort Larned, the Cheyennes requested that the plunder be deducted from their annuities. Military authorities at nearby Fort Riley were aware of the circumstances at all times, and evidence indicates that calculated exaggeration of the threat came from civilian contractors who were determined to confine the Kaws to their reservation for personal profit.[15]

Curtis, of course, was unaware of these details. But in later years, after he had achieved national fame, he never wearied of relating the difficult circumstances under which he had returned to Topeka, nor did he refrain from challenging those who suggested that he had left the reservation because of personal fear. In an interview shortly after he was elected vice-president, Curtis recalled: "We [the Kaws] wanted to appeal to the white man, and I could speak English. I was lithe and active, and young as I was, the Chief of the tribe thought I could be intrusted with the important message. I ran and walked for miles, summoning help for the besieged tribe. I at last got to Topeka, where relatives of my father lived, and I decided to stay with them for awhile. . . ."[16]

That Curtis returned to Topeka in 1868 there is no doubt. Less certain is his responsibility for warning outsiders of the alleged crisis at Council Grove. For one thing, federal troops were standing by with orders to intervene if the lives of non-Indians were threatened, and according to Kansas Governor Samuel Crawford, the request for state assistance was delivered to him at seven in the evening of the raid by "Jo Jim" (Joseph James), an adult Kaw half-blood interpreter who had been designated for the assignment by Agent E. S. Stover. Moreover, it is unlikely that full-blood Kaw Chief Ahlegawaho would have intrusted such an important responsibility to an eight-year-old eighth-blood whose residence on the reservation was anything but permanent. In any case, the incident contributed to Curtis's developing antipathy regarding the virtues of traditionalist, reservation life—an antipathy which was fortified later that year when his father joined with Governor Crawford's Nineteenth Kansas Cavalry for a campaign against the very tribe that had raided Council Grove.[17]

Excluding a moment of hesitation in 1874 as to whether he should go with the Kaws when they were removed to a diminished reservation in northern Indian Territory, Curtis's involvement with the Kaws or with Indian affairs in general was virtually nonexistent until he entered national politics two decades later. However, he remained on the Kaw annuity roll until 1878, when Kaw-Osage Agent Laban J. Miles dropped his name for having failed to reside on the Indian Territory reservation. This action was supported by Acting Indian Commissioner C. W. Holcomb, who ruled that Indians who wished to share in annuity distributions must be present at the distributions and that failing to do so was cause for their names to be dropped. Curtis, of course, could continue to enjoy the status of a legal Kaw, since one of his ancestors was so designated in the treaty of 1825.[18]

From the time he left the Kaw Reservation until he was well into his maturity Curtis was profoundly influenced by his Grandmother Curtis. She oversaw his public school education, taught him the virtues of sobriety, encouraged him to seek part-time jobs, and made sure he understood how vital the Republican Party was to everything decent in Kansas and in the nation. It was futile to oppose her, said Curtis's stepsister. "[I]f we strayed momentarily, by accident or inadvertence, from the fold of her orthodoxy, she needed only to remind us of our allegiance, which lasted to her death. [She] knew everything that was going on, and although the day of women in politics was yet distant, she doubtless had her say-so in many an important episode. . . ."[19] In short, it is difficult to imagine how the maturing environment of Curtis could have been more distant from the kind of life that his Kaw contemporaries were then experiencing in the Indian Territory, which, tragically, included nearly a 50 percent decline in population since removal.[20]

Among the jobs Curtis held prior to entering Topeka High School in 1876 was a stint as a jockey during the summer racing seasons. Apparently small in stature, well-coordinated, and an excellent rider since his reservation days, he was able to save considerable money and make important social contacts that would serve him well in the future. This experience also provided the means for operating a hack service and expanding his circle of political friends, many of whom took a fancy to the young mixed-blood. One of these was A. H. Case, a prominent Topeka attorney who had made Curtis's acquaintance during his jockey days, and it was with Case that Curtis read law while serving as office handyman and bill collector. By 1879 he was handling some of Case's minor court appearances, and by 1881, at the age of twenty-one, Curtis had passed the requirements for admission to the Kansas Bar.[21] Meanwhile, he became active in Republican political groups, where his propensity to listen carefully, work hard, analyze the workings of party machinery from the grassroots level up, and make devoted friends became his basic style. He also found time to organize a home-talent theatrical company to put on "Ten Nights in a Barroom" and thus attract attention to his interest in the explosive prohibition issue in Kansas. In addition, he engaged in real estate development, based on forty acres of half-blood land which he and his sister had inherited from their mother in North Topeka. The tract had a large debt on it, which Curtis cleared by dividing it into lots. Years later, he revealed with pride the success of the venture:

> I sold one-quarter of a block of land to a distillery and gave them one-quarter of a block. I did the same with a brewery and had a distillery and a brewery located in the southwest corner of the land. After this was done I turned the payments over to the bankers and soon had the mortgage and back taxes paid and after this was done I began to build small houses on the lots.[22]

It was his abstruse position on the prohibition issue that launched Curtis on his public career as Shawnee County Attorney in 1884 and established the political strategy that later worked so well in Congress. Shortly after Curtis had been elected to the U.S. Senate in 1907, a campaign observer noted that the Kaw Indian from Kansas had "never tasted liquor or smoked a cigar."[23] Other evidence supports the veracity of this observation.[24] An ardent supporter of prohibition on the national level, Curtis nevertheless stated, "I am free to confess I did not like the [Kansas] Prohibition law [of 1881] but I did believe it was the duty of every officer to do his best to enforce it."[25] As county attorney he did just that, in spite of the misguided belief of the illicit saloon-keepers (who had supported his election) that Curtis was a "resubmissionist" and one of their own. The dominant Republican Party in Kansas had come out solidly for prohibition, and after Curtis had virtually ended the flow of alcohol in Topeka, the party gave him its hearty support for reelection in 1886.[26] Thus did Curtis secure recognition as a politician who could get things done, who could support laws even though they might conflict with personal belief, and who had improved his social and economic status—all this merged with his humble Kaw beginnings. He had truly demonstrated that the rugged individualism so pervasive in American society at that time was not beyond the grasp of Indians.

The year 1889 was an important juncture in the emergence of Curtis as an Indian leader. He returned to his private law practice, accelerated the political activities that would lead to his election to Congress in 1892, and succeeded in having his name placed back on the Kaw roll in the Indian Territory.[27] Passage of the General Allotment Act two years earlier had provided the legislative tool for the final assault on Indian sovereignty, and the timing of its enactment coincided well with Curtis's awareness that his "progressive" performance as an Indian *individual* was one of his greatest political assets. The G.A.R. could call him "Our Charley"; constituents could pride themselves on having shaken his hand and discussed the Kansas weather; and his political opponents could ridicule him as a whispering palaverer, or worse, as an "Injun." But they missed the point. William Allen White, who thought he knew Curtis well, wrote to Curtis in 1925, "Looking over your career in a rather cool-blooded way, I should say you, externally, have a lot of the French and Indian, but internally, your governing spirit has been . . . New England."[28] His white blood notwithstanding, it was the external, and especially the Indian, identity that Curtis exploited so well, as is evident in a different observation made twenty years earlier.

> Although slightly less than one-quarter Indian, Curtis might from his features and his swarthy skin, be taken for a full-blood. "The Indian" he has been called, sometimes in hate, sometimes in admiration, throughout his political career. "Beat the Indian" was the battle cry in many a hard-fought campaign. But it was not enough to beat the Indian who has just reached a dominating place [as senator] in Kansas politics. Curtis has the wily persistence and dogged determination in a fight that marks him as a true son of his Kaw ancestors.[29]

Affirming such "wily persistence and dogged determination" reveals much about the mythology of the Kaw Indian who became Hoover's vice-president. As perceived, it suggests that step by step, with almost savage tenacity, the Indian from Kansas slowly but surely stalked his political prey so that ultimately it was his in 1928—the most noble achievement of his natural career. But this ignores his more important contribution while dealing with Indian matters from 1892 to 1907.

As noted, "Czar" Reed was impressed with Curtis's ability to move legislation off dead center, and for the conservative Republicans he played a useful behind-the-scenes role.[30] National issues, however, did not really concern him. "He had a rabble-rousing speech with a good deal of

Civil War in it," recalled White, "a lot of protective tariff, and a very carefully poised straddle on the currency question (which, I was satisfied—and still think—that he knew little about and cared absolutely nothing for). For his politics were purely personal. Issues never bothered him."[31] And later, at the time of the Cuban crisis of 1898, "Our Charley' knew nothing about the deeper currents of imperialism that were sweeping the world in the nineteenth century. He was out after votes to hold his job, and 'free Cuba' was a vote-getter."[32]

The one issue that did excite Curtis was Indians, not just because he was *an* Indian, but because he was a *progressive* Indian who by personal interest and public responsibility was determined to help complete the allotment revolution begun decades earlier—even as early as the one that his distant relatives had begun in 1825. The committee assignments he received indicate that his colleagues in the House were willing to cooperate to the utmost. He was assigned to the Committee on Territories, which had major responsibility for setting the scene for Oklahoma statehood; to the Committee on Ways and Means and the Committee on Public Lands, which were both important to Indian policy in general; to the Committee on Expenditures in the Interior Department, which Curtis chaired after 1897, and which exercised great power over the purse strings in Indian matters; and most important of all, to the Committee on Indian Affairs, which Curtis chaired after 1900, and which was involved in nearly every detail of the government's program of detribalization.

In 1900 Representative Curtis wrote to Interior Secretary Ethan Allen Hitchcock, "I have done more to secure legislation for the [Indian] Territory than all the others put together since the 54th Cong. [of 1896]."[33] This was neither exaggeration nor mere idle speculation, as informed people in the Indian Territory knew only so well. Said a Muskogee paper, "He [Curtis] is now not only the most powerful man in the House of Representatives in matters concerning this Indian country, but his influence is equally great with members of the Senate."[34] When questioned as to the key to his success, Curtis went straight to the point: "Single out a few of the most vital points, agree on them absolutely and then work for those alone."[35] The record bears this out.

The Indian Office files and other documents are abundant with the numerous details Curtis attended to with great dedication. He helped the town of Newkirk in Indian Territory obtain a free wagon bridge to

Kaw country across the Arkansas[36] he aided the Kiowas in their efforts to prevent neighboring tribes from making claims on their reservation lands,[37] and he brought pressure on the Bureau of Indian Affairs to have coal and asphalt revenues pay for the operation of the Chickasaw schools.[38] He sponsored numerous railroad bills in Congress for the Indian Territory, as, for example, a branch of the Katy through the Osage and Kaw reservations to Cowley County, Kansas,[39] and he wrote scores of recommendations for people (including relatives) seeking employment in Indian education.[40] He wrote letters of introduction to the Indian Bureau for merchants attempting to sell goods and services for use on Indian reservations[41]; he took great interest in Indian law enforcement, though essentially from the standpoint of economy in operations[42]; and he listened with sympathy to tribal councils who wished to press claims against the government.[43] Heirship problems, particularly those of minor children, were of great concern to him,[44] and he made regular visits to Indian Territory for talks with Indian leaders and white politicians, so much so that in later years he often was referred to as Oklahoma's third senator.[45]

With few exceptions, he used his position of power to influence the appointment of Indian service personnel sympathetic to his point of view, and he mixed politics freely in the process. For example, at Grayhorse and Hominy on the Osage Reservation in the Indian Territory and on the Prairie Potawatomi Reservation in Kansas, he insisted that trade privileges and inside information regarding the sale of surplus land be granted to individuals of Republican persuasion.[46] Fully aware of the power that newspapers could exert in promulgating the allotment revolution, Curtis saw to it that the Indian Bureau printed official notices in Republican newspapers in Kansas, Indian Territory, and elsewhere.[47] He recommended numerous Republicans for appointment as tribal attorneys;[48] he tampered freely in the appointment of tribal chiefs and business leaders who were prepared to cooperate with the government; and he showed little patience with those who tried to oppose him.[49] Perhaps no better tribute to his effectiveness in obtaining support for his program can be found than in an article printed in the Guthrie *State Capital* in 1903. Describing Curtis as the one most powerful figure in Congress on Indian matters, the *Capital* complained that "Kansas has the lion's share of the federal jobs in the Indian Territory—fully one-third more than any other state in the Union."[50]

At a different level, Curtis was closely tied to corporations involved in the exploitation of natural resources in Indian Territory. As early as 1897 it was reported that Curtis and the House Committee on Indian Affairs were in "total agreement" with Indian Commissioner William A. Jones's determination "to take hold of the problem in the Indian Territory. . . . There are now over 200,000 whites in Indian Territory. . . . They have made improvements worth millions of dollars and to talk of ejecting them and confiscating their property is nonsense."[51] Three years later, in commenting on a pro-oil amendment proposed by Curtis to the Cherokee allotment bill, the same newspaper stated, "The bill seems to indicate that Standard Oil Co. has a champion in Congress, and that he is doing his very best to protect his clients."[52] Less than a month later it was reported that "Congressman Curtis has again over rode [*sic*] the report of the sub-committee and introduced a section in the Cherokee agreement protecting Standard Oil in the Cherokee nation."[53] That same year evidence was brought forth that Curtis was using improper legal maneuvers to prevent the higher courts from tampering with corporate oil interests in the Indian Territory.[54]

As in Kansas, where he was heavily tied to the railroad interests, Curtis characteristically attempted to maintain a low profile.[55] In 1905, for example, during congressional hearings over the controversial 1.5 million dollar Indian Territory Illuminating Oil Company lease on the Osage Reservation, Curtis offered that "he knew very little about the implications concerning activity of oil interests upon Indian lands," whereupon the committee room broke up in laughter after one of Curtis's colleagues said, "[T]he Chairman of this [Indian Affairs] Committee is not excelled by any other member of Congress in drawing bills where he does not have knowledge of the subject."[56] Such humor aside, the fact is that Curtis was extremely well informed on the relationship between mineral exploitation and Indian policy, and that he worked hard for corporate interests to develop this resource. As an accomplished attorney he was knowledgeable on the complexities of corporate arrangement and strategy. He brought pressure on the Interior Department to award pipeline contracts to big business, and he displayed unusual ingenuity in sorting out and recommending exploration leases designed to eliminate competition in the burgeoning oil and gas fields south of Kansas.[57] So blatant were his actions in 1906 that the Interior Department, in a memorandum to President Theodore Roosevelt, categorically termed eighty-one Standard Oil-financed leases recommended by Curtis—covering 6,648 acres in the Cherokee Nation and reported to be valued in the vicinity of eight million dollars—as patently illegal.[58]

Such activity points to one of the two most important contributions that Curtis made as an Indian leader—the Curtis Act of June 28, 1898, or as it was officially known, "an act for the protection of the people of the Indian Territory, and for other purposes."[59] A number of tribes were excluded from authority of the General Allotment Act of 1887, including the so-called Five Civilized Tribes of Indian Territory. By virtue of the Indian Appropriation Act of March 3, 1893, Congress removed this exemption, and shortly thereafter President Grover Cleveland appointed a commission composed of chairman Henry Dawes, and associate commissioners Archibald S. McKennon and Meredith Kidd, to make allotments to the Five Tribes.[60] But because leaders of all tribes refused to have any dealings with the Dawes Commission (as it came to be known), Congress in 1896 granted additional authority for the commission to prepare the tribal rolls unilaterally, if, after the expiration of a ninety-day waiting period, the tribes refused to take action on their own.[61] By the Atoka Agreement of 1897 the Choctaws and Chickasaws capitulated, but with the Cherokees taking the leadership, the remaining three tribes did not. More stringent legislation was needed, certainly in the mind of Charles Curtis of Kansas.

Often at odds with the Dawes Commission,[62] Curtis was convinced that one man could "do more than the entire Commission,"[63] which is precisely what many of the Indians feared. The *Purcell Register* in Oklahoma Territory reported how "the smooth Cherokees sent ten thousand dollars to Charley Curtis's district in Kansas to be used in defeating him for the nomination in Congress."[64] According to the Vinita newspaper, which conceded that Curtis was the architect of the 1898 bill, Curtis was smug and confident that his will would prevail. He expected no amendments, boasted of how the House Committee on Indian Affairs was following his instructions to the letter, and announced, "The passage of this bill will be the beginning of a new era for that country."[65]

There is little doubt that the Curtis Act of 1898 had profound consequences. In addition to forcing the Seminoles, Creeks, and Cherokees to divide their lands in severalty, it abolished tribal law and courts; provided comprehensive guidelines for the legalization of townsites in Indian Territory—mostly to the disadvantage of the full-bloods; continued the power of the federal inspectors; established civil government for the Indian Territory; gave the Interior Department discretionary authority over oil and other mineral leases; and established the political setting for Oklahoma statehood nine years later.[66] A firm testimony to Curtis's legislative prowess was that the House easily passed the bill after less than three minutes of consideration. Many members were absent; others were yawning or sleeping on lounges. "An air of indolence prevailed," noted one observer.[67]

Announcement of the outcome brought angry responses in Cherokee country. Violence by full-bloods at Goingsnake courthouse in the Cooweescoowee District was tempered only after the sheriff was able to "send them off into the woods to try the contents of another bottle, while the judge sadly attended to business as provided by the Curtis Bill."[68] DeWitt Clinton Duncan, a mixed-blood Cherokee who wrote under the penname "Too-Qua-Stee," could say only that "this nefarious, tyrannical, Curtis law dishonors the social life of our people . . . and reduces all the noble fathers and mothers of our country to the moral condition of pimps and prostitutes."[69]

Four years later, after having played a major role in its drafting, Curtis prevented a last-ditch effort to block House consideration of the Cherokee Allotment Act by bringing personal pressure on President Roosevelt.[70] The mixed-blood Kaw from Kansas had demonstrated how the real world of power and politics operated.

By then Curtis had demonstrated another talent for Indian leadership—the efficient and untroublesome allotment of his own tribe. Because the Kaws did not come under specific authority of the Curtis Act or other congressional actions of the 1890s, it was left to the tribal agent to supervise the allotment process. In 1903, O. A. Mitscher recalled the situation on the Kaw Reservation when he had first assumed his duties as agent in 1901. "At the time the sentiment against allotment was almost unanimous, both among the full and mixed-bloods. Any person talking allotment was considered an enemy to the best interests of the tribe. . . . After being on the reservation a short time [I] came to the conclusion that it would be best for the Indian and best for Oklahoma to open this land for settlement."[71]

Mitscher's change of mind was less a reflection of personal conviction or changing tribal sentiment as it was the consequence of pressure brought to bear by a small group of mixed-bloods led by "General" William E. Hardy, a white "squaw-man" who had been officially adopted by the Kaws and appointed for life as secretary and treasurer of the Kaw National Council by Interior Secretary Ethan Allen Hitchcock.[72] Hardy's position on allotment was clearly at odds with the majority of the tribe, as is apparent from his statement to a Coffeyville newspaper declaring that "the roving disposition of his people will remain the same, no matter how much civilization does for them" and that "the next move of the full and half-bloods . . . will be to Mexico."[73] Hitchcock also appointed Kaw full-blood Washungah of the Picayune band as titular chief for life, but it was Hardy who was the effective political leader of the tribe. And to shore up his confidence was his nephew and chairman of the House Committee on Indian Affairs, Congressman Charles Curtis of Kansas.[74]

Over the years a legend has grown regarding the ease with which the Kaw tribe worked out the details of their allotment. By comparison to the Cherokees, the Osages, and literally scores of other tribes who at great expense and almost endless negotiation had to be literally forced to accept the inevitable, the Kaws accomplished the division of their lands with ease, very little expense to the government, and what one scholar has called "remarkable harmony."[75] This they did in 1902, but only because their situation was unique beyond comparison. With Curtis in power, Mitscher serving as government liaison, and Hardy as reservation manager, the outcome was never in doubt. Most of the developments have been described elsewhere, but for the present purpose a few details will serve to confirm Curtis's central role in Kaw allotment and to indicate how by his personal performance he was able to prove his "progressive" leadership to the outside world.[76]

Following a visit to the Kaw Reservation in the summer of 1901, Curtis wrote to the Indian Bureau that he feared certain unspecified developments "might delay changes contemplated by the Kaws." The same letter requested a new survey of the reservation in anticipation of allotment, and the retention of an unpopular Kaw clerk "until after the [land] selections [had] been made."[77] Shortly thereafter, the Indian commissioner received an unsolicited resolution from the Kaw council, requesting the visit of a Kaw delegation to Washington to talk over matters "peculiar to the Kaw Tribe of Indians both of land and money and now pending before the Department in Washington."[78] Within days, a letter arrived from Curtis in Topeka, reminding the commissioner that he had earlier made a verbal agreement to this action.[79]

By January 1902, Curtis was back in Washington. On the fifteenth he received an urgent letter from Washungah, stating, "I very much prefer a delegation to go to Washington rather than attempt a settlement here [on the reservation], for to submit matters here would only delay our purpose—so I ask that a delegation of 7 representative Kaw Indians be allowed to come and treat with the Government for final disposition of our matters."[80] Curtis personally selected the delegation that quickly came to Washington, and it was he who wrote the allotment document signed by the delegation of February 8, 1902. On July 1 of that year it was written into law. Since it had been agreed that the delegation's decision would be final, the document was never submitted to a general vote of the tribal membership.[81]

"When the Kaw lands were allotted recently," said a local newspaper, "Congressman Curtis, because of the fact that there is one-quarter [*sic*] Indian blood in his veins, was made the owner of a valuable tract of land in the reservation, sharing equally with members of the Kaw tribe. He also secured allotment for his children, and the Curtis family now owns about 1,800 acres of good land in the Arkansas valley."[82] General Hardy gave a different reason, which captured better the essence of his distinguished nephew's progressive Indian leadership:

> Since Curtis has been in Congress he has done great things for the Indian, not only the Kaws, but the Indian everywhere, whenever the opportunity offered. When the Kaw lands were allotted the general council of the tribe voted unanimously to place his name on the Kaw rolls of citizenship, allowing him to share equally with us our land. In this manner we made him an honorary member of the tribe and only in part repaid him for the work he had done for the Indians.[83]

Notes

1. *Time*, February 24, 1936.

2. A summary of Curtis's political career, especially for the vice-presidential years, is Marvin Ewy, "Charles Curtis of Kansas: Vice President of the United States, 1929–1933," *Emporia State Research Studies* 10 (December 1961). For the role of Dolly Curtis Gann in Washington society, see Dolly Gann, *Dolly Gann's Book* (Garden City, N.Y., 1933).

3. James C. Malin, "Charles Curtis," *Dictionary of American Biography*, vol. 22 (New York, 1958), p. 136.

4. William Allen White, *The Autobiography of William Allen White* (New York, 1946), p. 304.

5. Ewy, "Charles Curtis," pp. 22–23.

6. Ibid., pp. 18, 23, 49; *Coffeyville Daily Journal*, February 8, 1902.

7. Article 2, Charles Curtis Autobiography, Charles Curtis Papers, Manuscript Division, Kansas State Historical Society.

8. Article 1, ibid.

9. Charles J. Kappler, *Indian Affairs: Laws and Treaties*, vol. 2 (Washington, D.C., 1904), pp. 222–25.

10. Berlin B. Chapman, "Charles Curtis and the Kaw Reservation," *The Kansas Historical Quarterly* 15 (November 1947), p. 337; Malin, "Charles Curtis," p. 136; *Ponca City Daily Courier*, September 16, 1903; Kaw Indian Census Rolls, Pawnee Agency Miscellaneous Files, Records of the Bureau of Indian Affairs, Record Group 75 (hereafter cited as RG 75), Federal Archives and Records Center (hereafter cited as FARC), Fort Worth Texas (hereafter cited as FW).

11. William E. Unrau, *The Kansa Indians: A History of the Wind People, 1673–1873* (Norman, Okla., 1971), p. 34; Reverend John Rothensteiner, "Early Missionary Efforts among the Indians in the Diocese of St. Louis," *St. Louis Catholic Historical Review* 2 (1920), p. 79; Gann, *Dolly Gann's Book*, pp. 2–3; Wil-

liam E. Unrau, "The Mixed-Blood Connection: Charles Curtis and Kaw Detribalization," in Forrest Blackburn (et al.,) eds., *Kansas and the West: Bicentennial Essays in Honor of Nyle H. Miller* (Topeka, Kans., 1976), pp. 153–54.

The traditional interpretation is that Julie Gonvil's (Gonville's?) husband Louis was the son of Louis Pappan, Sr., who had come to the St. Louis area from Montreal in the late eighteenth century. Catholic marriage, baptismal, and burial records, however, suggest that Julie's father-in-law may have been Joseph Marie Pepin (dit Lachance, who married Josephine Gonville [Gonvil?], half-blood Osage daughter of Joseph Gonville [Gonvil?], and an unidentified full-blood Osage woman). If so, Julie and her husband Louis were blood relatives, and the Osage blood-quantum on the maternal side would have made Charles Curtis a three-sixteenths Kaw-Osage, as opposed to the traditionally accepted one-eighth Kaw. See appropriate entries in *Catholic Marriages, St. Louis, Missouri, 1774–1840* (St. Louis, n.d.), and *Index of St. Charles Marriage Registers, 1792–1863* (St. Charles, 1969), both based on the indices prepared by Oscar Collet and available in the Missouri Historical Society, St. Louis.

12. Gann, *Dolly Gann's Book*, pp. 1–3; "Born an Indian, Baptized a Catholic," *The Outlook* 149 (July 1928), p. 405; Ewy, "Charles Curtis," pp. 6–9.

13. On September 10, 1866, Kaw Agent Hiram W. Farnsworth reported to Central Superintendent Thomas Murphy, "I am satisfied that the condition of the tribe would be greatly improved if they were moved south [to Indian Territory], and greater facilities furnished them for farming and stock raising." *Annual Report of the Commissioner of Indian Affairs, 1866* (Washington, D.C., 1867), pp. 274–75. The Kaw removal treaty of 1866–1867 failed primarily because competing speculators could not reach a settlement satisfactory to all. For the complex maneuvering underlying the negotiations, see William G. Ewing to B. D. Miner, February 20, 1867, William G. and George Washington Ewing Papers, Manuscript Division, Indiana State Library, Indianapolis. For details of the abortive agreement itself, see "Articles of Agreement made and concluded at the City of Washington on the thirteenth day of February, one thousand eight hundred and sixty-seven between Lewis Bogy, Commissioner of Indian Affairs . . . and Chiefs of the Kansa [Kaw]," Documents Relating to the Negotiation of Ratified and Unratified Treaties with Various Tribes of Indians, 1801–1869, Unratified Treaties, 1866–1869, RG 75, T–494, R 9, National Archives, Washington, D C. (hereafter cited as NA).

14. Kappler, *Indian Affairs*, vol. 2, pp. 552–54; Unrau, *Kansa Indians*, pp. 208–9.

15. Ibid., pp. 209–12. Kickapoo Agent Franklin G. Adams was mainly responsible for the exaggerated reports that a bloody encounter would occur at

Council Grove. Writing to Indian Commissioner N. G. Taylor two months after the event, Central Superintendent Thomas Murphy stated, "Of course it is well known that Adams' report is not correct—the real factor is the desire of certain parties [notably Joab Spencer and James Mead] to keep the [Kaw] Indians confined for the issuing of rations." See Murphy to Taylor, August 5, 1868, March 11, 1869, and J. W. McMillan to Taylor, March 11, 1869, Letters Received by the Office of Indian Affairs (hereafter cited as LR), RG 75, Kansas Agency, M 234, R 367–368, NA.

16. *New York Times*, April 14, 1929.

17. Captain M. Howard to Captain Martin Mullins, July 8, 1868, LR, RG 75, Kansas Agency, NA; Samuel J. Crawford, *Kansas in the Sixties* (Chicago, 1911), pp. 288–89; Unrau, *Kansa Indians*, p. 211; Ewy, "Charles Curtis," p. 9; Mark Plummer, *Frontier Governor: Samuel Crawford of Kansas* (Lawrence, Kans., 1971), pp. 117–19.

18. While Curtis later claimed that in 1874 he had "a longing for the old [Indian] life," the advice of Julie Pappan prevailed, and Curtis severed his association with the Kaw tribe, at least for the present. See Ewy, "Charles Curtis," pp. 10–11. Statement of Laban J. Miles before Subcommittee of the House Committee on Indian Affairs, n.d., 1910, and C. W. Holcomb to Cyrus Bede, February 18, 1878, *Osage Enrollment, Hearings before a Subcommittee of the House Committee on Indian Affairs*, 61st Cong., 2d sess., (Washington, D.C., 1910), pp. 36, 91–92.

19. Ewy, "Charles Curtis," pp. 10–13; Gann, *Dolly Gann's Book*, pp. 1, 6.

20. Frank F. Finney, "The Kaw Indians and Their Indian Territory Agency," *Chronicles of Oklahoma* 35 (Winter 1957–58), p. 418. This shocking decline was part of a demographic pattern preceding removal to Indian Territory. Less than a year prior to Curtis's birth in 1860, the Kaw population stood at 1,037. By 1868 it had decreased to 825, and in the year prior to removal there was not one Kaw male over the age of fifty-five. According to a report from Agent Mahlon Stubbs in 1872, the Kaws were "absolutely destitute [and] living on a little corn and dead animals they can find lying around." See William E. Unrau, "The Depopulation of the Dheghia-Siouan Kansa Prior to Removal," *New Mexico Historical Review* 48 (October 1973), p. 320; and Mahlon Stubbs to Enoch Hoag, March 18, 1872, LR, RG 75, Kansas Agency, NA

21. Ewy, "Charles Curtis," pp. 11–14.

22. Article 3, Curtis Autobiography, Curtis Papers.

23. Sheffield Cowdrick, " 'From Saddle to Senate,' The Remarkable Career of Charles Curtis, a Kaw Indian," *The World Today* (March 1907), p. 314.

24. Ewy, "Charles Curtis," p. 54.

25. Article 7, Curtis Autobiography, Curtis Papers.

26. Ewy, "Charles Curtis," pp. 16–18. Important highlights of Curtis's spectacular career as a law-and-order man on prohibition and criminal prosecution in general are recorded in the *Topeka Daily Capital,* March 2; April 18; May 1, 3, 15; June 6, 11, 12, 16, 24, 30; July 15; August 21; and December 5, 1885.

27. *Topeka Daily Capital,* April 2, 18, 21; July 10; August 21, 1889; Statement of Laban J. Miles (1910), *Osage Enrollment,* pp. 91–92.

28. White to Curtis, May 19, 1925, William Allen White Papers, Series C, Box 66, Manuscript Division, Library of Congress.

29. Cowdrick, "'From Saddle to Senate,'" pp. 313–14.

30. Ewy, "Charles Curtis," p. 23.

31. White, *Autobiography,* p. 106.

32. Ibid., p. 305.

33. Curtis to Ethan Allen Hitchcock, n.d., Ethan Allen Hitchcock Papers, Private Papers Collection, RG 200, NA.

34. *Muskogee Phoenix,* August 9, 1900.

35. Ibid.

36. Curtis to Commissioner of Indian Affairs (hereafter cited as CIA), November 21, 1898, LR, RG 75, Land, NA.

37. *Muskogee Phoenix,* May 10, 1894.

38. Acting Commissioner of Indian Affairs to Secretary of the Interior, August 28, 1900, Records of the Office of Secretary of the Interior, RG 48, Box 73, Indian Territory Division, Special Files, NA.

39. H.R. 12069, Records of the United States House of Representatives, RG 233, Box 4416, Committee on Indian Affairs, NA.

40. Curtis to CIA, August 7, 1900, LR, RG 75, Education, NA.

41. Curtis to CIA, May 15, 1901, LR, RG 75, Finance, NA.

42. *Muskogee Phoenix,* March 26, 1896.

43. *Arkansas City Daily Traveler,* September 5, 1901.

44. Curtis to CIA, July 14, 1902, LR, RG 75, Land, NA.

45. *Muskogee Phoenix,* September 16, 1897; "Oklahoma Oil May Bring Riches to Indian Senator from Kansas," clipping, n.d., Charles Curtis Clipping Books, 1907–1923, Library Division, Kansas State Historical Society.

46. Curtis to W. A. Jones, September 14, 1897, LR, RG 75, Miscellaneous, NA; R. W. Johnson to CIA, September 2, 1902, and Curtis to W. A. Jones, September 15, 1902, LR, RG 75, Land, NA.

47. Curtis to CIA, December 6, 1900, LR, RG 75, ibid.; Curtis to CIA, July 15, 1901, LR, RG 75, Finance, NA.

48. Curtis to CIA, June 24, 1898, LR, RG 75, Land, NA.

49. Curtis to CIA, May 23, 1898, ibid.

50. *State Capital*, n.d., in Ethan Allen Hithcock Clipping Book, Hitchcock Papers.

51. *Vinita Indian Chieftain*, December 23, 1897.

52. Ibid., May 3, 1900.

53. Ibid., May 31, 1900.

54. Ibid., May 3, 1900.

55. Ewy, "Charles Curtis," pp. 26–27.

56. H. Craig Miner, *The Corporation and the Indian: Tribal Sovereignty and Industrial Civilization in Indian Territory, 1865–1907* (Columbia, Mo., 1976), p. 178.

57. Curtis to Ethan Allen Hitchcock (marked "Personal"), October 23, 1903, and Curtis to Hitchcock, March 30, 1905, Hitchcock Papers.

58. Curtis to Hitchcock, September 11, 1904; and Hitchcock to President Theodore Roosevelt, September 26, 1906, ibid.

59. Kappler, *Indian Affairs*, vol. 1, pp. 90–91.

60. Ibid., p. 498.

61. Ibid., p. 80.

62. For an example see Archibald S. McKennon to Henry Dawes, July 5, 1899, Box 52, Henry Dawes Papers, Manuscript Division, Library of Congress. Dawes's view that more than one-quarter blood quantum should be required to determine who was a legal Indian obviously did nothing to improve relations with Curtis. See Dawes to Director of the Census, November 11, 1899, Box 53, ibid.

63. *El Reno Americana*, October 29, 1898, in Hitchcock Clipping Books, Hitchcock Papers.

64. Quoted in *Vinita Indian Chieftain*, July 14, 1898.

65. Ibid., March 3, 1898.

66. Kappler, *Indian Affairs*, vol. 1, pp. 90–101.

67. *Vinita Indian Chieftain*, April 21, 1898.

68. Ibid., July 28, 1898.

69. Ibid., July 21, 1898.

70. *Muskogee Phoenix*, July 10, 1902.

71. *Kaw City Star*, September 18, 1903.

72. Ibid.

73. *Coffeyville Daily Journal*, n.d., quoted in *Muskogee Phoenix*, January 20, 1898.

74. *Kaw City Star*, September 18, 1903.

75. "Honorable Charles Curtis, American Indian Senator from Kansas," *The American Indian Magazine* 7 (August 1920), pp. 41–42; Chapman, "Charles Curtis," p. 348.

76. Unrau, "Mixed-Blood Connection" pp. 151–61.

77. Curtis to CIA, August 27, 1901, LR, RG 75, Land, NA.

78. Resolution of Wah-Shun-Gah ("X" his mark), Wah-Mo-O-E-Ke ("X" his mark), Forrest Chouteau, Willie Hardy, Mitchel Fronkier, and W. E. Hardy, Kaw Agency, I.T., August 24, 1901, LR, RG 75, Finance, NA.

79. Curtis to CIA, September 10, 1901, ibid.

80. Washungah (written in the hand of Forrest Chouteau, Acting Secretary of the Kaw Tribe) to Curtis, January 15, 1902, LR, RG 75, Land, NA.

81. Curtis to CIA, January 21, 1902, LR, RG 75, Special Files, NA; Chapman, "Charles Curtis" pp. 342–44.

82. *Kaw City Star*, September 18, 1903. The actual legal acreage was 1,676 acres. See Homestead Allotment of Kaw Indians, 1902, Pawnee Miscellaneous Files, FARC, FW.

83. *Kaw City Star*, September 18, 1903.

Essay on Sources

There is no comprehensive biography of Curtis. Marvin Ewy, "Charles Curtis of Kansas: Vice President of the United States, 1929–1933," *Emporia State Research Studies* 10 (December 1961), is a convenient summary of Curtis's political career, with emphasis on the vice-presidential years. Don C. Seitz, *From Kaw Teepee to Capitol: The Life Story of Charles Curtis, Indian, Who Has Risen to High Estate* (New York: Frederick A. Stoke, 1928), is a sloppy campaign sheet with numerous errors in fact and interpretation; while James C. Malin's essay on Curtis in the *Dictionary of American Biography,* vol. 22, supplement 2 (New York: Macmillan, 1958), p. 136, is a critical overview that, like Ewy, suffers from the absence of a substantial body of Curtis manuscripts.

The limited Charles Curtis Papers in the Kansas State Historical Society raise more questions than they answer; hence, the career of this prominent mixed-blood must be chronicled from congressional documents, Indian Office manuscripts, newspapers, and other private manuscript collections. Of the latter, the William Allen White Papers in the Library of Congress and the Ethan Allen Hitchcock Papers in the National Archives are of considerable importance. The Charles Curtis Scrapbooks, in the Newspaper Division of the Kansas State Historical Society, and the Kaw Indian Collection, in the Western History Collection of the Oklahoma Historical Society, provide considerable information, as do the Pawnee and Osage Miscellaneous Files in the Federal Records Center in Fort Worth, Texas. Among the most important articles on Curtis are: Berlin B. Chapman, "Charles Curtis and the Kaw Reservation," *Kansas Historical Quarterly* 15 (November 1947), pp. 337–51; Frank F. Finney, Sr., "The Kaw Indians and Their Indian Territory Agency," *Chronicles of Oklahoma* 35 (Winter, 1957–58), pp. 416–24; and William E. Unrau, "The Mixed-Blood Connection: Charles Curtis and Kaw Detribalization," in Forrest R. Blackburn et al., eds., *Kansas and the West: Bicentennial Essays in Honor of Nyle H. Miller* (Topeka, Kans., 1976); pp. 151–61. Dolly [Curtis] Gann, *Dolly Gann's Book* (Garden City, N. Y., 1933), is a chatty and uncritical account of selected aspects of Curtis's early life and public career.

6

Luther Standing Bear

"I would raise him to be an Indian"

Richard N. Ellis

Luther Standing Bear (1868–1939) enjoyed membership in a remarkable group of American Indian writers who, in the early decades of this century, wrote on a variety of themes, from autobiography to commentaries on Indian cultures and federal Indian policy. Collectively, they gave voice to Indian attitudes and opinions that had gone unheard and unsolicited for centuries in North America. Like Nampeyo in the realm of art, these writers gave names to Indian authors; they cut the trails so that others might follow.

Standing Bear, a Teton Sioux, was a contemporary of two other notable Sioux writers, Dr. Charles A. Eastman (Santee) and Gertrude Simmons Bonnin (Yankton). A comparison of the lives and careers of these three authors yields interesting and important distinctions.

Born in 1858 near Redwood Falls, Minnesota, Eastman came of age—like Standing Bear—during a period of increasing tension and violence between Indians and other Americans. Raised in a traditional culture to become a hunter-warrior, Eastman was nevertheless persuaded by his Christianized father, who had been pardoned by President Lincoln for his participation in the 1862 "Sioux Uprising," to enter the alien world of white society. A remarkably bright student, Eastman graduated from Dartmouth College and the Boston University School of Medicine. Later, he served as government physician at Pine Ridge Agency; as

Indian Inspector for the Bureau of Indian Affairs; and as Indian secretary for the YMCA. He also helped in founding the Boy Scouts of America, and he is most responsible for the incorporation of elements of Indian lore in that organization. Eastman wrote nine books and some achieved such popularity that they were translated into several different languages. Through his writing he hoped to demolish the wall of prejudice that separated Indians from whites. Because he was one of the best educated Indians of his generation, he had to contend with the very great burden of being the living symbol, in the eyes of non-Indian humanitarian reformers, of all that the Indian could accomplish once he had abandoned savagery and embraced civilization.

Gertrude Bonnin, or Zitkala-Sa (as she often signed her name), was born in 1876 at Yankton Reservation, Dakota Territory. The year of her birth marked the beginning of the final military conquest of the Plains Sioux. Although she learned quickly to distrust and resent whites, she nevertheless sought a formal education, despite her mother's wishes, attending Earlham College in Richmond, Indiana, and later the Boston Conservatory of Music. Her articles and poetry appeared in the leading, mass-circulation magazines of her day. Her most memorable book, American Indian Stories *(1921), depicted her childhood, her initial rejection and eventual acceptance of Christianity, and her changing attitudes toward whites. Like Eastman's autobiographies* (Indian Boyhood [1902] and From the Deep Woods to Civilization [1916]), *her memoir was romantic, describing the Indian way of life as a state of grace inevitably corrupted by the coming of the Euroamericans. Bonnin's account, however, was less detailed in its treatment of Sioux customs and more openly resentful of non-Indians.*

Luther Standing Bear, in marked contrast, was a member of the first class at Carlisle Indian School. Unlike Bonnin and Eastman, he never went to college; he acquired only a rudimentary education—which makes his later career as a writer all the more remarkable—and he learned a trade that proved to be useless once be returned to the reservation. He never achieved the same celebrity as did his two more famous Sioux contemporaries. They were the darlings of the Christian humanitarians who advocated assimilation; his was a more checkered career, which included performing in Wild West shows and appearing in Hollywood movies. Standing Bear gained an audience for his more elaborate ethnographies of Sioux culture during a period when assimilationists and their policies were in retreat. Whereas both Bonnin and Eastman believed that Indians should adopt white ways and sometimes retain only inchoate spiritual values from their heritage, Standing Bear championed the rights of traditionalists to live free from molesta-

tion by either the government or the reformer. Standing Bear's writings of the 1920s and 1930s would be echoed by other Indian authors who came to prominence in the 1960s and 1970s.

"Today the children of our public schools are taught more of the history, heroes, legends, and sagas of the old world than of the land of their birth while they are furnished with little material on the people and institutions that are truly American," wrote Luther Standing Bear to President Franklin D. Roosevelt in a 1933 letter in which he proposed a bill to require the teaching of American Indian history and culture in the nation's public schools.[1] In the same year, in *Land of the Spotted Eagle,* Standing Bear expounded on the role of native peoples in American history and on the need to preserve traditional cultures. That book called for a new attitude toward Indian people and forcefully recommended changes in United States Indian policy—recommendations that are similar to those made by Indian leaders in the 1960s and 1970s.

These reforms were advanced by Luther Standing Bear, whose full life included traditional Sioux society as well as education at the Carlisle Indian School in Pennsylvania; employment at John Wanamaker's famous department store in Philadelphia; various occupations on the reservation; participation in Buffalo Bill's Wild West Show; and work as a film actor, lecturer and writer. Although he wrote four books—two of them important, one of which is largely autobiographical—many aspects of his life remain unknown. Written late in his life, it is not surprising that *My People the Sioux,* which recounts autobiographical episodes, contains some errors and perhaps an inflated sense of family and self-importance. Similar criticism, however, can be applied to virtually all autobiographies; for memory is a faulty thing and few if any memoirs are self-denigrating in tone.

Even Standing Bear's time of birth is in dispute. According to his own account he was born in "the year of breaking up of camp" and the "month when the bark of the trees cracked," which he reported as December 1868. Bureau of Indian Affairs records, however, list the year of his birth as 1863 and that of his brother, Henry, as 1869; yet there is no reason to assume accuracy on the part of the government because there were no bureau officials among his people at that time.[2]

Standing Bear was a Lakota or Teton Sioux; and though he claimed to be an Oglala, one of the Teton sub-tribes, he was undoubtedly a Brulé. According to his own account he lived at the Spotted Tail Agency and Rosebud Reservation, home of the Brulés, and returned there after attending school at Carlisle. His father later moved to Pine Ridge, the Oglala reservation, and Luther ultimately followed suit. Confirmation of his Brulé identity comes from George Hyde, who collected oral traditions and utilized written records for his studies of the Sioux. Hyde identified the elder Standing Bear's band as "the Wears Salt Band" of the Brulés and found that he was listed on agency rolls as a mixed-blood. Documents for the 1889 land allotment agreement list the elder Standing Bear as a Brulé, and allotment records describe his son Luther Standing Bear as three-quarters Sioux and one-quarter white.[3]

Standing Bear was born into a prominent Brulé family—for his father was undoubtedly a band leader—and he was raised in traditional Sioux culture, a culture that he would see under attack during his lifetime. Significant culture change had occurred by the time he returned from Carlisle, and cultural deterioration continued under the influence of United States Indian policy. While some acculturation had begun with the adoption of white goods such as weapons, implements, and horses, it was not until the 1860s, the decade of Standing Bear's birth, that the Teton Sioux were forced to confront the United States government and its policies. True, Indian agents had already been appointed, and conflict had come with the senseless Grattan Massacre, caused by white stupidity, and the subsequent campaign by William Harney that included a defeat of the Brulés at Ash Hollow; but in the 1860s a permanent American military presence developed in the country of the Tetons.

It was a decade of deceptive warnings to the Sioux, for while the army came in force it also proved to be ineffectual. Military expeditions in the valley of the upper Missouri and to the West in 1863 and 1864 failed to bring a decisive victory over the Tetons, and the elaborate Powder River campaign in 1865 was a failure. Efforts at treaty making were destroyed by the military occupation of the Bozeman Trail in present-day Wyoming, until Red Cloud's war caused the government to abandon the region. It was not until the controversial Fort Laramie Treaty of 1868 that the Great Sioux reservation was created, and agencies, including the Spotted Tail Agency, were established.

These were significant years for the Tetons, for in addition to constant military presence, there were Indian agents, missionaries, a growing white population, and an increased determination by the government to "civilize" reservation Indians through a program of forced acculturation. The flare-up of conflict in 1876, with the Sioux victory at the Little Big Horn, sealed the fate of the Tetons, for the army drove them to the reservation and kept them there. Thus, in the first years of Standing Bear's life, the Sioux lost their freedom and became subject to a program of cultural annihilation that was designed to strip away Indianness and to "Americanize" the Tetons and other native peoples.

Standing Bear describes this transformation in his first book, *My People the Sioux*, without mentioning the battles with the army, except for the Custer fight in which his father participated. He focuses instead on aspects of his youth and traditional Teton culture. His name was Ota Kte, or Plenty Kill, because his father had killed many Indian enemies. During his youth the Brulés had a big battle with Pawnees, in which many enemies were killed and some captured. During the same period he successfully participated in his first and only buffalo hunt, a high point in the life of a young Teton male. He was also a member of a war party that set out to attack the Poncas but was recalled by tribal elders before completing its mission.

Yet this was a period of transition. While Standing Bear was raised to become a hunter and warrior, he also witnessed the impact of the white presence. His band spent some time near the agency; and his father was a member of a delegation to Washington, returning dressed in a Prince Albert coat, a stiff shirt, and a silk hat which soon was used to carry water.[4] It was also a time of white buffalo hunters and the dramatic reduction of the great herds that brought a dependence on government rations. When Standing Bear saw his first cattle—"spotted buffalo," the Sioux called them—he was struck by their foul smell, and later, upon noticing that whites at the agency were bald, he wondered if they got that way from eating beef. Other rations included flour and green coffee beans. The Sioux did not make bread and were not instructed in the use of flour, so they threw it away and used the sacks to make shirts. They had to learn, too, that the coffee beans had to be roasted and ground, though they did not have coffee mills. Coffee was bitter; they called it *pejuta sapa*, or black medicine. Thinking that it would be better if it were more bitter, his mother added pepper to the coffee. It was also a time of contact with white people such as missionaries, although, according to Standing Bear's memoir, "along with them came the bootleggers."[5]

Reservation life brought even more drastic modification of Sioux culture, as virtually every important cultural aspect was attacked by a government determined to eliminate the old ways. Disappearance of the buffalo herds brought basic economic change and dependence on the government, which meant that both cultural traits associated with the buffalo and the major economic activities of adult males began to disappear. Raiding and warfare were prohibited, reducing the significance of warrior societies and closing to young men such as Standing Bear a major avenue for economic, social, and political advancement. Missionaries attacked traditional religion as "pagan," and the government banned the Sun Dance, the most important religious ceremony of the Tetons. Supported by Indian police and ultimately by the army in the exercise of nearly totalitarian powers, Indian agents often withheld rations as a means of forcing the Sioux to follow instructions. Perhaps most significant of all was the effort to destroy the authority of traditional chiefs as a method of reducing cultural integrity.

Reservation Sioux faced these and other pressures in the late 1870s and thereafter; but young Luther Standing Bear was thrust into the midst of another aspect of the acculturation program when he became a member of the first group of Indian students to attend the new Indian school at Carlisle, Pennsylvania. In 1879 the government tried to recruit children for the school, and young Standing Bear decided to go. He was influenced perhaps by his father's decision that fighting would gain nothing for the Sioux and that they would have to learn the ways of the whites; but Standing Bear also longed to do something courageous. "It occurred to me," he later wrote, "that this chance to go East would prove that I was brave if I were to accept it." He had been taught that it was better to die young on the battlefield than to die of old age, and he fully expected death. He had no idea of what a school was; he thought "we were going East to die."[6]

The trip to Carlisle seemed to confirm that expectation. At the moment of departure on a Missouri River steamboat, some of the children, including Standing Bear's sister, chose not to go. Some of the older boys thought of jumping ship. Soon they were taken from the steamboat "to a long row of little houses standing on pieces of iron which stretched away as far as we could see," and which suddenly began to move. This was their first experience with *Maza Canku*, or Iron Road, known to whites as a railroad train. As they traveled on, they feared that the whites planned to kill them by taking them "to the place where the sun rises, where they would dump us over the edge of the earth." Many times during the trip, the older boys sang brave songs to keep up their courage, but they arrived safely at the old cavalry barracks at Carlisle.[7]

The school planned and directed by Richard Henry Pratt was to become the most famous of the Indian schools. It was a pilot project which would make education an important element in the program of acculturation. Pratt, an army officer who had commanded Negro troops and had been responsible for Indian prisoners in Florida, was convinced that Indians could and should be educated, and his school was dedicated to the goal of fitting Indian people into white society. "In Indian affairs I am a Baptist," he once said, "because I believe in immersing the Indians in our civilization and when we get them under holding them there until they are thoroughly soaked."[8] As a result, he planned to teach them to read and write in English, to learn a trade, and to acquire discipline. At Carlisle, Indian children were thrust out of their own worlds and into the white world, where even the so-called outing system, a summer program which placed Indian children in white homes, as designed to bring them into a closer association with the cultue of white America.

For Standing Bear and the other Sioux children, a perception of the strangeness of white culture began immediately. The school was not prepared for their arrival, and they were placed in dormitories that lacked beds and other furnishings. They dined on bread and water in the morning and bread, meat, and coffee at noon. "How lonesome the big boys and girls were for their far-away Dakota homes where there was plenty to eat." Eventually the food got better and they were provided with mattresses of straw.[9]

As instruction commenced, the children were called to a blackboard with writing on it. Each word was a white man's name, and each child picked a name with a pointer. Standing Bear chose the name Luther, which was then sewn on his back. After he had learned to write his name, the teacher wrote the alphabet on his slate and he sat trying to decipher what it meant; but "no one was there to tell me that the first letter was 'A' and the next 'B' and so on." The next day, the teacher "talked to me in English, but of course I did not know what she was saying." Eventually the interpreter was brought in to explain the alphabet.[10]

Attendance at Carlisle also meant a change of appearance, for long hair and traditional clothes symbolized traditional culture. "The Transforming, the 'civilizing' process began. It began with clothes," he wrote. "Never, no matter what our philosophy or spiritual quality, could we be civilized while wearing the moccasin and blanket. The task before us was not only that of accepting new ideas and adopting new manners, but actual physical changes and discomfort has to be born uncomplainingly until the body adjusted itself to new tastes and habits." They were given pants, coats, vests, farmer's boots, and other items that felt "cumbersome and awkward"; they had difficulty deciding whether pants buttoned up the back or front. They also received red flannel underwear, which caused "actual torture" and was remembered by Standing Bear as the worst thing about life at Carlisle. It was so bad that he risked breaking the rules by wearing it only for inspection. Each child also was permitted to select the religious denomination that appealed to him; on Sunday inspection was held, followed by attendance at Sunday school in town.[11]

In addition to academic training, each boy was taught a skill. Standing Bear was trained as a tinsmith, and he made cups, coffeepots, and buckets that were issued to reservation Indians. On returning home, he found that the trade was of no benefit because "the Indians had plenty of tinware that I had made at school."[12] Requests to abandon the trade and to go to school all day long were rejected. A skill of slightly more value lay in learning to play the cornet and participating in the Carlisle band, for the band performed at the ceremony opening the Brooklyn Bridge and at other locations in New York.

A student's life at Carlisle was carefully regulated and designed to eliminate Indianness. At times it brought embarrassment and humiliation; occasionally it created situations that were ludicrous. For example, in an effort to instill a sense of competition, a teacher asked a student to read aloud a paragraph for criticism by other students. Standing Bear read without errors, but the teacher questioned if his reading had been perfect. He read the paragraph again and again and again, until the eleventh time when "everything before me went black and I sat down thoroughly cowed and humiliated for *the first time in my life* and in front of the whole class!"[13]

Because English was the only language permitted at Carlisle, Standing Bear could not communicate with his visiting father, who spoke only Lakota, until he had received permission from Captain Pratt. After touring eastern cities, his father told him that the whites "keep coming like flies" and that it was necessary to learn their ways to be able to live with them. His father's visit stimulated the young Carlisle student.[14]

Standing Bear took his father's advice and became a model student, twice returning to Sioux country to recruit more students, and the second time making the trip alone. Along with Robert American Horse, Maggie Stands Looking, and a few others, he decided to remain at Carlisle when the first group of Sioux students returned home, a decision that led to his employment at the Wanamaker department store in Philadelphia.

When Luther Standing Bear returned to his reservation, he had received something of an education; he had learned a trade that proved useless to him; he had acquired practical experience in a store; and he had gained familiarity with the white world. He returned resplendent, dressed in the latest style of clothing; he "felt quite 'swell' in them," although later he laughed when he remembered his appearance. He returned to a reservation where the old life had changed. "It was," he wrote "like the Garden of Eden after the fall of man."[15]

Standing Bear was more fortunate than most of the returning students, who went home with only a superficial education and a trade that was usually of no value. He could not employ his tinsmithing, but he had a recommendation from Pratt which led to immediate employment as an assistant teacher at a salary of three hundred dollars a year. Bureau of Indian Affairs employees were supportive of the young teacher and described him as "diligent and faithful, persevering and trustworthy"; a "very competent mixed blood."[16]

The years at Rosebud brought a number of changes to Standing Bear's life. His father had bought a house, and having watched the whites dine and wishing his son to have the same benefit at home, he directed the family on how to set the table. Luther was served his meal at the table, and after he had finished the rest of the family sat on the floor to eat. More significant, however, were Luther's marriage to Nellie De Cory, a mixed-blood, and the agreement to permit allotment of the reservation. Luther explained land allotment to his father, who then spoke in favor of the agreement and soon thereafter moved to the Pine Ridge Reservation to select his allotment. The father was at Pine Ridge and Luther was living at Rosebud during the Ghost Dance troubles and the tragedy at Wounded Knee. It was a shocking event for the young teacher. "It made my blood boil. I was ready myself to go and fight then," he wrote. "There I was, doing my best to teach my people to follow the white men's road—even trying to get them to believe in their religion—and this was my reward for it all!"[17]

When Standing Bear visited Pine Ridge to receive a first-hand account of the slaughter from his brother, a scout for the soldiers, he was encouraged to move there by the new agent, whom he had known at Carlisle. Now that his entire family was living at Pine Ridge, he made the move and clerked at an uncle's store before taking over a new government school in Allen, South Dakota. In succeeding years, he bought a ranch and then moved to the agency, where he worked in a store, clerked for the agent, and assisted the minister.

In 1902, he was managing a store in Allen when he was encouraged by friends to apply for a job with Buffalo Bill's Wild West Show. Standing Bear was hired as interpreter and, accompanied by his wife and child, joined the troop at Rushville, Nebraska, continued to New York, and then traveled to England where they performed for the king. By his own account, he was in charge of the Indian contingent during the eleven-month tour to England.

In 1903 Standing Bear again agreed to join Buffalo Bill Cody. As the Indians prepared to depart Rushville, two members of the contingent decided not to go because they had dreamed that something bad would happen. Several days later Standing Bear was sitting in the last car of the railroad train chugging across Illinois when a train approaching at high speed smashed into it. A number of Indians were killed, and Standing Bear and others were seriously injured; their participation in Cody's show was over.

According to his account in *My People the Sioux*, Standing Bear was selected as chief in 1905 to replace his deceased father.[18] If this is true, he did not actively fill the role for very long, for in succeeding years he resided on the reservation only intermittently. A major concern during this period was the acquisition of land. Standing Bear filed for his allotment and also sought allotments for his children. In correspondence with the Indian Office, he declared that he had filed a claim for his daughter Jessie soon after her birth in June 1904. The child died, he stated, in

August 1905; and he wanted confirmation of the allotment. His claim was denied because the allotting agent reported that the child actually had died in August 1904, and that Standing Bear had not applied for allotments for himself and his children until May 1906; but as late as 1911, the agent stated, Standing Bear had sought congressional help to acquire the land in question.[19] In that year he also sought an allotment for his new wife, the former May Splicer, a three-quarter-blood Mohawk woman who had been born in Syracuse, New York, and educated at the Lincoln Institute in Philadelphia. They had been married in Sioux City, Iowa, in 1907, and in the succeeding four years they had lived in Walthill, Nebraska. Standing Bear sought to have his wife enrolled as an Oglala and then to get approval of an allotment for her; but that application was denied by the Indian Office because the Oglala tribal council refused to adopt her as a member of the tribe.[20]

During this period Standing Bear did receive his allotment, and after some difficulty, he received title to the land, which gave him the right to do with it as he wished. He recorded that he believed the title would give him his freedom from Indian Office control because it would give him his citizenship. He sought the assistance of Thomas Sloan, an educated member of the Omaha tribe who was a practicing attorney and who would become prominent in national Indian issues. But it was only by presenting himself in the office of the Commissioner of Indian Affairs and virtually camping in the doorway that Standing Bear gained his objective.[21]

Although he resided off the reservation—in Sioux City where he worked briefly for a wholesale dry goods company, and then at Walthill, Nebraska—Standing Bear continued to take an interest in reservation affairs. In 1911, the same year in which Standing Bear sought an allotment for his wife, Indian Inspector James McLaughlin, formerly an agent on one of the Sioux reservations, was sent by the Interior Department to Pine Ridge to obtain approval for the sale of unallotted lands in Washabaugh County, South Dakota. A bill had been introduced into the Senate to that effect. McLaughlin found the residents of Pine Ridge unanimous in their opposition to the bill because allotment in the county had not been completed and they had not yet received any benefits from the surplus lands opened in Bennett County during the previous year. McLaughlin met with Oglala leaders, noted their opposition, and also advised them that Congress had the power to open their surplus lands by legislation and without their consent.[22]

Fear of such a development caused discussions in the Oglala tribal council and initiated a protest against opening additional lands on the reservation. A petition, "purported to have been signed by all the adult males of the reservation," was sent to Washington to prevent the opening of Washabaugh County; and a delegation consisting of Judge Fast Horse, Jack Red Cloud, Charles Turning Hawk, and Jacob White Eyes was selected to present their opposition in person. Although Standing Bear was eager to participate and wished to be a member of the delegation, he was rejected by the council; he then announced his intention of proceeding to Washington at his own expense. Superintendent John Brennan accused him of wanting to come to Washington with the intention of "butting in" on the meeting with the Commissioner of Indian Affairs. Writing on behalf of the duly chosen delegation, Brennan reported that Standing Bear was a "common disturber and was repudiated by the Oglala Council," and that the delegation wished him excluded from the meeting.[23]

This is undoubtedly the event mentioned by Standing Bear in *My People the Sioux,* where he recounts that tribal leaders invited him to Pine Ridge for consultation. He agreed to represent their interests in Washington, he reported, but the superintendent, who resented the fact that Standing Bear had gone over his head and obtained title to his allotment, convinced the Indians that Standing Bear was seeking to advance himself and that he would only make trouble for the Sioux. "They were afraid to go against the agent's wishes," he wrote, "and, when the test came, I was voted out. . . ."[24]

Perhaps the combination of this action and the rejection of his wife's application for enrollment and allotment, along with ill health, caused Standing Bear to seek work elsewhere. He was employed briefly at the 101 Ranch in Oklahoma; then, finding the heat in Oklahoma too intense, he wrote to film producer Thomas Ince. Ince sent funds to cover transportation, and in 1912 Standing Bear journeyed to California to join the group of Indians working at Ince's studio. Thereafter, he worked in a number of films, including some westerns starring William S. Hart. He also appeared in a play, *The Race of Man,* in New York. He joined the lecture circuit, speaking on Indian affairs, instructed Boy Scouts and Girl Scouts, and owned a concession in Venice, California.

Late in life he turned to writing and produced four books, all published by Houghton Mifflin: *My People the Sioux* (1928), *My Indian Boyhood* (1931), *Land of the Spotted Eagle* (1933), and *Stories of the Sioux* (1934). *My Indian Boyhood* and *Stories of the Sioux* were written for children, with the objective of increasing their knowledge and appreciation of Indian life. While the other books were also intended to bring increased understanding of Indian people and their cultures, they were written for a broader audience and were more significant.

My People the Sioux, edited by western historian E. A. Brininstool, is largely autobiographical, taking Standing Bear from his training as a typical Lakota youth to his long association with white culture beginning at Carlisle and ending with his life in California, far from the reservation and its culture. It is particularly important for providing an Indian account of life at Carlisle, and it is unique in presenting information on the life of an Indian living off the reservation early in the twentieth century. Unfortunately, there are important gaps in this account, particularly relating to his marriages and to his activities in Los Angeles.

If *My People the Sioux* is autobiographical with some mildly critical comments on federal Indian policy, *Land of the Spotted Eagle* was both a statement on the value of Lakota life and a ringing attack on past and present Indian policy. "White men," he wrote, "seem to have difficulty in realizing that people who live differently from themselves still might be traveling the upward and progressive road of life." For whites the Indian was a savage, "meaning that he is low in thought and feeling, and cruel in acts; that he is a heathen, meaning that he is incapable . . . of high philosophical thought concerning life and life's relations."[25] And so whites demonstrated little brotherly love or understanding.

With the editorial assistance of Melvin Gilmore, curator of ethnology at the University of Michigan, and his niece, Warcaziwin, Standing Bear set out to change these misconceptions and to present a positive description of Lakota culture. What resulted is an account of the virtues of Sioux life, virtues that are often contrasted to weaknesses in white culture.

> We did not think of the great open plains, the beautiful rolling hills, and winding streams with tangled growth, as 'wild.' Only to the white man

> was nature a 'wilderness' and only to him was the land 'infested' with 'wild' animals and 'savage' people. To us it was tame. Earth was bountiful and we were surrounded with the blessings of the Great Mystery. Not until the hairy man from the east came and with brutal frenzy heaped injustices upon us and the families we loved was it 'wild' for us. When the very animals of the forest began fleeing from his approach, then it was that for us the 'Wild West' began.[26]

While Indians were natural conservationists, whites were not. If Indian culture was in harmony with nature, whites became "the symbol of extinction for all things natural to this continent."[27]

Standing Bear stressed the values, harmony, and freedom in traditional Lakota culture, sometimes overstating his case while he criticized the white's effort to remake Indians into his own likeness.

> Food, which had always been procured through the exercise of great energy and industry, was doled and rationed to him; clothing, which so fitted his imagination and environment, was replaced with garments incongruous and, for him, injurious to health; for the cleanly, well-aired tipi . . . he was given the army tent and wooden shacks. Even his spiritual life was disarranged, his religious ceremonies, songs and dances forbidden and in some cases stopped by order, thus filling him with resentment. Everything that was natural and therefore healthful, was displaced with things unsuitable, foreign, and unfitted.[28]

To expect Lakotas to prosper under such conditions was shortsighted. "Had conditions been reversed and the white man suddenly forced to fit himself to the rigorous Indian mode of life," he wrote, "he might now bear the stigma of 'lazy' if, indeed, he were able to survive at all."[29]

Published in 1933 at the beginning of the Indian New Deal, with its fresh emphasis on the value of traditional Indian cultures, *Land of the Spotted Eagle* found a receptive audience and was reviewed favorably. However, it was in the last two chapters that Standing Bear made his strongest statement about the status of American Indians and Indian-White relations in the United States. He expanded upon ideas presented previously in an article in *American Mercury*, in which he reacted to conditions at the Pine Ridge Reservation noted during several recent visits.

Standing Bear had found the Sioux in a deplorable condition, physically and spiritually, as a result of U.S. policies. Their land base had been destroyed; their economy was in a shambles; and, despite government rations, they were starving. Their culture had been attacked and weakened, and the reservation was now virtually a prison. "Even the law has forsaken him, and the Indian today is not only unheard and unheeded, but robbed, pillaged, denied his heritage, and held in bondage." Even faith in traditional religion had been destroyed.[30]

> It is this loss of faith that has left a void in Indian life—a void that civilization cannot fill. The old life was attuned to nature's rhythm—bound in mystical ties to the sun, moon and stars; to the waving grasses, flowing streams and whispering winds. It is not a question . . . of the white man 'bringing the Indian up to his plane of thought and action.' It is rather a case where the white man had better grasp some of the Indian's spiritual strength.[31]

Responsibility for the sad state of affairs on Indian reservations lay with the whites. There was no Indian problem created by the Indians.

> The attempted transformation of the Indian by the white man and the chaos that has resulted are but the fruits of the white man's disobedience of a fundamental and spiritual law. The pressure that has been brought to bear upon the native people, since the cessation of armed conflict, in the attempt to force conformity of custom and habit has caused a reaction more destructive than war, and the injury has not only affected the Indian, but has extended to the white population as well. Tyranny, stupidity, and lack of vision have brought about the situation now alluded to as the 'Indian Problem.'[32]

The final abuse was to label Indian people as "savages," but that was the "greatest salve" that the white race had been able to apply "to its sore and troubled conscience."[33]

Whites needed to learn the values of Indian culture and to appreciate the place of the Indian in the nation's history, but basic policy changes designed to preserve the Indian heritage were also necessary, for "in denying the Indian his ancestral rights and heritages the white race is but robbing itself."[34] Although John Collier's Indian New Deal supported traditional culture, religion, and arts, Luther Standing Bear was ahead of his time in his recommendations. He opposed "far-removed boarding-schools" and suggested a dual educational program that included instruction in Indian life as well as white education. "I say again," he wrote, "that Indians should teach Indians; that Indians should serve Indians, especially on reservations . . . " He proposed a school of Indian thought, instruction in tribal arts and crafts, and the employment of Indian historians, not only to instruct Indian children in their own history but also to incorporate the history of Indian America into the public school curriculum. The training of Indian doctors, nurses, engineers, architects, dentists, and lawyers would provide skilled Indians to serve Indians on reservations.[35]

In the 1933 letter that Standing Bear wrote to President Roosevelt, he suggested legislation which would provide that the study of the "history, culture, arts, and society of the American Indian be made a part of the regular curriculum of the schools of the United States." Such legislation was never introduced into Congress and such a change in the educational system did not occur in his lifetime.[36]

Luther Standing Bear died in 1939 while working on the film *Union Pacific*. He had led a varied and interesting life, moving from pre-reservation life to the first class at Carlisle, to England with Buffalo Bill, and ultimately to Hollywood. When he returned to the reservation after the Carlisle years, he discovered that he could not fit in because he could not "endure existence under the control of an overseer." He wrote: "I developed into a chronic disturber. I was a bad Indian, and the agent and I never got on."[37] And so he left the reservation to act in films, to lecture on Indian life, and ultimately to write books to give a non-Indian audience a greater appreciation of Indian life and history.

Other Indians attended Carlisle and other Indian schools or worked in the motion picture business, or joined the lecture circuit, but there were few Indian authors. It was his books that set Standing Bear apart. *My People the Sioux* provides a rare insight into changes in Sioux life, Indian education, and the life of an urban Indian in the early twentieth century. There were Indians more educated than Standing Bear; among them anthropologist Arthur C. Parker, attorney Thomas Sloan, and medical doctors Carlos Montezuma and Charles Eastman. Standing Bear was not a part of that better educated group, but he was more representative of those who had received a modicum of education and then found reservation life to be unacceptable. He expressed what many Indians felt, and that is what makes his books unique.

Through his lectures and his work with children, Standing Bear presented a positive image of Indian life. He undoubtedly served as something of a role model for Sioux children on and off the reservation. However, he reached a larger audience when his books appeared in the late 1920s, a time of intense criticism of federal Indian policy, and in the early 1930s, when the Indian New Deal was in its infancy. He presented forceful Indian views of the treatment of native people without the stridency of a Carlos Montezuma, and he offered concrete recommendations that would be echoed by other Indian spokesmen some forty years later. Thus, he proposed a bill to require the teaching of Indian history and culture in the public schools. In his later years Standing Bear was drawn increasingly to the culture of his youth; consequently, he stressed the need to preserve the cultures of Indian people. "So if today I had a young mind to direct to start on the journey of life and I was faced with the duty of choosing between the natural way of my forefathers and that of the white man's present way of civilization, "he wrote, "I would, for its welfare, unhesitatingly set that child's feet in the path of my forefathers. I would raise him to be an Indian!"[38]

Notes

1. Standing Bear to Roosevelt, May 2, 1933, 22628–1933–013, Central Correspondence Files, 1907–39, Record Group 75, Records of the Bureau of Indian Affairs, National Archives, Washington, D.C. (hereinafter cited as CCF).

2. Standing Bear probably was born in the mid-1860s. In 1931, he stated that the exact year of his birth was unknown. Luther Standing Bear, "The Tragedy of the Sioux," *American Mercury* 24 (November 1931), p. 273.

3. George E. Hyde, *Spotted Tail's Folk: A History of the Brule Sioux* (Norman, Okla., 1961), p. 288n; *Senate Executive Document No. 51*, 51st Cong., 1st sess., pp. 51, 242; McGregor to Collier, January 16, 1935, 63456–1934–Pine Ridge–034, CCF.

4. Luther Standing Bear, *My People the Sioux* (Lincoln, Nebr., 1975), pp. 69–70.

5. Ibid., pp. 71–72, 74, 59; Luther Standing Bear, *Land of the Spotted Eagle* (Lincoln, Nebr., 1978), p. 57. Standing Bear wondered how whites could eat beef: "We had, in the beginning, found the smell of the white man quite obnoxious, but at the first contact with his cattle we held our noses."

6. Standing Bear, *My People the Sioux*, p. 124; *Land of the Spotted Eagle*, p. 68.

7. Standing Bear, *My People the Sioux*, pp. 128–32.

8. Richard H. Pratt, *Battlefield and Classroom: Four Decades with the American Indian, 1867–1904*, ed. Robert M. Utley (New Haven, Conn., 1964), p. 335.

9. Standing Bear, *My People the Sioux*, p. 134.

10. Ibid., pp. 138–39.

11. Standing Bear, *Land of the Spotted Eagle*, p. 232.

12. Standing Bear, *My People the Sioux*, p. 146.

13. Standing Bear, *Land of the Spotted Eagle*, pp. 16–17.

14. Standing Bear, *My People the Sioux*, pp. 149–52.

15. Ibid., pp. 190–91.

16. Dorchester to Commissioner of Indian Affairs (hereafter cited as CIA),

August 3, 1891, and Wright to CIA, May 18, 1892, Letters Received, 1881–1907, Records of the Bureau of Indian Affairs, National Archives, Washington, D. C.

17. Standing Bear, *My People the Sioux,* p. 224.
18. Ibid., pp. 273–76.
19. See 22371–1912–Pine Ridge–313, CCF.
20. See 91258–1911–Pine Ridge–053, CCF.
21. Standing Bear, *My People the Sioux,* pp. 278–82.
22. McLaughlin to Secretary of the Interior, October 27, 1911, 20780–1912–Pine Ridge–056, CCF.
23. Brennan to CIA, February 23, 1912, and Hauke to Judge Fast Horse, et al., March 7, 1912, in ibid.
24. Standing Bear *My People the Sioux,* pp. 282–83.
25. Standing Bear, *Land of the Spotted Eagle,* p. xv.
26. Ibid., p. 38.
27. Ibid., p. 166.
28. Ibid., p. 167.
29. Ibid., p. 168.
30. Ibid., p. 229.
31. Standing Bear, "Tragedy of the Sioux," p. 277.
32. Standing Bear, *Land of the Spotted Eagle,* p. 248.
33. Ibid., p. 251.
34. Ibid., p. 255.
35. Ibid., pp. 252–54.
36. Standing Bear to Roosevelt, May 2, 1933, 22628–1933–013, CCF.
37. Standing Bear, "Tragedy of the Sioux," p. 273.
38. Standing Bear, *Land of the Spotted Eagle,* pp. 258–59.

Essay on Sources

The major sources for information about Luther Standing Bear, for his views on Teton culture, and for his observations of history and Indian-White relations are his books: *My People the Sioux* (Boston, 1928; reprint, Lincoln, Nebr., 1975); *My Indian Boyhood* (Boston, 1931); *Land of the Spotted Eagle* (Boston, 1934; reprint, Lincoln, Nebr., 1978); and *Stories of the Sioux* (Boston, 1934). Of these, *My People the Sioux* and *Land of the Spotted Eagle* are most significant. Both include important biographical material, and taken together they are the most important sources for knowledge of Standing Bear's life. They also provide Standing Bear's assessment of United States Indian policy and its impact as well as recommendations for policy reform. The latter book closes with a chapter entitled "What the Indian Means to America," which clearly states those reform proposals. Some of those also can be found in his essay, "The Tragedy of the Sioux," in *American Mercury* 24 (November 1931), which was written in reaction to conditions that he observed during a visit to the Pine Ridge reservation. That essay undoubtedly stimulated the growing movement for Indian reform that led to the Indian New Deal during the presidency of Franklin D. Roosevelt because it was one of a series of articles critical of government management of Indian affairs that appeared in national magazines in the 1920s and early 1930s.

Correspondence from Standing Bear and about his activities is also scattered throughout the records of the Bureau of Indian Affairs located in the National Archives in Washington, D.C., and in the Federal Archives and Records Center in Kansas City, Missouri.

Important books that deal with Sioux history or places and events that touched Standing Bear's life include: George E. Hyde, *Spotted Tail's Folk* (Norman, 1961); James C. Olson, *Red Cloud and the Sioux Problem* (Lincoln, Nebr., 1965); Robert M. Utley, *The Last Days of the Sioux Nation* (New Haven, 1963); and Richard H. Pratt, *Battlefield and Classroom: Four Decades with the American Indian, 1867–1904*, edited by Robert M. Utley (New Haven, 1964).

7

Designing Woman

Minnie Kellogg, Iroquois Leader

Laurence M. Hauptman

Minnie Kellogg (1880–1949) was born among the Oneidas of Wisconsin who had been removed from New York during those years when Maris Pierce had organized efforts on behalf of the Six Nations to retain their homelands. Like Charles A. Eastman and Gertrude Bonnin, and unlike most "educated" Indians of her generation, she did not attend Indian schools but instead matriculated at white institutions. It was through her education that she became involved in various reforms during the first decade of this century, the highpoint of progressivism in the United States.

In April 1911, she was invited by Fayette M. McKenzie, Christian idealist and professor of economics and sociology at Ohio State University, to join five other prominent Indians at McKenzie's Columbus home to discuss the formation of a pan-Indian association. They formed themselves into the American Indian Association and called for a general convention of Native Americans to meet the following autumn (serendipitously on Columbus Day) at Columbus, Ohio. At the convention, this time more broadly represented geographically and by tribe, the group of well-educated, acculturated professionals—traditionalists were not invited—formed themselves into the Society of American Indians, in an effort to more sharply distinguish themselves from the white-dominated Indian defense or-

ganizations like the Philadelphia-based Indian Rights Association. The society pledged itself to Indian "self-help," to be achieved through what the members termed "race consciousness," and the discovery of "race leadership," a search that presumably began at just such a gathering of educated and progressive Indians. Concern for the Indian in particular and for humanity in general inspirited their gathering.

Kellogg presented a paper, "Industrial Organization for the Indians," in which she elaborated upon her view of Indian self-sufficiency and, remarkably, anticipated proposals of the Indian New Deal which would be established almost a quarter-century later. However, despite certain similar views, Kellogg would prove to be a vociferous opponent of Commissioner John Collier during the depression decade.

Unlike the leadership of the Society of American Indians, she never considered herself to be a "New Indian"; instead, she claimed that she was an "Old Indian" adjusted to new conditions. She continually decried the destruction of traditional Indian lifeways, insisting that Indian values should be preserved. Rather than concentrate her efforts in the Society of American Indians, however, she was drawn more fully after 1911 into the life of the Wisconsin Oneidas. And, as the following essay shows, she squandered her talents in fights that embroiled her in controversy. Tragedy, a word that has been trivialized through improper usage, is nevertheless apt when applied to Minnie Kellogg's life.

Minnie Kellogg, born Laura Miriam Cornelius, was one of the most important and tragic figures in recent American Indian history. She influenced important events in the national arena as well as in the local Iroquois communities in Canada and the United States. Kellogg was one of the founders of the Society of American Indians and of the modern Iroquois land-claims movement. Every scholar doing fieldwork among the Iroquois, from the time of J. N. B. Hewitt onward, encounters her name and her legacy in documents on Iroquois factionalism, land claims, religion and revitalization movements, and Indian views of Washington and Ottawa policies. Although cited in the early 1920s for her noteworthy accomplishments as a writer, linguist, and reformer of Indian policy, no study of her remarkable career exists in print. This essay will focus on one major aspect of her important life, namely, the factors that made her a recognized leader in the Iroquois polity in the first half of the twentieth century.[1]

Kellogg was a dynamic speaker who could sway large audiences. She was the dominant personality in a major Iroquois secular movement that had revitalizationist overtones. She conformed to what the anthropologist William N. Fenton has observed about Iroquois leadership:

> The prophet who would succeed among the Iroquois must speak in ancient tongues, he must use the old words, and he must relate his program to the old ways. He is a conservator at the same time he is a reformer. All of the Iroquois reformers have been traditionalists. This is one of the reasons that Iroquois culture has endured so long.[2]

In an extraordinary way, Kellogg could transcend her highly educated background to convey her ideas to largely rural and uneducated Indians. To white audiences and to her well-educated colleagues in the Society of American Indians, she frequently quoted from Franz Boas, G. Stanley Hall, and William James to support her points about Indian race equality and mental capacities. To reservation communities, she spoke in "ancient tongues," and with traditional metaphors, of the glory of the eighteenth-century League of the Iroquois, which she attempted to reconstruct; of the lessons of Indian elders and their wisdom; and, of course, of the overriding concerns of Indian people to win back their lands.

Despite her exceptional gifts—a brilliant mind, beauty, self-confidence, unusual oratorical abilities, and her educational attainments—Kellogg is also the most controversial Iroquois leader of the twentieth century. It is clear from her many bizarre involvements that either she misused her prodigious talents or was incapable of carrying out all the extraordinary designs she had for her people's betterment. Although acknowledged today as a major force and as a brilliant person, she is accused by Iroquois elders of swindling them out of hundreds of thousands of dollars in her abortive efforts to bring their land claims to fruition; of creating debilitating factionalism that impeded tribal development for decades; and even of contributing to the loss of her own tribal landbase at Oneida, Wisconsin, through her schemes that ultimately impoverished Indians.[3] Moreover, though never convicted of a felony, she was arrested on at least four separate occasions on a series of charges relating to her activities. Unfortunately, because of her questionable ethics and her inability to carry out what she espoused, Kellogg is blamed today for all that went wrong in Iroquois history during the interwar period from 1919 to 1941.

Consequently, her life has the sense of tragedy: she wanted to use her extraordinary abilities to help her people but ended up being accused by them as a common outlaw.[4]

Kellogg's family was, in part, a major reason for her leadership in Iroquois affairs. Laura Miriam Cornelius, the daughter of Adam Poe and Celicia Bread Cornelius, was born on the Oneida Indian Reservation in Wisconsin on September 10, 1880. As a baptized member of the Episcopal Church of the Holy Apostles, the most important religious as well as political institution among the Wisconsin Oneidas, she was a descendant of those Indians who had sought their Christian "ecclesiastical salvation" in the West under the leadership of Reverend Eleazer Williams. She was directly related to Chief Daniel Bread, a major nineteenth-century Oneida leader in New York and Wisconsin, who was known for his powerful oratorical skills; and to Chief Skenandore, the last of the New York chiefs, who had led the tribe's emigration to Wisconsin and who also had a reputation as an orator. It is important to note that Skenandore remained a force in tribal affairs until his death in 1897, well after Cornelius's coming of age.[5]

Cornelius was born into a society in cultural flux, people crying out for a prophet. The uprooting of the Oneidas from New York contributed to structural changes in politics and society. Politically divided into three separate factions since their days in New York—the First and Second Christian and Orchard parties—the Oneidas replicated their divisive history upon arriving in Wisconsin in the 1820s and 1830s. Other changes were also evident. By the end of the nineteenth century, clan affiliation had become a less important factor in Oneida politics. In the same period, encouraged by outside white influences and missionaries especially, the Oneida social structure became patrilineal, evolving from the traditional Iroquois matrilineal model.[6]

Even before the Dawes General Allotment Act of 1887, the Oneidas were faced with uncontrolled timber stripping of their lands, serious soil erosion, low leasing arrangements, and increased consumption of alcohol. On June 13, 1892, the 65,000-acre Oneida Reservation was finally allotted with the issuance of a total of 1,524 allotments and 20 trust patents to the Indians. In 1918, a federal "competency" commission began issuing fee patents to Oneidas of less than one-half Indian blood in order to quicken the pace of assimilation. Oneida lands soon became subject to taxation, resulting in new and impossible tax burdens, foreclosures, and subsequent tax sales of property. Land speculators encouraged Oneidas, largely uneducated rural people, to fall into debt by borrowing money or by mortgaging their homesteads to buy musical instruments, carriages, and livestock—all of which they generally did not need. Some of their homes were subsequently lost through their inability to pay back loans and in outright swindles in which whiskey was employed.[7] Hence, by 1934, the Oneidas owned less than ninety acres; they had lost more than 95 percent of their lands and were one of the two tribes most devastated under the Dawes Act.[8]

Although Cornelius's upbringing occurred in a society in which clan importance and sex roles had been significantly transformed by outside pressures, her self-assuredness was based, in part, on ancient Iroquois respect for clan mothers and women's overall major involvement in behind-the-scenes political activities. Iroquois women traditionally did not generally make their mark through oratory, and they did not usually address meetings of the League as Kellogg did later in her life. Nevertheless, women could and did speak at local councils. According to one anthropologist, "the strength of the League and of the women in it also depended on its local character." She added: "That is, although intertribal meetings were held and were occasions of great importance and solemnity, decisions were made and approved on a local basis, thus allowing for the influence of women who tended to remain in the villages."[9] As a highly educated woman and one familiar with Iroquois history, she used traditionalism at all stages of her remarkable career to establish her right to speak, to win over audiences, and to generate political influence and power.

Unlike many of her contemporaries on the reservation, Cornelius managed to avoid the usual educational route to distant Indian boarding schools at Carlisle and Hampton. She was educated at Grafton Hall, a private boarding school at Fond du Lac administered by the Episcopal Diocese. The school was within sixty miles of her home at Seymour, Wisconsin, and provided a setting that included mostly non-Indian women, which was far different from the segregated regimen of military discipline in far-off Indian boarding schools.[10] Later in her life, in condemning Indian education under the auspices of the Bureau of Indian Affairs, Cornelius reflected on her education and credited her father for his "wonderful foresight" in sending her to Grafton Hall.[11]

> I had been preserved from the spirit-breaking Indian schools. . . . My psychology, therefore, had not been shot to pieces by that cheap attitude of the Indian Service, whose one aim was to 'civilize' the race youth, by denouncing his parents, his customs, his people wholesale, and filling the vacuum they had created with their vulgar notions of what constituted civilization. I had none of those processes of the Bureaucratic mill in my tender years, to make me into a 'pinch-back white man.' Had it been imposed upon me, I am certain something would have happened to it then.

After receiving a classical education, she was graduated with honors in 1898. Interestingly, her graduation essay, "The Romans of America," was a study that traced the "analogy between the Iroquois Confederacy, or Six Nations, to the ancient Roman Empire."[12] One writer has commented that her abilities were inherited and that her success at Grafton was attributable to her noteworthy ancestry. An equally important conclusion is that her pride in her Iroquois roots provided her with a strong measure of self-confidence that served her well all her life.

This pride in her Indian upbringing was frequently revealed. She was unquestionably one of the best orators among the Iroquois of her generation, speaking effectively in both English and Oneida. She is credited with being the best native speaker of her generation.[13] The ability to converse in proper syntax bestows an Iroquois with the power to influence and impress audiences which is still used for political advantages among the Six Nations. This is especially true at Oneida, Wisconsin.[14] It is evident in early observations of Cornelius made by others as well as in her own writings that she was both aware of Iroquois oral traditions and proud of her Iroquois heritage.[15]

Her later education included two years in Europe, funded in part by her own performances as a "show Indian," and study at a series of major institutions of higher education: Stanford University, Barnard College, the New York School of Philanthropy (later the Columbia University School of Social Work), Cornell University, and the University of Wisconsin. She attended Barnard for no more than a year and a half but made a distinct mark on her colleagues. Cornelius wrote a short story for the college's literary magazine.[16] She also inspired the following comment in the *Mortarboard,* the college yearbook: "Her heart's desire, to uphold the honor of her ancient race."[17] Hence, it is clear that during these years she had already determined to work on behalf of her people. Whether as a result of an unstable personality, her strong Progressive muckraking style, or her fervent advocacy of women's rights which led on one occasion to an arrest during a protest demonstration, Kellogg drifted from one college to another in the twelve years following her graduation from Grafton Hall.[18]

Like many Iroquois before or after her, Cornelius attempted to speak for indigenous peoples as a whole. This ethnocentric characteristic of expression has frequently led Iroquois to presume to voice the concerns of all Native Americans in international convocations from New York to Geneva, Switzerland. Consequently, during her career, she became involved not only in the affairs of the Six Nations but also in those of the Blackfeet, Brothertown, Cherokee, Crow, Delaware, Huron, Osage, and Stockbridge Indians.[19] Her crusading and relentless agitation, which led to trouble with the law and to arrests in Oklahoma in 1913 and in Colorado in 1916, also prompted her to assist reform-minded Indians in founding the Society of American Indians in 1911. It may be suggested that Cornelius's role was no mere coincidence but a cultural manifestation since Iroquois on both sides of the United States–Canadian border frequently have been at the forefront of new Indian nationalist movements in the twentieth century—among them, the Indian Defense League of the Americas; the American Indian Federation; the National Congress of American Indians; the National Indian Brotherhood; the Great Lakes Inter-tribal Council; and the American Indian Movement (Red Power).[20] As politically savvy people with strong beliefs in tribal sovereignty and treaty rights inculcated from childhood, the Iroquois became involved in nationalist organizations very early. Among the original theorists behind the Society of American Indians were three Iroquois: Arthur C. Parker, Dennison Wheelock, and Laura Miriam Cornelius.

The Society of American Indians, originally called the American Indian Association, held the second organizing meeting of its executive committee at the Cornelius home in Seymour, Wisconsin, on June 20 and 21, 1911. The meeting was attended by two prominent Oneida attorneys, Chester P. Cornelius and Dennison Wheelock, as well as by four other members of the organization. The participants discussed general rules of the organization; planned their first national convention at Columbus, Ohio, in October; arranged for publicity and invitations to tribal delegates; established a constitution and bylaws committee; and issued a statement outlining the objectives of the society.[21]

Although she served as secretary of the executive committee and later as vice-president on education, Cornelius's views of Indian progress apparently were incompatible with those of the American Indian Association as a whole. Although she was in total agreement with the association's belief in the Indians' ability and inherent right to "defend all rights and just claims of the race" and to promote Indian dignity through self-help, she disagreed completely with the paternalistic expression drafted at her home: "While the Association and its founders most sincerely appreciate the splendid elements and achievements of the old-time Indian culture and the methods by which early conditions were met, it realizes most keenly the inefficacy of these methods in meeting the conditions of modern times."[22] Cornelius's speeches indicate that she broke with the society over this point. Unlike white reformers and even many members of the Society of American Indians, she wanted to blend the wisdom of the elders of the reservation into the education of Indian children. Writing in the *Quarterly Journal* of the Society of American Indians in 1913, she insisted, in language which is quite modern in tone, that

> Culture is but the fine flowering of real education, and it is the training of the feeling, the tastes and the manners that make it so. When we stop to think a little, old Indian training is not to be despised. The general tendency in the average Indian schools is to take away the child's set of Indian notions altogether, and to supplant them with the paleface's. There is no discrimination in that. Why should he not justly know his race's own heroes rather than through false teaching think them wrong? Have they not as much claim to valor as Hercules or Achilles? Now I do not say here that everything he has natively is right or better than the Caucasian's. Not at all, but I do say that there are noble qualities and traits and a set of literary traditions he had which are just as fine and finer, and when he has these, or the sake of keeping a fine spirit of self-respect and pride in himself, let us preserve them.[23]

After citing the anthropologist Franz Boas as her authority on the equal mental capacity of Indian and Caucasian, she added that the Indians' power of abstraction, oratorical abilities, and sense of humor were three areas which could be incorporated into current Indian education in the United States. Unlike many of her Indian contemporaries in the Progressive Era, she honored the wisdom of ancient tribal leaders and their lessons inculcated in childhood as a vital reality in her life.[24]

By 1911, the white press compared Cornelius and other early leaders of the society to Booker T. Washington in their calls for self-help and the uplift of the "Indian race." After the society's Columbus meeting in 1911, the *New York Tribune* hailed Cornelius as a scholar, a social worker, "one of the moving spirits in the new American Indian Association," and "a woman of rare intellectual gifts."[25] Yet, because of her sharp break with the organization's leadership, her role in the Society of American Indians was peripheral at best. She emphasized the need for self-sufficiency and independence—much like the view from the modern-day Onondaga Longhouse—although her own model for this endeavor was based on the Mormons. Much of her rhetoric paralleled the self-help plans of the age; however, Cornelius went against the grain in her elaborate designs for reservation development and in her view of reservations and reservation Indians as generally positive.

To Cornelius, the ideal for the Indian was not simply the imitation of white society but the creation of planned industrial villages, which she considered a "hard-headed, practical scheme which is not dependent upon charity to carry it out."[26] Why should Indians, she asked, model themselves upon a white society that produced child labor, sweatshops, unsanitary and unsafe working conditions, and concentration of capital and political power in the hands of a few? In her speech at the society's first convention in 1911, she advocated transforming reservations into self-governing industrial villages (based on the Garden City idea) by using the Mormon concept of communistic cooperation and organizing along Rochdale lines with a provision prohibiting any individual from obtaining 51 percent of the voting stock. What Cornelius meant was that Indians, through their own hands, would contribute their labor to the community's improvement. Just as the Mormons bypassed the rake-off of "the contractor, the banker, the bonding company and the promoter," the Indians would also succeed without money because they would also capitalize labor. The community itself would set the rules and ensure against laziness by fixing the amount of labor required of its tribal members.[27]

Cornelius insisted that industrial organization for the Indians should be designed "along the lines of organization for himself and by himself—organization of those things which shall control his livelihood and which shall be based on a special consideration for his needs."[28] Instead of forcing him to become a white man, give the Indian the skills and opportunity to transform his reservation into a self-sustaining community. After all, she maintained, "I cannot see that everything the white man does is to be copied."[29] The key was to "reorganize the opportunities of the Indian at *home.* [her emphasis]" The Indian possessed many assets— land, labor, the devotion to outdoor life. The conditions of labor in the outside world were inferior to those conditions that the Indian could establish for himself. As a Progressive Era reformer, Cornelius insisted that with the help of experts, development of Indian reservations could be achieved. They would design the best industry adapted for each reservation, which would take into account Indian diversity. The townsite for the "industrial village" would be chosen next and would serve all the people equitably. In a rather typical Iroquois way, Cornelius concluded that the Indian could teach the white man a thing or two and "avoid the things that are killing off the majority of the laboring population in the country among the whites."[30]

Cornelius's designs for the Iroquois were equally intriguing. In one of her first plans, the "Cherry Garden" experiment, she developed what she claimed was a strategy of self-sufficiency for her Oneida tribesmen. The rich cherry-growing area of their Wisconsin homeland was to be the economic salvation of those poor Indians. Through the hard work and cooperative efforts of the Oneidas, who rarely agreed on anything because of serious factional discord, Cornelius hoped to develop a large tract that would transform her people into "self-supporting and prosperous" members of society.[31] Despite her significant work, Cornelius's role in the society ended abruptly, and after 1913 she was no longer listed as a member of the organization.[32] The historian Hazel W. Hertzberg has perceptively observed that the quick dismissal of her ideas about reservation development at the 1911 convention may have disturbed those Indians in the society who believed that the reservation was a "transitional stage in Indian development."[33]

Her marriage in 1912 to Orrin Joseph Kellogg, a Minneapolis attorney, appears to have further alienated her from the society's leadership, although little information is available about her husband except his claim to distant Seneca ancestry and his relationship to his wife's Indian concerns. In 1913, the Kelloggs were arrested in Oklahoma on charges of fraud and for impersonating federal officials in their investigations of the Osage oil leases and the Indian school at Pawhuska. At the time, they had the support of Thomas Sloan, the noted attorney and officer of the Society of American Indians, who had asked them to help him in his capacity as a special examiner hired by a congressional committee.[34] Although not convicted in Oklahoma, the Kellogs' overall political activism and involvement seems to have generated scorn from society members employed in the Indian service and from conservatives in the society. It is also apparent that Minnie Kellogg, as she was known, was never a follower and had difficulty working with other vocal members in the society whose programs she questioned. Although she remained active in Indian affairs, lobbying before Congress during the Wilson administration, her involvment in Indian nationalist organizations ended by World War I.[35]

In 1920, Kellogg published her major work, *Our Democracy and the American Indian: A Comprehensive Presentation of the Indian Situation as it is Today*. Here, she once again revealed her sharp differences with other Indian critics of Indian policy. The so-called Lolomi plan, which had been outlined as early as 1916 in testimony before Congress, suggested that Indian affairs be separated from the everyday seedy side of hack politicians and their politics as well as from the corrupt and inefficient administration of the BIA. The management of Indian affairs, she insisted, should be placed in the hands of a gigantic trust headed by men of national and international standing who would serve as experts and consultants in the administration, development, and protection of Indian wealth.[36] The reform sentiment of the Progressive Era, with its emphasis on city managers and the gospel of efficiency, was now applied to the development of Indian reservations.

In the book, she leveled her major criticism against the Indian service in the United States. Yet she also worked out a plan of action, unlike her radical Indian contemporary Dr. Carlos Montezuma, an acculturated Yavapai who merely called for the abolition of the BIA. Although the plan called *Lolomi*—a Hopi term meaning "perfect goodness be upon you—," was largely a diatribe against the BIA, it built on her earlier designs for self-sufficiency. She blamed the Indian Bureau's "school for sycophants" for packing Indian tribal councils, "destroying natural leadership in the race," pauperizing Indians, and fostering dependence.[37] In using the Iroquois Confederacy, of course, as her model for pre-BIA Indian independence and self-sufficiency, she insisted that "Indians have been denied their appreciation of their *place in history*, their noble primitive stock and their advanced philosophy of life" by a "Bureau who wishes to create factions among the tribes" and whose "ware-house *[sic]* Indians" are its executors. "Our solidarity will be threatened by them just so long as you do not wake up and refuse to allow them to represent you."[38] She reserved most of her ammunition for her attacks on BIA-managed boarding schools, which she insisted were injurious to Indians, destroying individuality, exploiting student labor, and producing a subservient type of Indian. In their place, the Lolomi plan would carry the "school to the field or the home. Not being dictated to by politics, it will secure only sympathetic instructors who know what they are about and whose service terminates when they cannot produce the desired results."[39] Sycophants and employees of the Indian service who managed to obtain their positions after losing their footing in other areas would be rooted out. Instead of pauperizing Indians and fostering dependence by "making a pinchback white-man of the Indian,"—one of her favorite phrases—the Lolomi plan would help create self-sufficiency among reservation communities by adopting her earlier plan of synthesizing the Mormon model of cooperative labor and organization, the capitalization of labor, and the Garden City plan.[40]

Kellogg reserved her grandest design of all for the Iroquois. It involved her efforts in the 1920s and 1930s to resurrect and reconstruct the structure and operation of the eighteenth-century League of the Iroquois. Again advocating the Lolomi policy, she envisioned the transformation of the Iroquois reservations into self-governing, thrifty, industrious, and self-sustaining settlements with comfortable houses. In the process, Indian self-respect would be achieved through a concerted effort to restore "the pride of the Indian heritage, and to instill in the red man the proud consciousness of his race."[41] At the heart of her plan was the effort to win back between six and fifteen million acres of land, which she insisted was taken fraudulently from the Iroquois by New York State and by land speculators between 1784 and 1838. Her strategy was to win a favorable decision in the courts, which would allow the Iroquois a sizable restored landbase for economic development and for the political restoration of the League's ancient greatness.[42]

One of the more interesting sidelights of this episode was Kellogg's rather strange relationship with J. N. B. Hewitt, the Iroquois ethnologist of the Smithsonian Insitution's Bureau of American Ethnology. From 1920 to 1932, although each distrusted the other, both sought information and other favors relating to their particular research. Hewitt, attempting to complete a manuscript on the laws and ritual of the League of the Iroquois, needed Kellogg's help in gaining access to informants and information on reservations. Kellogg viewed Hewitt as a valuable contact, asking him for manuscripts about the League and attempting to win his support for her plans by writing to him about her ideas for a comparative study of the Iroquois languages and for an Iroquois grammar and dictionary. She frequently invited him to use her homes at Oneida, Wisconsin, and later Nedrow, New York, as a base for his fieldwork; she even went so far as to suggest her willingness to take care of his living expenses while he was at Onondaga. To Kellogg, in need of legitimizing both her efforts and her power, Hewitt, the leading scholar on the Iroquois of his generation, was an essential ingredient in her schemes.[43]

Hewitt, of Tuscarora ancestry, "played her along" for twelve years and consciously tried to tread lightly as an anthropologist working among highly factionalized societies. Nevertheless, he eventually dismissed her grand design to resurrect the pre–Revolutionary War Iroquois Confederacy. He insisted that her plan was impractical and was very critical of some of her efforts which he thought bastardized the ancient traditions of the Six Nations. He took strong exception to her stationery listing George Thomas as "presiding sachem" of the League of the Six Iroquois Nations because, Hewitt informed her, the proper word for Thomas's title was "royāe'r" and not the Algonquian word *sachem*.[44] He also objected to the listing of six tribal organizations within Kellogg's league, which he maintained could not "claim or be regarded as the source and repository of the organic laws and authority of each separate tribe. Without such tribal organizations it is a mockery of words to speak of the League of the Six Nations of New York at the present time." He also condemned her for using in her stationery the phrase, "Grand Council Fire, Indian Village, Onondaga National Domain, North America"; he believed that the use of the word *domain* was incorrect since the federal–Iroquois Treaty of Canandaigua of 1794 made the land in question a reservation in accordance with the "harsh implications of the Treaty of Fort Stanwix." In conclusion, he insisted that her "illustrated letterhead has a sinister import to me because it portrays as a reality the mere phantom of what has been, is not now, and long ago had gone into perdition."[45]

Kellogg was able to win support for her plans for the Iroquois from diverse communities because her activities emphasized solidarity with traditionalist politics, culture, and values. Traditional approaches to Iroquois medicine and attempts to resurrect the clan system were also encouraged. Through her understanding of the symbols of Iroquois traditional existence, she established her headquarters at the Onondaga Reservation, the historic capital of the League, in order to reconstruct the old political offices of the Confederacy. Despite Hewitt's pessimism and scorn, Kellogg and her party were able to gain influence and power on every reservation from Oneida, Wisconsin, to St. Regis. Kellogg went so far as to revive Oneida chiefly titles associated with matrilineal lineages, to bring Longhouse leaders from Onondaga to Wisconsin to conduct a council, and to "arrange" a visit to New York by Iroquois traditionalists for the purpose of overseeing the installation of nine "sachems." Combined with these efforts were her strong emphasis on the purity of spoken Oneida and her able and highly respected oratorical skills.[46] Equally important was her keen ability to articulate the traditional Iroquois belief in sovereignty based upon treaty. In testimony before a Senate committee in March 1929, she clearly set forth this overwhelming Iroquois concern:

> Here are a group of Indians [Iroquois], 16,000 in all, occupying some 78,000 acres in reservations in New York or colonized in small groups in western states and Canada. Their legal status is peculiar to Indian relations. They have a treaty with the United States Government which gives them the status of an independent protectorate of the United States under this treaty of 1784, confirmed and added to in the treaty of 1789. They are a protected autonomy, with the title of original territory vested in them. In spe-

cific language, the U.S. ceded all right and title to them to territory they reserved to themselves out of their Iroquois domain in return for their ceding all right and title in the Ohio Valley to the United States Government.[47]

Two events gave Kellogg the opportunity to think of reconstructing the League. On March 3, 1920, the United States Circuit Court of Appeals for the Second Circuit, in *United States* v. *Boylan*, an ejectment proceeding involving the removal of Oneidas living on a thirty-two-acre tract of land and the partition of the land for use by non-Indians, found that the Oneidas were a federally recognized tribe and that New York State courts had no jurisdiction to dispose of their property without the consent of the United States.[48] This hard-won Indian victory gave Kellogg and the Iroquois hopes for other victories in the courts.

In August 1920, the Everett Commission—a New York State Assembly committee formed in 1919 to examine "the history, the affairs and transactions had by the people of the state of New York with the Indian tribes resident in the state and to report to the legislature the status of the American Indian residing in . . . New York"—began holding hearings. After nineteen months, which included on-site inspections of Iroquois reservations in Canada and the United States, Chairman Edward A. Everett of Potsdam issued a report in 1922 which largely reflected his opinion and that of the commission's researcher and stenographer, Lulu G. Stillman. The report concluded that the Iroquois as Six Nations were legally entitled to six million acres of New York State, having illegally been dispossessed of their title after the Treaty of Fort Stanwix in 1784. This report, however unrepresentative of the commission, helped to stimulate Iroquois efforts to regain their lands by legal means; and these efforts brought Kellogg to the fore.[49]

In the 1920s, Kellogg took advantage of these stirrings. She, her husband, her brother, and her many followers collected money in every Iroquois community—in New York, Oklahoma, Wisconsin, Ontario, and Quebec—with the intention of using it for a great Iroquois claim of up to eighteen million acres of land in New York and Pennsylvania. Her husband's legal background notwithstanding, much of the money collected—a considerable sum especially since much of it came from economically hard-pressed Indians—was never used for the intended purpose and was never returned to the contributors. The Indians were told that if they did not contribute they would not be eligible for the claims when they were awarded. Kellogg and her followers had several methods of collection in the pursuit of such claims. They gave tax receipts or due bills, which indicated that the contributor was entitled to 10 percent interest and 40 percent bonus when the money was "recovered in our claim against the State of New York." They also formed claims clubs on nearly every Iroquois reservation in the United States and Canada, charging dues for membership or levying a tax on each person of approximately a dollar and a quarter per month. Long after the Kelloggs' final legal appeal in pursuit of the claim ended, she and her followers were still collecting money. Although the exact extent of their fund-raising cannot be ascertained—it was perhaps as high as several hundreds of thousands of dollars—the record of numerous Indian protests filed with the Interior and Justice departments about the Kelloggs' activities as well as the bitter memories of the incident, which survive with today's Iroquois elders, confirm that many contributors lost their savings and property.[50] In an interview conducted in 1970, Oscar Archiquette, the noted Wisconsin Oneida leader, has provided the best description of her activities:

> Then Minnie Kellogg, in 1921, insisted: 'Oh, she said, I am working on the New York claim now. You will have your money before the snow flies—give me $10. Oh, give me $25. You will make more than the other guy. Give me $25.' You know that lady, she collected $60,000 cash. That's on record at the Bureau of Indian Affairs. Minnie Kellogg, she is perhaps a 7th cousin of mine. I figure she is the smartest Oneida woman that ever walked in a pair of shoes. Oh she was smart—but in the wrong way. Oh, she could have been a big help to us Indians. . . . In 1921, an educated Oneida lady [Minnie Kellogg] called a general meeting of Oneidas near Duck Creek Bridge, Brown County, Town of Hobart. The meeting concerned the New York land claim which we Oneidas have and never were paid for. She told us that it was necessary for us to go back to the old Indian ways of having chiefs as legal representatives for the Oneida Nation. She did manage to have a good number of Oneidas to attend the meeting where she took the authority of installing chiefs, and, of course, she had to collect money for expenses traveling back and forth to New York while working on this claim. One of her appointed chiefs was her treasurer, and he could not read or write, although he was smart enough to have property. My brother said, 'I could give sweet talk, too, and collect money

> from the Indians.' Not only did she collect from Oneidas, but also from the Stockbridge Indians and the Brothertowns, and a number of white business people in Green Bay. She also collected money in Canada and gave Indian dances in Germany, getting money for the Indians. . . . Our highly educated Oneida lady called another general meeting, after the meeting in 1921, perhaps in 1923. I was present at this meeting. She opened the meeting in English and Oneida and told us she had made arrangements for the attorney who was from New York to come to Oneida and tell us about our claim. He was from Wise and Whitney law firm of New York. . . . But it did substantiate the Oneida lady's talk as to our claim in New York to a certain extent. She was also telling us that the Six Nations were never paid for the land taken by St. Lawrence Power, and that she was going to work on that claim, too. And, of course, she mentioned that we had a lot of money coming. She might have had three or four meetings in Oneida with her sweet talk, and she went around in a way re-registering Oneidas for so much payment to her, or more like an investment, and a printed receipt given to the victim, written on it: '10% Interest, plus 40% Bonus.' Not all the Oneidas believed her. This lady without question had college education and it is claimed that her English was next to perfect. I can say that her Oneida language was perfect. . . . Her last haul of money from poor Oneidas in Oneida, Wisconsin was perhaps in 1928 or so when she told her victims that they would be getting lots of money before the snow falls. The snow has fallen many times, but not the money.[51]

Despite these and other accusations, Kellogg's role in bringing to court the momentous land-claims case, *James Deere* v. *St. Lawrence River Power*, initiated in 1925, makes her a significant person worthy of study, for she helped to define one of the Iroquois positions in this matter well into the future.[52] In November 1922, Kellogg attended a meeting of the Indian Welfare League in Albany, in which Assemblyman Everett was chastized by both Indian and non-Indian reformers for his report, including his actions which allegedly stirred up false hopes among Indians about the land-claims issue. In a column in the *Knickerbocker Press*, Kellogg reacted to the meeting by defending Everett and claiming that she belonged to no welfare societies "because they seem to me to leave the Indians in a worse condition than they found them in." She added that the real question was not the workings of the Everett Commission but the legal status of the Six Nations. To her, the Treaty of Fort Stanwix of 1784 gave the

Iroquois Confederacy independence; however, the "only way to put the Six Nations on an economic footing was to obtain the rights inherent" in that treaty.[53] Less than a week later, Kellogg, her brother, and the soon-to-be prominent James Deere sent Everett a letter endorsing his report, condemning the Indian Welfare League, and making an offer to retain his legal services in future litigation.[54]

The Deere case was brought before the United States District Court for the Northern District of New York. The litigation was a test case, a class-action suit, on behalf of the Iroquois Confederacy. Everett and the New York City law firm of Wise, Whitney, and Parker (Carl Whitney was Everett's nephew), represented James Deere, a Mohawk, in his ejectment proceedings against the St. Lawrence River Power Company, a subsidiary of Alcoa, and seventeen other occupants of this one-square-mile parcel of land. The power company hired the eminent statesman Charles Evans Hughes to argue the motion. Hughes soon maintained that the case should be dismissed on technical grounds, claiming that there was no federal question involved and consequently the court had no jurisdiction in the matter. The plaintiffs insisted that an 1824 treaty between the St. Regis Indians and New York State, which allowed for the sale of the disputed land to the state, was null and void because no single tribe of the Six Nations Confederacy had such authority and because only the federal government and the Six Nations Confederacy could write such agreements at that time.[55] Although the case was partially an outgrowth of efforts by Everett and Stillman, the Deere case was primarily a manifestation of Kellogg's attempt to win recognition for her reconstituted version of the League.[56]

During the lengthy deliberations in the Deere case, Kellogg, her husband, and Wilson K. Cornelius were arrested in Canada in 1927. They were charged with alleged conspiracy to defraud and of obtaining fifteen thousand dollars by false pretenses from members of the Iroquois living on reserves in Quebec and Ontario. At the trial in Montreal, the Kelloggs argued that the money was collected to help rehabilitate the Indian, to gain his independence, and to create "a sense of nationhood" through plans to recover millions of acres of land in New York and Pennsylvania. The Royal Canadian Mounted Police, on the other hand, accused them of obtaining subscriptions by false pretenses at Oka, Caughnawaga, St. Regis, Lorette, Munsey, and other Canadian reserves.[57]

Despite the apparent cooperation of the BIA—the Indian Bureau sent an expert witness to testify against the Kelloggs—the defendants were cleared of all charges by the court; nevertheless, they were deported from Canada.[58]

During the proceedings of the trial in October, the United States District Court dismissed the Deere case because of what it insisted was the court's lack of jurisdiction in the matter.[59] Everett's death in 1928 and later fruitless appeals in the Deere case proved fatal to Kellogg's grand design. Her last major thrust toward reconstitution of the eighteenth-century League came in 1929 when she testified at a major hearing of the United States Senate. Once again, she spoke in proud terms of the Six Nations; of her reconstruction plans for their economic, political, and spiritual revival; of her hatred for the BIA, who she now accused of spreading "propaganda, pernicious propaganda, criminal propaganda" against her as well as against the Iroquois as a whole; of her claims to lands in New York and Pennsylvania; and of her opposition to the building of a dam at Onondaga which would condemn part of the reservation. In packing the hearing with her supporters, her aim was to lobby for Senate pressure on the Justice Department to intervene on the side of the Indians in the Deere case. At the hearing, Orrin Kellogg maintained: "We are here to get the Senate committee to look into the wrongs that have been done to the Six Nations of New York. We want them to make a survey of conditions up there and recommend to the United States Government . . . that they intervene and settle this question for all time to come."[60] Despite Kellogg's appeals, the Senate refused to act.

The land claims issue and Kellogg's efforts to reconstitute her version of the League led to increased factionalism among the Iroquois. Every Iroquois reservation in the United States and Canada was affected. Onondaga was a case in point. For over a decade, two rival councils, one a Kellogg council headed by George Thomas and the other the traditional existing hereditary council headed by Joshua Jones, vied with each other for power. In reality, the major issue was Minnie Kellogg herself and whether she had a right to speak for the Six Nations. Her enemies maintained that she had no right to a voice in Iroquois affairs because her people, the Oneidas, had lost their place when they migrated to Wisconsin; she claimed, however, that the Six Nations remained intact and that the Oneidas had been forcibly pushed out of their territory in New York and consequently their status as a member of the Six Nations remained unchanged. Eventually, in 1927, she lost a suit for control of the tribal funds of the Onondaga Nation. Nevertheless, her rival council attempted to operate, however secretively, well into the 1930s.[61] One Oneida described Kellogg's activities in 1930: "She does not hold her councils on any other reservation in New York State at the present time; she holds her councils in the Onondaga Hotel, or some place like that. She selects her own officers, secretaries, treasurers, and field agents who go about the reservation."[62]

The New Deal Era was the final death knell of the Kellogg Party. For better or worse, the federal government's work-relief programs increasingly tied the Indian to far-off Washington. Instead of a few thousand dollars, as was true in the 1920s, the federal government poured hundreds of thousands of dollars into Iroquoia. The Kellogg vision of self-help and self-sufficiency went out the window, along with the views of rugged individualism of Herbert Clark Hoover. The community action programs of the New Deal, though not accepted universally, had the blessing of the majority of the Iroquois. Pie-in-the-sky grand designs about reconstructing the ancient League or winning back eighteen million acres meant less to the Iroquois when they had an administration in Washington providing them with employment and allowing them to revive their arts, their language, and their pride in being Iroquois. By taking care of their immediate needs, the federal government actually contributed to the co-optation of the claims movement.[63]

Although Kellogg continued to operate throughout the 1930s in opposing Commissioner John Collier's policies and holding fast to her own rehabilitation program, few Iroquois listened.[64] By the 1940s, she was a broken woman who had outlived her time in history and dissipated both her fame and the money that had come with it. Ironically, the woman who had pushed for self-help and self-sufficiency was living by 1947 on welfare in New York City; she died in obscurity soon after.[65]

Kellogg's apparent obsession with elaborate master plans to rehabilitate the economic and political systems of Indian societies led her to believe that she was the only one capable of achieving these goals. As a secular leader of a mass movement with a messianic message of redemption, she could win large numbers of Indian people to her causes, but only at a price to her well-being. She drove herself relentlessly, and on at least one occasion, she was institutionalized for depression. In her early life, her uncompromising style was reflected in her inability to stay at any one university for any length of time. Moreover, in the last two decades of her life, long after she had been repudiated by the Indian and non-Indian worlds, she lost touch with reality, clinging to ideas that had no hope of materializing.[66]

Minnie Kellogg, however, was not simply a neurotic accident in Iroquois history. Although she never fulfilled the expectations of her followers, she was a leader in the context of Iroquois culture and history. In the factional world of Indian politics, she promised her followers the political offices of her version of the League of the Iroquois. She also promised land that would be won through Indian claims assertions in the courts. In return, she received significant amounts of money and political support and power. The mutual interaction of Kellogg and her followers lay not simply in the power arena but also in other areas. Despite her sophistry and her inability to provide both moral stewardship and the total transformation of the Iroquois polity, she dealt with questions of Iroquois treaty rights and sovereignty as well as with other fundamental aspirations, needs, and values of her people.[67]

The Kellogg movement was no mere scam, nor was it a fleeting episode in Iroquois history. It was a revolution. Writing in the context of Oneida ethnohistory, which can broadly be extended to the Iroquois as a whole, anthropologist Jack Campisi has perceptively observed:

> Nonetheless, the actions of the Kelloggs encouraged Oneida identity and a sense that the various bands were one people, different in culture, history, and language from the other Indian groups. The Kelloggs encouraged communication among the Oneida bands and increased the awareness of their common heritage. And lastly, the Kelloggs kept active a series of contacts with the state and national governments relative to the status of the Oneidas. The Oneidas existed as a problem because they made themselves one.[68]

The Kellogg movement, and more particularly Minnie Kellogg, fooled too many Iroquois for too long a period to be dismissed too quickly. Despite chicanery, Kellogg helped transform the modern Iroquois, not back into an eighteenth-century League, but into major actors, activists, and litigants in the modern world of twentieth-century Indian politics.

Notes

1. *Who Was Who In America with World Notables*, vol. 5 (Chicago, 1973), p. 387. Kellogg was the author of several books, booklets, and plays that are no longer available today; these include *The Lost Empire; The Trail of the Morning Star; Eagle Eye; Indians Reveries;* and *Gehdos of the Lost Empire.* The research for this article was funded in part by grants from the Research Foundation of the State University of New York, the American Philosophical Society, and the National Endowment for the Humanities. An earlier version of this paper was presented on October 8, 1982, at the Iroquois Conference at the Institute of Man and Science, Rensselaerville, New York. Professor Jack Campisi shared with me his unique understanding of Oneida history. He deserves special acknowledgement; this essay could not have been written without his encouragement.

2. William N. Fenton, "The Iroquois in History," in *North American Indians in Historical Perspective*, ed. Nancy O. Lurie and Eleanor B. Leacock (New York, 1971), p. 131. Some of Kellogg's message of "redemption" parallels the ideas of the so-called Thunderwater movement that was active on Iroquois reservations in Canada from 1914 to 1927, although the connection between the two movements is nebulous. Interview with Ernest Benedict, St. Regis Reservation, Cornwall Island, September 10–11, 1982.

3. Interviews with Norbert Hill, Sr., October 18, 1978; Frank Danforth, October 20, 1978, Oneida Wis.; Jim Schuyler, October 20, 1978; Anderson Cornelius, October 21, 1978; and Melissa Cornelius, October 21, 1978, Oneida, Wis. Interview with Ruth Baird, October 20, 1978, Green Bay, Wis. All of the people interviewed are respected elders of the Oneida Tribe of Wisconsin. Melissa Cornelius was Minnie Kellogg's first cousin. Transcribed interview with Oscar Archiquette by Dr. Robert W. Venables, October 20, 1970, Shell Lake, Wis.

4. Kellogg is frequently accused of being responsible for the land sale in which the Oneida Indian School property at the core of the Oneida territory was

sold to the Catholic Diocese of Green Bay. She, in fact, attempted to save the school property. Jack Campisi, Field Notes, 1972 (in possession of Campisi, SUNY-Albany). The property today is the Sacred Heart Seminary, Oneida, Wis.

5. *The Episcopal Church's Mission to the Oneidas* (Oneida, Wis., 1899), pp. 27–38.

6. The best ethnohistory of the Oneidas of Wisconsin is Jack Campisi, "Ethnic Identity and Boundary Maintenance in Three Oneida Communities" (Ph.D. diss., State University of New York, Albany, 1974).

7. Ibid.; and Laurence M. Hauptman, *Iroquois and the New Deal* (Syracuse, N.Y., 1981), pp. 70–74.

8. United States Congress, Senate Subcommittee on Indian Affairs, *Hearings on S. Res. 79: Survey of Conditions of the Indians in the U.S.;* 71st Cong., 1st sess., vol. 5 (Washington, D.C., 1930), p. 1930; Graham D. Taylor, *The New Deal and American Indian Tribalism: The Administration of the Indian Reorganization Act, 1934–1945* (Lincoln, Nebr., 1980), p. 6.

9. For an excellent analysis of women's historic role among the Iroquois, see Nancy Bonvillain, "Iroquoian Women," in *Studies in Iroquoian Culture,* ed. Nancy Bonvillain (Rindge, N.H., 1980), pp. 47–59.

10. *The Episcopal Church's Mission,* p. 38. Professor Floyd Lounsbury of Yale University, who was in charge of the WPA Oneida Language and Folklore Project, was told by Oneidas in 1939 that Kellogg suffered and faced white prejudice as a result of being "the only Indian at Grafton Hall." Personal Correspondence, Floyd Lounsbury, October 8, 1982, Rensselaerville, N.Y.

11. Laura Cornelius Kellogg, *Our Democracy and the American Indian* (Kansas City, Mo., 1920), pp. 38–39.

12. *The Episcopal Church's Mission,* p. 38.

13. Interview of Ernest Benedict, September 10, 1982. St. Regis Indian Reservation; Personal Correspondence, Floyd Lounsbury; interview with Archiquette by Venables.

14. Hauptman, *Iroquois and the New Deal,* p. 80.

15. *The Episcopal Church's Mission,* pp. 38–39; Kellogg, *Our Democracy and the American Indian,* pp. 17–24.

16. Patricia K. Ballow to Laurence M. Hauptman, October 22, 1982, in possession of the author. Ms. Ballow is the archivist of Barnard College. "Special Student" Bursar's Receipt No. 2725, February 6, 1906, for Laura M. Cornelius, Barnard College Archives. Laura M. Cornelius, "Overalls and the Tenderfoot: A Story," *The Barnard Bear* 2 (March 1907), pp. 5–18. The author thanks Ms. Ballow for her help in this research.

17. *The Mortarboard: The Yearbook of Barnard College, Columbia University, Published by the Class of 1908* (New York, 1907), p. 142.

18. Campisi, Field Notes, 1972. Kellogg, the Progressive Era reformer, worked to expose poor conditions in Milwaukee's tenements; was a muckraking investigator of Osage leases and the Indian school at Pawhuska, Oklahoma; objected to some of the conditions caused by the nonregulation of certain American industries; and favored the work of the key Progressive Era think-tank, the New York Bureau of Municipal Research. Kellogg, *Our Democracy and the American Indian*, pp. 44–45, 84–88. Laura M. Cornelius, "Industrial Organization for the Indian," Society of American Indians, *Report of the Executive Council on the Proceedings of the First Annual Conference, Oct. 12–17, 1911* (Washington, D.C., 1912), pp. 46–49.

19. Kellogg, *Our Democracy and the American Indian*, p. 17 passim to end. Akwesasne Notes, *A Basic Call to Consciousness: The Hau De No Sau Nee Address to the Western World, Geneva, Switzerland, 1977* (Rooseveltown, N.Y., 1978). Also, see any issue of *Akwesasne Notes*, 1968–1982. Janey B. Hendrix, "Redbird Smith and the Nighthawk Keetowahs," *Journal of Cherokee Studies* 7 (Fall 1983), pp. 83–85.

20. For example, Clinton Rickard (Indian Defense League of the Americas); Alice Lee Jemison (American Indian Federation); Louis R. Bruce, Jr. (National Congress of American Indians); Ernest Benedict (National Indian Brotherhood); Norbert Hill, Sr. (Great Lakes Inter-tribal Council); Alcatraz (Richard Oakes); Wounded Knee, 1973, and the Longest Walk, 1978 (Oren Lyons).

21. Society of American Indians, *Report of the Executive Council on the Proceedings of the First Annual Conference*, pp. 8, 10–15.

22. Ibid., pp. 14–15.

23. Laura Cornelius Kellogg, "Some Facts and Figures on Indian Education," *The Quarterly Journal* 1 (April 15, 1913), p. 37.

24. Ibid., pp. 36–46.

25. William A. DuPuy, "Looking for an Indian Booker T. Washington to Lead their People," *New York Tribune*, August 27, 1911.

26. Cornelius, "Industrial Organization for the Indian," p. 50.

27. Ibid., pp. 43–55.

28. Ibid., p. 44.

29. Ibid., p. 48.

30. Ibid., p. 50.

31. DuPuy, "Looking for an Indian Booker T. Washington."

32. Although listed as the Vice-President on Education of the Society of American Indians in 1913, her name is missing from the membership lists provided in the proceedings of the society's annual meetings in 1914 and thereafter; nor is she represented as an author in the *Quarterly Journal (American Indian Magazine)* after that time.

33. Hazel W. Hertzberg, *The Search for an American Indian Identity: Modern Pan-Indian Movements* (Syracuse, N.Y., 1971), p. 61.

34. "What Has Become of Investigators," *Tulsa Daily World,* October 5, 1913; "Alleged Swindlers of Indians Caught," *Tulsa Daily World,* October 12, 1913. The *Tulsa Daily World,* on October 5, 1913, claimed that Mrs. Kellogg was for years involved in questionable collection schemes allegedly for the benefit of poor Oneidas and other Indians. For the Osage in this period, see John Joseph Mathews, *The Osages: Children of the Middle Waters* (Norman, Okla., 1961), pp. 774–84; Bill Burchardt, "Osage Oil," *Chronicles of Oklahoma* 41 (Autumn 1963), pp. 253–69.

35. Her differences with other Indians can be seen in Kellogg, *Our Democracy and the American Indian,* pp. 60–61. For Montezuma, see Peter Iverson, "Carlos Montezuma," in *American Indian Leaders: Studies in Diversity,* ed. R. David Edmunds (Lincoln, Nebr., 1980), pp. 206–11. Arthur C. Parker was another member of the society who had little to do with his Iroquois colleague Laura Cornelius Kellogg. M. Friedman to Arthur C. Parker, June 12, 1913, Arthur C. Parker Manuscripts, Rush Rhees Library, University of Rochester. For Parker, see Hazel W. Hertzberg, "Nationality, Anthropology and Pan-Indianism in the Life of Arthur C. Parker (Seneca)," *Proceedings of the American Philosophical Society* 123 (February 1979), pp. 47–72.

36. Kellogg, *Our Democracy and the American Indian,* pp. 40–41, 60–63, 92–97.

37. Ibid., pp. 52–53.

38. Ibid., pp. 28–29.

39. Ibid., p. 93.

40. Ibid., pp. 96–99.

41. Ramona Herdman, "A New Six Nations: Laura Cornelius Kellogg Sees the Old Iroquois Confederacy Re-established on a Modern Business Basis," *Syracuse Herald,* November 6, 1927, p. 11.

42. Ibid.; "Six Iroquois Nations File Suit for Ownership to 6,000,000 acres in State," June 12, 1925, Warren H. Norton Scrapbooks, "Indians, 1916–1927," Onondaga Historical Association, Syracuse, N.Y.; "Expects Decision Soon on Huge Indian Claim: Ottinger Says St. Regis Suit is Test Case Involving Lands Worth $3,000,000,000," *New York Times,* February 27, 1926.

43. J. N. B. Hewitt to Laura Cornelius Kellogg, May 19 and June 4, 1920, April 17, 1926, July 9, 1932; Kellogg to Hewitt, February 16, 1925, May 31, 1927, May 17, 1932; Hewitt to Chief David Russell Hill, March 26, 1928, April 21, 1929, J. N. B. Hewitt Manuscripts, No. 4271, Box 2, National Anthropological Archives, Smithsonian Institution (hereafter cited as SNAA).

44. Kellog to Hewitt, May 17, 1932, ibid.

45. Hewitt to Kellog, July 9, 1932, ibid.

46. Campisi, "Ethnic Identity and Boundary Maintenance," pp. 152–53.

47. U.S. Congress, *Hearings on S. Res. 79*, vol. 12, p. 4858.

48. *U.S.* v. *Boylan*. 265 F 165 (1920).

49. New York State Assembly, "Report of the Indian Commission to Investigate the Status of the American Indian Residing in the State of New York, Transmitted to the Legislature, March 17, 1922 (unpublished manuscript version), pp. 303–324.

50. See notes 3 and 4, above. Kellogg tax receipt in author's possession. "Final Notice: to all Oneidas who may participate in the New York Claim," December 31, 1925, Bureau of Indian Affairs (hereafter cited as BIA) Central Files, 1907–1939, No. 9788–1923–260, P. 1, New York, RG 75, NA. Freeman Johnson (Tonawanda Seneca) to Commissioner of Indian Affairs (hereafter cited as CIA), April 7 and 20, 1927; Jonas Schuyler (Oneida) to Commissioner Charles Burke, January 7, 1927; William Skenandore (Oneida) to CIA, July 9, 1926, BIA Central Files, 1907–1939, No. 9788–1923–260, P. 2, New York, RG 75, NA. Interview with Chief Irving Powless, Sr., May 15, 1979, Onondaga Indian Reservation.

51. Interview with Archiquette by Venables. Hewitt claimed that at the Six Nations Reserve in Ontario, the Kelloggs solicited eighty thousand dollars for the claim. Hewitt to M. W. Stirling, June 25, 1932, Bureau of American Ethnology Manuscripts, Letters Received, 1909–1950, Box 45, "J. N. B. Hewitt, 1929–1937," SNAA.

52. New York State joined the case later as one of the defendants. 32 F 2d. 851 (1927).

53. Quoted in Helen M. Upton, *The Everett Report in Historical Perspective: The Indians of New York* (Albany, N.Y., 1980), pp. 77–104.

54. Ibid., pp. 114–15.

55. Ibid., pp. 124–29.

56. Cf. ibid. Upton fails to understand Kellogg's overall importance in Iroquois politics during the 1920s and gives too much credit to Assemblyman Everett and Lulu Stillman. Mrs. Stillman, an extraordinary person in her own right, later became the legal advisor to the Iroquois from the early 1930s until her death in 1969.

57. "Three Go on Trial in Six Nations Case," *New York Times*, October 4, 1927; "National Status of Iroquois is Again Discussed," *Montreal Gazette*, October 6, 1927, and "Verdict in Indian Case This Afternoon," *Montreal Gazette*, October 13, 1927, both found in Hewitt Manuscripts, No. 4271, Box 2, SNAA.

58. F. G. Tranberger to Commissioner Burke, with attached memorandum, November 2, 1927 (date received), BIA Central Files, 1907–1939, No.

9788-1923-260, N.Y.,P.2,RG75,NA. The attached BIA memorandum reads: "As Kelloggs have been very troublesome to the Six Nations Confederacy Indians in the United States and to the United States Department of the Interior and Department of Justice, also the Post Office Department, it is probable that all trouble can be eliminated *by obtaining the conviction of these persons in the Canadian courts* [emphasis mine]."

59. "$2,000,000,000 Suit of Indians Rejected," *New York Times*, Oct. 25, 1927.

60. U.S. Congress, *Hearings on S. Res. 79*, vol. 12, p. 4879.

61. Campisi, "Ethnic Identity and Boundary Maintenance," p. 442. " 'Fighting Squaw' Defends Rights of Oneida Tribe as Members of Six Nations," March 14, 1924, p. 106; "Principals in Row Over Six Nations Leadership," October 12, 1924, p. 47; "Indian Affairs Bureau Warns Six Nations as to Rights on State Claim," November 21, 1924, p. 32; all found in Warren H. Norton Scrapbooks, "Indians, 1916–1927," Onondaga Historical Association, Syracuse, N.Y.

62. Quoted in Campisi, "Ethnic Identity and Boundary Maintenance," pp. 442–43.

63. Hauptman, *Iroquois and the New Deal*, pp. 1–18, 30, 70–87, 177–83.

64. "She [Kellogg] is entirely dissatisfied with anything that John Collier may do, and does not want to discuss tribal affairs with him saying that they are not under his jurisdiction. . . ." Henry Kannee Memorandum for Miss Barrows, September 14, 1937, President Franklin D. Roosevelt Manuscripts, OF 6–C, FDR Presidential Library, Hyde Park, N.Y. Kellogg had written to Senator Royal Copeland on August 5, 1937, and Copeland forwarded his letter to M. H. McIntyre on August 14, 1937. McIntyre refused to allow Kellogg to see Roosevelt. McIntyre to Kellogg, August 25, 1937, President Franklin D. Roosevelt Manuscripts, OF 296. Collier warned people of Kellogg's "collection schemes." Circular letter on "Activities of O. J. and L. C. Kellogg," undated (1933?), J. N. B. Hewitt Manuscripts, No. 4271, Box 2, SNAA; John Collier to Mrs. Charles E. Reynolds, October 7, 1935, BIA Central Files, 1907–1939, No. 40728–1933–051 New York, RG 75, NA.

65. Campisi Field Notes, 1972; interview with Archiquette by Venables; interview with Ernest Benedict. Evidence of Kellogg's fallen position can be found in Records of the New York Agency 067 Tribal Relations, Box 3, RG 75, NA.

66. Kellogg appears to have been suffering from manic depressive behavior. Joseph Mendels, *Concepts of Depression* (New York, 1970), pp. 19–33. After the death of her mother, Kellogg entered a sanitarium: "Our sorrow bothered my sister and myself completely, and I have even had to go to a sanitarium of late to be able to go on with our terrific job of re-habilitating our wonderful Six Nations into their former mode of government." L. C. Kellogg to J. N. B. Hewitt, Feb-

ruary 16, 1925, J.N.B. Hewitt Manuscripts, No. 4271, Box 2, File: Kellog News-clippings, et al., SNAA. Interview with Ernest Benedict.

67. Minnie Kellogg was both a transactional as well as a transformational leader in the terminology of James MacGregor Burns. See Burns, *Leadership* (New York), 1978, pp. 4–5.

68. Campisi, "Ethnic Identity and Boundary Maintenance," p. 443.

Essay on Sources

The secondary literature on Laura Cornelius "Minnie" Kellogg is quite thin. Consequently, the researcher must rely on Kellogg's own published writings, several major archival collections, general works on the Oneida Indians, court and legislative testimony, and newspaper accounts. The Oneida Tribe of Wisconsin has for many years searched for her historical, legal, and linguistic papers which were apparently destroyed.

The best place to begin to understand Minnie Kellogg and her world would be to visit Oneida, DePere, Green Bay, and Seymour, Wisconsin, in order to speak to tribal leaders and elders as well as to visit the Oneida Indian museum. The reader would also find Kellogg's writings most helpful; see *Our Democracy and The American Indian* (Kansas City, Mo., 1920) and her article in the Society of American Indians' *Quarterly Journal* 1 (April 15, 1913). The researcher would find the Society's *Proceedings of the First Annual Conference, Oct. 12–17, 1911* (Washington, D.C., 1912) an important source on Kellogg's early Indian nationalistic activities.

Several archival collections contain significant Kellogg correspondence and/or correspondence about the Kellogg Indian land claims movement; see the J. N. B. Hewitt and the Bureau of American Ethnology papers at the National Anthropological Archives of the Smithsonian Institution and Record Group 75, BIA Central Files, 1907–1939, at the National Archives. Another major primary source on Kellogg is her testimony before the U.S. Congress, Senate Subcommittee on Indian Affairs. Hearings on S. Res. 79: *Survey of Conditions of the Indians in the U.S.*, 71st Cong., 1st sess. (Washington, D.C., 1930), Part 5.

For the best work on Oneida Indian history, see Jack Campisi, "Ethnic Identity and Boundary Maintenance in Three Oneida Communities" (Ph.D. diss., State University of New York, Albany, 1974), and his summary "Oneida" in Smithsonian Institution, *Handbook of North American Indians*, ed. William C. Sturtevant and Bruce G. Trigger (Washington, D.C., 1978). Moreover, in order to comprehend Kellogg, it is essential to understand the Iroquois sense of nationalism and sovereignty. The best works on this subject are: Barbara Graymont, ed., *Fighting Tuscarora: The Autobiography of Chief Clinton Rickard* (Syracuse, N.Y., 1973) and Laurence M. Hauptman, *The Iroquois and the New Deal* (Syracuse, N.Y., 1981). To understand how Iroquois nationalism fits into the context of a larger American Indian nationalism, see Hazel W. Hertzberg, *The Search for an American Indian Identity: Modern Pan-Indian Movements* (Syracuse, N.Y., 1971). For a contemporary Iroquois view of sovereignty, see any issue of *Akwesasne Notes* or its publication, *A Basic Call to Consciousness: The Hau De No Sau Nee Address to the Western World, Geneva, Switzerland, 1977*(Rooseveltown, N.Y., 1978).

There is a great need for more historical research on the Iroquois land-claims movement. For a survey of Oneida land claims history, see Philip O. Geier, III, "A Peculiar Status: A History of Oneida Indian Treaties and Claims: Jurisdictional Conflict Within the American Government, 1775–1920" (Ph.D. diss., Syracuse University, 1980). Campisi's work, cited above, is essential reading on this subject. Helen Upton's *The Everett Report in Historical Perspective: The Indians of New York* (Albany, N.Y., 1980) contains some information about the land-claims movement in the 1920's; however, a researcher would find it more useful to read the original unpublished Everett Report: New York State Assembly, *Report of the Indian Commission to Investigate the Status of the American Indian Residing in the State of New York, Transmitted to the Legislature, March 17, 1922*, a copy of which can be found at the Akwesasne Museum of the Mohawk Nation in Rooseveltown, New York. Two court decisions are also essential for an understanding of the Oneidas and their land claim: *U.S.* v. *Boylan*, 265 F 165 (1920); and *James Deere* v. *St. Lawrence River Power*, 32 F 2d 851 (1927).

Newspapers of the period focused on Kellogg and her movement. These include the *New York Times*, the *Montreal Gazette*, the *Tulsa World*, and the *Syracuse Herald*. The most important article found about Kellogg is Ramona Herdman, "A New Six Nations: Laura Cornelius Kellogg Sees the Old Confederacy Reestablished on a Modern Basis," in the *Syracuse Herald*, November 6, 1927.

8

Peterson Zah

A Progressive Outlook and a Traditional Style

George M. Lubick

In 1969, the Navajo Council's Advisory Committee recommended that the tribe hereafter use the term Navajo Nation *as a reminder to its members and non-Indians alike that both "the Navajo People and Navajo Lands are, in fact, separate and distinct." History supported such a view, the council proclaimed, because long before the United States came into being the Diné existed as a distinct ethnic, cultural, and political group; once the "New Men" arrived in the Southwest, Navajo sovereignty was further buttressed by treaties wherein Congress and the Supreme Court recognized the inherent Navajo right of self-government. Navajo nationalism, embodied in the emergence of the tribal council in this century, grew and changed in response to external pressures, particularly to the desires to exploit Navajo resources and to internal conflicts, such as those between the more traditional Navajos like Chee Dodge and the "progressives" represented by J. C. Morgan and his Returned Students Association.*

As for the internal conflicts, regardless of the lines of opposition, Navajos have generally manifested the desire to acquire greater control over their social, political, and economic lives. As Peter Iverson has written in "The Emerging Navajo Nation," the election of Peter MacDonald in 1970 as tribal chairman mirrored the mood of Navajo nationalism. From the time of his first inaugural through his reelection to an unprecedented third term as chairman in 1978, MacDonald

gave notice that his administration would seek greater sovereignty. The Diné would protect what was rightfully theirs and claim what was rightfully due to them. MacDonald also stressed self-sufficiency so that Navajos would no longer depend upon the skills of others to develop their economy and meet their society's needs.

The 1970s, however, were years of turmoil. Not only were there political scandals in Navajo tribal government, but the Navajo-Hopi land dispute raised the most troublesome questions about Navajo national sovereignty. The dispute had its origin in the withdrawal from "settlement and sale" of 2,508,800 acres from the public domain by executive order of December 16, 1882. The land was "set apart for the use and occupancy of Moqui [Hopis] *and such other Indians as the Secretary of the Interior may see fit to settle thereon." At the time of its withdrawal many Navajos resided on this land. Later, some of the reserve became assigned exclusively to the Hopis, and the remainder, about 1.8 million acres, became known as the Joint-Use Area.*

In the late 1970s, thousands of Navajos whose families had resided on this land for generations were threatened with immediate eviction, while others accepted "relocation." One such family from the Joint-Use Area was that of Peterson Zah (born 1937). While recognizing the exclusive rights of the Hopis to their reservation, the necessity of tribal resource development, the expansion of health and educational services, and cooperation with local, state, and national governments, Zah, unlike Peter MacDonald, ceaselessly voiced concerns for the traditional, least acculturated members of the tribe, and for the necessity of preserving that traditionalism which for untold generations had reminded the Diné to walk in beauty. His election as tribal chairman in 1982 represented an attempt by Navajos to adapt to the exigencies of modern society, and at the same time, to maintain their tribal heritage—a tendency that is shared by an increasing number of tribes in the 1980s.

The 1970s were years of intense activity throughout the Navajo Reservation. At the beginning of the decade, Navajos turned back Raymond Nakai's bid for a third term as tribal chairman and elected instead the articulate, well-educated Peter MacDonald. By the end of the decade, MacDonald's name would be synonymous with modern Indian leadership. His twelve-year tenure in the chairman's office was characterized by programs designed to achieve the elusive goals of Navajo self-determination and self-sufficiency. To reduce the tribe's dependence on outside sources, his administration fostered programs to stimulate employment, to develop tribal enterprises, and to teach Navajos new skills. Keenly interested in the preservation of the tribe's cultural heritage, MacDonald sought to extend control over education through the creation of a Navajo Division of Education, an agency that began operating early in his first term.

Development of the tribe's mineral resources received MacDonald's special attention; and under his leadership, the tribe negotiated leases with such corporate giants as El Paso Natural Gas and Exxon, in a concerted effort to obtain equitable royalties from the exploitation of Navajo uranium and coal and to provide employment for Navajos. In 1975, MacDonald was among the founders of the Council of Energy Resource Tribes. Funded by corporate and federal grants, CERT used its expertise to help Native Americans develop their mineral resources for their own benefit.

MacDonald's development policies were, of necessity, long-range programs, but, in the meantime, tribal government could count on federal money to finance a variety of social services on the reservation. Particularly during MacDonald's first administration, Washington provided the Navajo reservation with generous funding.

MacDonald's energy policies generated opposition in some quarters, and critics of his administration openly protested during his second term as chairman. But his adversaries remained ineffectual, and MacDonald won reelection to a third term in 1978 by a comparatively wide margin. His goals did not change perceptibly over the years, and in his third inaugural address in January 1979, he returned to themes enunciated eight years earlier. "We must claim what is ours—actively and aggressively," he told the inauguration audience. Further, he emphasized the need to strengthen tribal unity and then exhorted Navajos to "dream great dreams" and dare to put them into action.[1]

By the early 1980s MacDonald had reached the peak of his power and influence. His reputation extended well beyond the reservation boundaries, and he was recognized as one of the country's most powerful Indian leaders. At the same time, the Navajo Nation was enjoying an unaccustomed degree of economic success. Despite high unemployment on the reservation and drastic cuts in federal programs by Ronald Reagan's administration, the tribe recorded "probably the best financial year in its history" in 1981. Revenues exceeded expenditures by more than 27 million dollars—the result of the deregulation of petroleum which led eventually to increased royalties for the tribe.[2]

MacDonald also had stimulated the cause of self-determination among Navajos. His tribal counsel, George Vlassis, credits him with establishing the Navajos as an important political force in Washington, D.C. His major contribution, Vlassis contends, was to show Washington that "there was no way anybody could just buy him lunch and send him home." MacDonald shares a similar assessment of his place in modern Navajo history and regards as one of his greatest accomplishments his efforts to gain for Navajos the respect and dignity they deserve.[3]

In less than two years, however, MacDonald's seemingly unassailable political hold on the reservation had been breached. In his 1982 campaign for a fourth term as chairman, he encountered the soft-spoken head of DNA–Peoples' Legal Services, Peterson Zah, an opponent fully as articulate as the incumbent and equally charismatic. DNA *(Dinébeiina Nahiilna Be Agaditahe),* the federally funded legal services organization on the reservation, had been immensely popular since its inception in 1967, and as head of the program since 1972 Zah had developed an extensive constituency among rural and traditionalist Navajos. Equally important, he proved to be a forceful, energetic campaigner, presenting MacDonald with his most serious political challenge since 1970. Zah's supporters never doubted his ability to defeat MacDonald, but few people anticipated the extent of his victory on November 2, 1982. As late returns trickled in from remote chapter houses, they confirmed that Zah had defeated "the most powerful Indian leader in America" by nearly five thousand votes.[4]

Zah, then forty-five years old, represented a unique blend of the traditional and progressive in modern Navajo culture. Journalists who covered the 1982 campaign typically noticed only the obvious, modern side of Zah and focused on his university education, his successful administration of the legal services program, and his promises to reform and reorganize Navajo government. Yet Zah's ideas and goals were shaped by the much more subtle forces of Navajo tradition—the beliefs and values that grew out of his background in the remote, traditional community of Low Mountain in the central part of the reservation.

During Zah's boyhood and youth, Low Mountain had little contact with the outside world and was sometimes neglected by the Navajo tribal government as well. The area had been the center of opposition to government programs, and during the stock reduction programs of the 1930s it was considered antagonistic, if not hostile, toward non-Indians. Its residents practiced some dry farming but were primarily stock raisers. Zah's father had not completed his education, and his mother received no schooling. She was an accomplished weaver, however, and her blankets were sometimes the only source of income for the family. The family's home was located in the Navajo-Hopi Joint-Use Area, where Zah's family had lived amicably with the neighboring Hopis, occasionally trading a sheep for Hopi grain and other produce.[5]

Roads were virtually nonexistent around Low Mountain, and the few owners of cars and trucks found their vehicles to be expensive and unreliable forms of transportation. The nearest highway at Chinle, Arizona, was fifty miles distant. Keams Canyon, twenty-five miles southwest of Low Mountain, was the site of the nearest trading post, and Zah's family frequently made the two-day trip by horse and wagon to purchase such staples as coffee, sugar, and flour. The journeys were the family's only contact with the outside world, and for young Zah they were invariably special occasions. At the Keams Canyon and Piñon trading posts, Zah later recalled, he saw for the first time "how other people lived and was amazed at the 'looks' of non-Indians."[6]

Low Mountain changed little until Navajo G.I.s returned home after World War II, bringing with them stories of the progress and conveniences of American society as well as an appreciation for the value of education. While some of the old men around Low Mountain discussed the positive aspects of education, Zah remembered, the community hesitated to embrace the concept completely. In their contacts with the federal government, Navajos had seldom been asked for their opinions; most often they were told what to do. Education, many of them knew, meant that children were taken from their families and sent to distant boarding schools. Young Zah was subjected to the process, separated from his family at the age of nine and placed in a school more than one hundred miles away.[7]

Although Low Mountain Navajos remained divided about the need for education, Zah's own feelings were strongly influenced by educated relatives who worked as teachers and guidance counselors for the Bureau of Indian Affairs. Several of his aunts and uncles spent the school year at

BIA institutions in Flagstaff, Arizona; Brigham City, Utah; and Chemawa, Oregon; returning to Low Mountain during the summer months. "I dreamed of the day I would be able to do the same thing," Zah later wrote, "and I wanted to get as much education as I could and later return to the reservation to help the Navajos as my relatives were doing."[8]

Determined to pursue his dream, Zah left Low Mountain to enroll in the Phoenix Indian School, and following his graduation in 1958 continued his education at Phoenix College where he earned an associate of arts degree. In 1963 he received a bachelor's degree in education from Arizona State University. In 1964, his first job took him back to the Navajo Reservation where he worked as a vocational education instructor for the Area Redevelopment Administration at Window Rock High School. The following year, Zah was back at Arizona State University to supervise the training of volunteers for the VISTA program.

In the mid-1960s the Navajo Reservation enjoyed the benefits of a number of Lyndon Johnson's "Great Society" programs. The Office of Economic Opportunity, in particular, had a profound impact on the Navajo Nation through its various social and antipoverty programs. The tribal council authorized Navajo participation in the Community Action Program in 1964, and early the following year the Office of Economic Opportunity approved the tribe's request for funds to establish the Office of Navajo Economic Opportunity. Peter MacDonald, who had recently returned to the reservation, assumed the position of director of ONEO. Under his leadership, ONEO expanded to include programs for community development, Head Start, migrant and agricultural placement, alcoholism rehabilitation, and recreation and physical fitness, among others. ONEO's Legal Aid and Defender Society was established in 1967, and it eventually developed into an independent entity known by its initials DNA for *Dinébeiina Nahiilna Be Agaditahe.* The Navajo phrase translates as "Attorneys Who Contribute to the Economic Revitalization of the People."[9]

MacDonald used his control of ONEO to catapult himself to the center stage of Navajo political life.[10] DNA would serve a similar function for Peteson Zah, who joined the organization in May 1967 as an assistant to the director Ted Mitchell. The fledgling legal services group lacked even an office in its early days, and Zah's first task involved the acquisition of office space for the DNA staff of lawyers and court advocates.

Since a suitable structure was not available, Zah and his associates acquired lumber from local sawmills and constructed the building themselves. Despite its Spartan beginnings, DNA immediately filled an obvious need on the reservation, providing legal assistance for Navajos with an income of less than 3,500 dollars. And from the beginning, DNA was a grass-roots endeavor, as local chapters elected agency committees, who, in turn, chose the board of directors.[11]

The organization's first years were stormy ones as opposition to Mitchell's appointment entangled the legal services program in controversy that ended only with Mitchell's resignation in 1970. In addition, Tribal Chairman Raymond Nakai openly opposed DNA, and his supporters on the tribal council continually harassed the new organization. According to one DNA official, Nakai did not like the people DNA hired, and some tribal officials identified DNA with Ralph Nader's "Raiders," assuming that its employees were "summer vacation reformers." DNA also drew criticism from forces off the reservation. Irritated by its suits against reservation trading posts and the Gallup Indian Ceremonial, Sen. Barry Goldwater denigrated DNA by referring to it as a group of "young, inexperienced lawyers who have infested the Navajo Reservation." During the 1969 Senate debate on the economic opportunity program, Goldwater introduced an amendment to give the tribal council control over the legal services office. Fortunately for DNA, Senators Edward M. Kennedy and Walter Mondale successfully mobilized support to defeat the amendment.[12]

Despite such resistance, DNA could point to substantial success. It became popular with Navajos as soon as it began to assist people with their legal problems. Its offices at Shiprock, Crownpoint, Tuba City, Chinle, and Window Rock were each supplied with two attorneys, two counselors, and two interpreter-investigators. By the fall of 1968 it employed eighteen lawyers, many of them graduates of the prestigious law schools at Harvard, Yale, Columbia, Stanford, and elsewhere. Between April 1967 and July 1968, DNA served over 7,900 clients; by 1970 its case load reached nearly 12,000. Over the three years of its existence, it had been involved in 27,400 cases. Its community education programs reached over 15,000 residents at chapter, community, and school meetings, where DNA employees discussed, in Navajo and English, such topics as legal services, preventive law, and consumer and community education.[13]

Peter MacDonald's election as Navajo tribal chairman in 1970 guaranteed DNA's survival; indeed, the new chairman gave the organization his wholehearted support. Leo Haven succeeded Ted Mitchell as director and guided DNA until 1972, when Zah assumed control. Although he lacked formal legal training, Zah practiced in tribal courts and took all appellate cases for DNA. He also helped train tribal court advocates, young Navajos proficient in basic court procedures, and participated with them in complicated litigation.[14]

Among DNA's most controversial suits were those directed against operators of reservation trading posts. Few Navajos could count on a regular income, and traders had traditionally extended them credit in exchange for sheep, blankets, and other produce. Navajo customers accepted the traders' terms, usually unaware of hidden charges and powerless to combat high interest rates. Zah particularly resented the resulting "economic bondage" of Navajos to post operators. "I have a burning hate for the traders," he admitted, pointing out that "these bastards have been taking advantage of my people, the Navajos." In 1971, DNA lawyers filed a class action suit against the Piñon Trading Post and secured an out-of-court settlement for 32,500 dollars. Its personnel then helped Piñon residents organize a consumer's cooperative, the first of several such enterprises to grow up on the reservation. For Zah, the cooperative store represented a way "to cut out the traders" and allow Navajos to control their economic affairs.[15]

Outside the reservation, DNA championed consumer rights for Navajos against bordertown merchants from Gallup to Flagstaff. Among its most common activities was representation of Navajos whose vehicles had been repossessed by automobile dealers. One of DNA's suits produced a ruling that required auto dealers to obtain written consent from tribal courts before entering the reservation to repossess a vehicle, and thereafter some of the conflicts were eliminated. But as late as 1978, approximately 10 percent of all DNA cases still concerned repossessions.[16] DNA achieved its greatest victory in 1973, when the United States Supreme Court ruled in *McClanahan* v. *Arizona State Tax Commission* that Navajos were exempt from paying state income tax on wages and salaries earned on the reservation. The decision, according to Zah, was "a landmark tribal sovereignty case," not only for Navajos but for all Native Americans.[17]

DNA's success brought Zah national recognition in 1972 when the Native American Legal Defense and Education Fund selected him as its first president. Shortly afterward, he was chosen to serve on the executive committee of the National Legal Aid and Defender Association. His selection by the national organizations attested to the success of DNA and the growing reputation of its director. Under his guidance, DNA's advocacy of the rights of local Navajos had challenged tribal, state, and local governments and eventually would take on such energy companies as Exxon. The entire experience was exciting for Zah and his DNA staff, providing a unique opportunity to work with people at the local level. "I felt their needs and problems," he explained. "We really didn't care who was on the other side."[18]

In 1973, Zah and his legal services program faced the loss of OEO funding and were also challenged by a new legal organization, Lawyers for Navajos, Incorporated, which sought to supplant DNA on the reservation. Zah's organization triumphed in both instances. An out-of-court settlement with OEO secured its funding for the rest of the year, and the tribal council strongly supported DNA against the Lawyers for Navajos. With passage of the National Legal Services Bill in early 1974, DNA was assured of continued financial support, and Lawyers for Navajos simultaneously lost its bid to operate the reservation's legal services program. DNA changed its name in accordance with the new legislation, becoming DNA–Peoples' Legal Services and expanding its program to encompass legal aid to the neighboring Hopi Reservation.[19]

During the next several years, Zah was at the center of Navajo political life. In May 1976, he took leave from his DNA post to organize the "Walk for Better Government"—a protest march in response to a wave of rumors and allegations generated by a Justice Department investigation of the Navajo Housing Authority and audits of tribal finances authorized by the tribal council. In fact, the audits found no evidence of financial malfeasance, and only one member of the housing authority, Pat Chee Miller, was found guilty of any crime. But the publicity emanating from the investigations raised serious questions about the integrity of tribal government and undermined the faith of many Navajos in that institution.

On May 18, the opening of the tribal council's spring session, a column of "Navajo People Concerned for their Government" walked from the Window Rock Civic Center to the council chambers to present a list of recommendations. Speaking for the contingent, Zah told members of the council that the news stories about corruption had caused Navajos to wonder about their tribal government. Indeed, many were embarrassed by the whole affair. The source of the problem, according to Zah, was not the tribal chairman or any person but the cumbersome, ineffective governmental structure that had been established years earlier by the Bureau of Indian Affairs. "Instead of looking for a new man or a new woman to run the Tribal Government," he argued, "I think it is time to look for a new Tribal Government." The existing institution was not accountable to the Navajo people, and Zah was particularly concerned that council members had not discussed the scandals at local chapter meetings.[20]

The marchers' first recommendation called for a task force to reorganize the government. And Zah asked also for a committee to investigate the tribe's administrative organization, financial status, and current resources. In closing he warned, "We must change the whole system of government in terms of checks and balances especially in relation to policies and expenditures of the tribe."[21] The May march and Zah's address brought no immediate action from either MacDonald or the tribal council, but the affair demonstrated the extent of dissatisfaction among Navajos. Equally important, Zah emerged as an important reform advocate, and he set forth ideas about government reorganization that would surface again in a few years. In the meantime, Navajos endured another investigation of tribal affairs when a Phoenix grand jury in 1977 subpoenaed tribal chairman Peter MacDonald. Navajos in this instance rallied to the chairman's defense, and the tribal council appropriated seventy thousand dollars for his legal defense. After only a week of hearings, MacDonald was acquitted, and the Navajo Nation's era of scandals finally ended. The audits, investigations, and indictment had disrupted tribal government and clearly limited MacDonald's ability to address important issues, but he seemingly lost little of his political support. Indeed, he may have benefited politically from the ordeal of his indictment.[22]

MacDonald determined to campaign for an unprecedented third term in 1978, though a dozen candidates, including several former political allies, were ready to challenge him in the primary election. Peterson Zah's name was mentioned frequently as a possible opponent of MacDonald, but the DNA director remained determined to avoid the 1978 race. He still had goals for DNA which he hoped to fulfill, and he was also deeply committed to his family following a July 1977 fire that had destroyed their home. Evidence suggested that the fire had been caused by arson, and Zah believed that it was connected to DNA's legal battles with the tribe and energy companies.[23]

Still, Zah impressed some Navajos as MacDonald's strongest challenger. By May 1978 a campaign committee had been organized, and bumper stickers promoting his candidacy had appeared around the reservation. Zah continued to argue that he could better serve the Navajos through DNA, and in June he explicitly stated that he would not run for chairman. "I believe in better government," he remarked, "but what is the position from which to do this?" The main issue confronting Navajos according to Zah, was the need for a new system of government. And while he had spoken out frequently about the need for reorganization, he cautioned his supporters that such statements did not reflect any motivation to run for chairman.[24]

In the ensuing election, MacDonald swept by his primary opponents and went on to defeat Raymond Nakai in the November general election. Zah could afford to wait to enter tribal politics. He was only forty-one years old in 1978 and already had gained widespread recognition throughout the reservation. Several more years as director of DNA would only enhance his reputation, and conflicts over mineral development and the land dispute with the Hopis promised to involve his legal-aid network extensively.

The dispute between the Navajos and Hopis reached a critical stage in 1974 when Congress passed the Navajo-Hopi Land Settlement Act, which was followed three years later by the partition of the former Joint-Use Area between the two tribes. In 1978, estimates indicated that 4,800 Navajos living on land granted to the Hopis would have to relocate, while a small number of Hopi families would need to abandon their homes on Navajo land.[25] MacDonald had vigorously opposed the Land Settlement Act since its passage. When possible, he had sought to delay implementation of its provisions, hoping eventually to see the measure repealed. In his 1979 inaugural address he damned the "involuntary uprooting" of thousands of Navajos. "A nation that cries tears for Palestinian refugees, Cuban refugees, for Hungarian and Vietnamese refugees, for political refugees, has no business creating a class of Navajo refugees—homeless, displaced, uprooted, and sentenced to die in exile," MacDonald stated, "just because a few Congressmen and Senators have decided for their own peace of mind that the dispute must be settled now, once and for all."[26]

The intent of the Land Settlement Act had not been the creation of a new class of refugees, but Navajos understandably viewed the relocation of thousands of residents with alarm. The law provided relocation benefits for the heads of families and made provisions for replacement homes, but such measures did not make relocation more palatable. The task of overseeing the relocation process fell to a federal commission, the Navajo and Hopi Indian Relocation Commission, located in Flagstaff. By September 1978 the commission had relocated sixty-four Navajo families, most of whose members were in their thirties and had attained some education.[27] The group was hardly representative of the Navajo population in the former Joint-Use Area.

MacDonald relied on the tribe's lawyers in negotiations with the Hopis and the federal government, while he doggedly continued his attempts to have the law repealed. In reply to Representative Morris Udall's contention in 1980 that both tribes had reconciled themselves to the law, MacDonald pledged to pursue every possibility for repeal, vowing, "We will not rest, we will not be satisfied, we will not stop our efforts until the homes and lives of the Navajo people in this area have been preserved."[28] Such language was reassuring to some, but Navajos living on the contested Hopi land perceived few improvements in their situation. Earlier court decisions had ordered the reduction of livestock in the former Joint-Use Area and also required that both tribes approve of any new construction projects. The Hopis were reluctant to approve Navajo requests, and the Navajos intensely resented this "freeze" on improvements of homes, schools, and roads.[29]

DNA was one of the few tribal organizations to aid residents directly, and its lawyers challenged grazing restrictions, stock reductions, and unfair compensation payments in behalf of local stock raisers. They also assisted those who contemplated moving by helping them secure relocation benefits. A 1977 grant from the Department of Health, Education, and Welfare enabled DNA to focus some of its attention on the needs of the elderly and to provide them with assistance in coping with relocation. Through DNA's involvement in the daily lives of the area's residents, Zah and his staff acquired an extensive knowledge of the plight of Navajos throughout the former Joint-Use Area. Equally important, DNA's activities produced a measure of satisfaction for the area's frustrated residents.

The land dispute and relocation issue were particularly poignant for Zah. He had grown up in the area and still retained close family ties there. Until passage of the 1974 Land Settlement Act, Navajos and Hopis had lived peacefully, and few Hopis in the area were anxious to see Navajo residents forced to relocate. Zah maintained that the land dispute was a creation of the federal government, and not an issue precipitated by either tribe. He realized, too, that any hostility between Navajos and Hopis would benefit the energy companies, which were interested in the area's mineral deposits. Control of the deposits by the smaller and weaker Hopi Tribe could prove especially beneficial for the corporations. In either case, Zah was convinced that both tribes were being used by outside interests.[30]

Zah's connections with the former Joint-Use Area and his understanding of its special problems were important factors in his decision to enter the 1982 primary election campaign. During informal announcements at chapter houses in the area in January 1982, he argued that "a chairman with a deep understanding and concern for that area" could repair many of the damages that had been caused by the land dispute. He cited its lack of health facilities and school buildings, its inadequate roads, and its poor water and utility services as results of the government's freeze on construction projects. Zah acknowledged that Navajos had not created the problems, but he criticized the tribal government's lack of concern for the needs of the area's residents in the years following the 1977 partition of the land.[31]

Zah proposed no panacea for the complex issue, but his long, personal friendship with Ivan Sidney, the recently elected Hopi tribal chairman, offered some hope for a solution. The escalating costs of the relocation program, he added, might induce Washington to accept a solution worked out by the new tribal chairmen.[32]

Zah's friendship with Sidney and its implications for a favorable resolution of the land dispute remained a constant feature in Zah's campaign. "Two leaders who have respect for one another can start anew and afresh on an old problem," he told audiences at White Cone and Whippoorwill in February. When Zah formally announced his candidacy later in the month, he invited Sidney to attend the rally at his home chapter at Low Mountain. The Zah and Sidney families had been friends for years, and the two tribal leaders had known each other since their student days at Phoenix Indian School. The invitation caused Sidney some concern, but he eventually accepted. "From there I had an interest," he later told a reporter, adding that MacDonald's reelection would mean "a lot more fighting" over the disputed land.[33]

By the spring of 1982 the relocation of Navajos had received widespread attention from scholars, journalists, and other writers. The intense strain of relocation on older, traditional Navajos was discussed in *Land and Religion at Big Mountain* and *A Sociocultural Assessment of the Livestock Reduction Program in the Navajo-Hopi Joint Use Area,* by anthropologists at Northern Arizona University. Thayer Scudder's *No Place to Go: Effects of Compulsory Relocation on Navajos,* a study requested by the Navajo-Hopi Land Dispute Commission, appeared in 1982; and *The Second Long Walk: The Navajo-Hopi Land Dispute,* by former *Navajo Times* and Gallup *Independent* reporter Jerry Kammer, had been published two years earlier. Scudder was perhaps the strongest proponent of repealing the 1974 law, arguing that its revocation would reduce the "human costs" of relocation for some five thousand Navajos. In addition, repeal would be more consistent with United States policy concerning the Indian Self-Determination Act, and it would also eliminate the growing financial burden for the federal government.[34]

In May 1982, Roger Lewis of the Navajo and Hopi Indian Relocation Commission aroused public interest when he described relocation as a "tragic, tragic thing" and added that he sometimes felt that the commission was "as bad as the people who ran the concentration camps during World War II."[35] Lewis's comments, along with earlier descriptions of the hardships caused by relocation, provided the impetus for the new discussions that focused on transfers of land between the two tribes as a means of reducing the number of relocatees. Tribal negotiating teams, headed by MacDonald and Sidney, met in Albuquerque in June to consider boundary adjustments. But the talks collapsed abruptly when MacDonald and his aides failed to appear at a scheduled meeting with the Hopis, although the group was meeting in a nearby room. In the ensuing blast of recriminations, all hope for an immediate negotiated settlement was lost.[36]

MacDonald's indiscretion, for which he eventually apologized to Sidney, provided Zah with an opportunity to attack his opponent, and he suggested to a campaign audience that the incumbent chairman was perhaps tired, having spent a dozen years in office. "How can we resolve anything if our chairman doesn't even show up to talk, especially when the talks are about reducing the number of Navajos who must be relocated," he asked. Zah was certain of his ability to discuss issues with Sidney, he pointed out, adding that "therein lies the hope for negotiations."[37]

During the campaign, Zah also relied on his reputation as a reformer and argued forcefully for reorganization of tribal government. MacDonald, Zah maintained, had lost sight of the basic needs of Navajos in his pursuit of "power and politics." In contrast, Zah pledged to return authority to the tribal council and to local communities. He also attacked MacDonald's lack of concern for education, and proposed a uniform system of education on the reservation. Navajos, he maintained, needed to decide the direction of their children's education, and he advocated a tribal education agency to oversee the instruction of youngsters "in what is best to the Navajo people—Navajo culture and language" in a well-rounded curriculum.[38]

Like MacDonald, Zah was a proponent of Navajo self-sufficiency and viewed taxation of energy companies as a means to foster economic independence. But Zah was keenly aware of the concerns of local residents living near mining sites on the reservation. DNA had defended them over the years and had amassed an extensive stock of information about the impact of mineral exploitation on local communities. Therefore, Zah proposed that, in the future, mining companies must first confer with local landowners, "grass roots, hogan-level Navajos," before taking their proposals to the tribal government at Window Rock.[39]

Throughout the campaign, both MacDonald and Zah were affected by the dismal economic plight of the reservation. High unemployment among Navajos hampered Zah's efforts to raise money, and his campaign staff was composed largely of volunteers. MacDonald had to defend his administration against critics of the high unemployment rate, but he remained a formidable candidate. During twelve years as chairman, he had attracted an extensive following and could point to a credible record of achievement. And as the incumbent candidate he could count on additional advantages. Consequently his supporters anticipated a primary victory of several thousand votes. MacDonald finished first among the candidates in the August primary election, but his margin over Zah proved to be exceedingly thin. Zah trailed the incumbent by less than 1,000 votes—20,083 to 19,086.[40]

In the ensuing general election campaign, Zah adhered to the strategy developed in the previous months. He selected Edward Begay, a popular politician from the eastern portion of the reservation, as his running mate and also gained the support of Wilbert Willie, Jack Jackson, and Larry Isaac, all of whom had been candidates in the primary. MacDonald chose Frank Paul to run with him, and Raymond Nakai added his endorsements to their cause.

Zah continued to stress his long friendship with Ivan Sidney as a special advantage in resolving the land dispute. He also used the two months before the November general election to develop his plans for tribal government reform and reorganization. Tribal authority, he argued, needed to be decentralized. According to his plan, the agencies and chapters would receive tribal funds and staff members to take care of local needs, while larger towns on the reservation moved toward township status, supplied with sufficient tribal funds for community improvements and similar responsibilities. Reform of the tribal government at Window Rock required the establishment of separate executive, legislative, and judicial branches of government.[41]

The theme of decentralization also characterized Zah's approach to developing the tribe's mineral resources. His emphasis was on planned development, with special attention to local needs and interests. MacDonald, Zah pointed out, "likes to do big things, bring in big companies to do big things." In contrast, Zah's energy policy was designed to promote orderly use of resources. He remained committed to taxing energy companies operating on the reservation, and he pledged to use the proceeds to create employment programs, to provide aid to elderly Navajos, and to fund scholarships for students.[42]

In the primary election, Zah successfully attracted the votes of young Navajos, and he courted them again during the next two months. "I don't like the brain drain syndrome," he told a student audience at Navajo

Community College. Zah encouraged Navajos to pursue a college education but was concerned that few found jobs on the reservation. His administration, he promised, would make room for educated young men and women in tribal government. The Council for Navajo Women had supported Zah in the primary campaign, and he recognized the need to open opportunities for women in tribal government. His appointment of Claudeen Bates Arthur as his campaign policy adviser suggested that his administration would bring women into important positions in Navajo government.[43]

A particular asset for Zah was his ability to exploit the growing dissatisfaction with MacDonald's twelve-year administration. Many Navajos remembered that in 1970 MacDonald was an acknowledged grass-roots leader. "But now he's on a pedestal," one Navajo explained to a reporter. "In twelve years he has rubbed people the wrong way." Several of the candidates in the primary campaign had voiced similar criticisms. Jack Jackson, for example, complained that the tribal council seemingly operated "at the whim of one person—Peter MacDonald." Women, too, had developed grievances against the incumbent; the Council for Navajo Women, in particular, was disillusioned with his administration. Many local Navajos also resented the fact that when MacDonald visited chapter houses he was escorted by a bodyguard of tribal policemen.[44]

Zah's long association with DNA–Peoples' Legal Services was a distinct advantage. As its director he was well known throughout the reservation, and DNA had the reputation as one of the few organizations that was responsive to the needs of grass-roots Navajos. "We seem to get involved in everything that happens here," one of its officials remarked. *The Navajo Times* echoed the same sentiment, pointing out that "on the Navajo reservation just about everyone knows about DNA. Either they have been clients themselves or someone in their family has used the DNA service."[45] Zah had gained additional recognition as leader of the "Navajo People Concerned for their Government" in the 1976 confrontation with MacDonald's allegedly scandal-ridden administration.

MacDonald's advisers remained content to stress the accomplishments of his administration and worked to hold together the constituency that had worked so effectively since 1970. Occasionally, a MacDonald aide complained that the *Navajo Times* had not given the incumbent adequate coverage or that the Gallup *Independent* sought to "throw the election to

Zah." But the MacDonald camp remained generally optimistic. Zah's support in the primary had been "soft," one of MacDonald's supporters reasoned, adding that the chairman had the upper hand and the momentum to achieve an "easy victory."[46]

There would be no such victory for MacDonald in 1982. In the general election, Zah gathered widespread support throughout the reservation and put together substantial margins in the larger chapters and at the Chinle, Fort Defiance, and Shiprock agencies to upset MacDonald by five thousand votes. In chapters in the former Joint-Use Area, he recorded a narrow victory over the incumbent. Zah also attracted young voters, who turned out in large numbers for the general election. These "alienated factions," as one analyst described the youth vote, had lost all faith in MacDonald during his third term and found an exciting leader in Zah.[47]

For Zah, the victory "completed a true grass roots effort to end years of unresponsive, unbalanced government." While politicians and others puzzled over the election results, Zah moved quickly to implement the programs he had advocated for the previous ten months. Within a few weeks he had assembled a committee on government reorganization to recommend major changes in tribal government. Out of its discussions came suggestions for reform in forty areas of tribal government. Jack Jackson, a member of the reorganization committee, described its meetings as a "historic occasion," the first time that Navajos had met to discuss the kind of tribal government they wanted.[48]

Government reorganization emerged as a prominent theme in Zah's inaugural address on January 11, 1983, when he introduced the theme of a "new Navajo partnership" to meet the needs of the tribe. The new chairman envisioned a close relationship between his office and the tribal council, but authority was not to be centralized in Window Rock. "We will decentralize the government so that local issues are decided by local communities," he told the audience. The structure of tribal government was also in need of change, according to Zah, and he proposed the separation of powers among the three branches of government.[49]

Resolution of the land dispute with the Hopis required a new understanding with the neighboring tribe. Throughout the history of the conflict, Zah maintained, lawyers from the outside had exercised too much control and had caused the traditional Navajo-Hopi relationship to deteriorate. "A little feast in the shade of a tree, and a lot of understanding would have taken us further toward a positive solution," he explained. In an effort to end the dispute, he emphasized that he and Sidney were committed to working together on areas of common concern.[50]

Resource development on Navajo land also required a new approach, and Zah announced that current leases with "unrealistic royalties" would be reviewed immediately. Rather than spending millions of dollars to hire outside law firms, the new chairman adhered to a campaign pledge to employ Navajo professionals.[51] When negotiations with energy companies began in the spring of 1983, the tribe was represented by the staff of the tribe's Minerals and Resources Department and members of Zah's own office.

The optimistic inaugural address with its promises of reform reflected the euphoria of Zah's election. But his State of the Navajo Nation address on January 25 was a much more realistic assessment of conditions on the reservation. Zah acknowledged that his reforms would be difficult to accomplish because of the severe effects of the recession. High unemployment remained a problem, and the Reagan administration's budget reductions had meant a corresponding cutback in programs and grants for the reservation. At the end of 1982, the tribe was running a deficit of approximately 25 million dollars for fiscal year 1983, and Navajo Agricultural Products Industries and Navajo Forest Products Industries had accrued millions of dollars in debts. Navajo Community College needed 1.5 million dollars for the current academic year and more for the following year, and the tribe owed the U.S. Labor Department over 7 million dollars. Even the current budget was in serious jeopardy, Zah lamented.[52]

One remedy for the tribe's financial difficulties was through renegotiation of existing leases with energy companies to increase royalty payments to the tribal government. Zah had long pledged to review such unfair leases, and his administration initiated the policy in April 1983, when the tribal council rescinded agreements with Chuska Energy and Development Company and Dineh Bii Resources—both Navajo-owned companies. Leases with the companies had never gone into effect, but tribal officials were certain that they could obtain better returns for the tribe. Negotiations with other companies would soon follow, and Zah asked the tribe's Justice Department to develop plans for a severance tax to provide an additional source of tribal income.[53]

In the meantime, Zah's reform of tribal government had been elaborated. The new chairman proposed the establishment of an Office of Legislative Affairs, which included three subdivisions—an expanded Office of the Legislative Secretary, an Office of Intergovernmental Affairs, and an office devoted to writing bills for eventual presentation to the tribal council. During Peter MacDonald's administration, the tribal council agenda was circulated only on the day of the council sessions. In contrast, the Office of Legislative Affairs would have authority to print the agenda two weeks prior to council meetings, thereby encouraging representatives to discuss agenda items with local residents well before the council met. Zah's goal of establishing a close partnership with local Navajos was reflected in the department devoted to preparing bills; it was designed to allow anyone to introduce a bill on any subject in the tribal council. The Office of Intergovernmental Affairs was essentially a liaison office to coordinate communications between Window Rock, Washington, D.C., and state capitols. Shortly after the measure had been announced, Zah and Begay visited chapter houses to stimulate local participation in the new administration's policy of partnership, stressing the need for local initiative.[54]

Perhaps the most dramatic aspect of Zah's administration concerned his frequent meetings with Ivan Sidney. The talks between the two tribal leaders, even their celebrated "historic negotiations" in Albuquerque in March, provided no solution to the land dispute, and both men realized that resolution of the problem was a long-term objective. But through their cooperation and obvious mutual respect, Zah and Sidney stimulated a sense of optimism among Hopis and Navajos. "We feel that we've got 100 per cent progress when we just sit at the same table today," Sidney said of the meetings in Albuquerque. Impressed by the good will generated by the tribal leaders, several Navajo chapters passed resolutions of appreciation for Zah's efforts, and the Hopi tribal council added its endorsement of Sidney's endeavors. Their early talks led to joint efforts to improve roads connecting the reservations and a common request that the BIA cease impounding livestock in the disputed area for ninety days and allow residents to make minor improvements in their dwellings.[55]

Much of the success attributed to Zah and Sidney resulted from a basic change in Navajo policy. Jeff Begay of the Navajo Tribe's Justice Department, and a staff assistant to Zah, explained that the new approach to resolving the land dispute focused on minimizing the number of Navajos forced to relocate—"to work within the constraints and minimize the hardship impacts." By calming Hopi fears of repeal of the 1974 legislation, Zah's policy enhanced the course of negotiations and opened new areas of cooperation. By the end of March, both tribal councils had passed a joint resolution advocating construction of a road between the Hopis' Second Mesa and Black Mesa on the Navajo Reservation. BIA support for their proposal encouraged Zah and Sidney to consider additional cooperative endeavors to improve health and educational facilities.[56]

When Zah summarized his administration's accomplishments after its first one hundred days, he pointed to substantial achievements as a result of cooperation with Sidney. Congress had appropriated money for a Hopi high school at Keams Canyon to educate youngsters of both tribes, and funds had been committed for the construction of medical clinics in the disputed area for the use of Hopi and Navajo residents. The route for the Black Mesa–Second Mesa road, the "Turquoise Trail," had been approved by Arizona state authorities, and its construction eventually would benefit both tribes. Future talks, Zah hoped, would lead to Navajo-Hopi cooperation against energy companies operating on Indian land. A joint committee had been proposed to negotiate with Peabody Coal, and the Navajo chairman anticipated that continued cooperation would provide both tribes with an equitable return for exploitation of their mineral resources. Energy companies like Peabody had used the land dispute to the detriment of Navajos and Hopis, Zah stated, and consequently they paid royalties of only fifteen cents to thirty-two cents per ton of coal.[57]

Zah's administration had produced other important results as well. The North Central Accreditation Association approved the Navajo Division of Education as an accreditation agency, and the tribe received additional federal funds from the 1982 Highway Improvement Act and the Emergency Jobs Bill. But the reservation's endemic economic problems remained unsolved, and the 1983 budget deficit represented an additional burden. New, equitable royalties from energy companies might alleviate the worst of the financial crisis eventually; in the immediate future, Navajos had to accommodate themselves to additional reductions in federal programs by the Reagan administration.

No one realistically expected Zah's administration to resolve the tribe's economic problems or the land dispute in its first few months in office.

Zah acknowledged as much in his inaugural address, noting that the problems facing the Navajo Nation had taken years to create and the solutions also would require years of hard work. In his first one hundred days, however, Zah had stimulated some changes in Navajo attitudes about government. His real accomplishment had been to establish the foundation for the kind of government he had envisioned for years and described in campaign speeches and tribal council addresses. Its theme was cooperation, or "partnership"—the term Zah preferred—and reflected his own "people-oriented" approach to tribal government. Much of Zah's public career, beginning with his association with DNA, had rested on his desire to reach and meet the needs of grass-roots Navajos.

He shared with his predecessor, Peter MacDonald, an intense pride in the Navajo heritage and a willingness to foster programs to stimulate both nationalism and self-sufficiency. But his style separated him dramatically from MacDonald. Soft-spoken and articulate, he preferred to visit chapter houses and agencies, drawing ideas from all parts of the reservation. He was equally determined to attract young Navajos into service to the Navajo Nation, convinced that young Navajo professionals "possess the intellectual ability and the dedication necessary to administer the entirety of tribal government affairs."[58] Gaining respect for Navajos had influenced his tribal policies, including relations with energy companies. Zah expected to gain higher royalties from such companies, but he was equally concerned about the attitudes of corporate officials. "We are looking for people who will have in mind respect for Navajos and our land," he told a Phoenix reporter. Zah vowed not to wait long for officials to contact the tribe, pointing out that "we will actively solicit partnerships, and make our own proposals."[59]

While no definitive judgment of Zah's success can rest on a discussion of a one-hundred-day career, it appeared in the fall of 1983 that the "new Navajo partnership" was working. Relations with the Hopis were better than they had been in perhaps several decades, and his administration remained optimistic about the renegotiation of leases. The initial reform of tribal government had begun, and Zah had brought tribal government to local Navajos. Major economic problems remained, however; and those issues, it appeared, would likely determine Zah's political future and the well-being of the Navajo Nation as well.

Notes

1. Navajo Nation, Navajo Film and Media Commission, Third Term Inaugural Address of Peter MacDonald, January 9, 1979, p. 2. On MacDonald's administrations, see Peter Iverson, *The Navajo Nation* (Albuquerque, 1983).

2. *Navajo Times,* September 22, 1982.

3. *Arizona Magazine* (Phoenix *Arizona Republic*), May 8, 1983, p. 10; *Navajo Times,* November 10, 1982.

4. Gallup, New Mexico, *Independent,* November 3, 1982.

5. Robert A. Roessel, Jr., "Tragedy at Low Mountain," in *Indian Communities in Action,* ed. Robert A. Roessel, Jr. (Tempe, Ariz., 1967), p. 60; Peterson Zah, "A Personal Presentation and Evaluation of Community Development at Low Mountain," in *Indian Communities in Action,* p. 120; *Dineh: The People—A Portrait of the Navajo,* Western World Productions, 1976 (documentary film).

6. Zah, "A Personal Presentation," p. 121.

7. Ibid., pp. 121–22.

8. Ibid., pp. 122–23.

9. Peter Iverson, "Peter MacDonald," in *American Indian Leaders: Studies in Diversity,* ed. R. David Edmunds (Lincoln, Nebr., 1980), pp. 224–25.

10. Iverson, *Navajo Nation,* p. 126.

11. *New York Times,* January 14, 1983; for a discussion of DNA's early years, see Iverson, *Navajo Nation,* pp. 91–100.

12. *Navajo Times,* June 8, 1978.

13. Ibid., September 10, 1970; June 8, 1978; Iverson, *Navajo Nation,* pp. 94, 99.

14. *DNA in Action,* September 30, 1972, p. 2.

15. *Dineh;* Iverson, *Navajo Nation,* pp. 134, 171.

16. *Navajo Times,* June 8, 1978; and April 6, 1978; Gallup *Independent,* January 25, 1983.

17. *Navajo Times,* July 14, 1982.

18. *New York Times,* January 14, 1983; *DNA in Action,* January 7, 1972, p. 9.

19. *Navajo Times,* June 7, 1973; June 14, 1973; July 5, 1973; June 6, 1978; June 28, 1973.

20. Ibid., May 6, 1976; May 20, 1976; June 8, 1978.

21. Ibid., May 20, 1976.

22. Iverson, *Navajo Nation,* p. 208.

23. *Navajo Times,* July 7, 1977; October 6, 1977; *New York Times,* January 14, 1983.

24. *Navajo Times,* June 22, 1978.

25. Navajo and Hopi Indian Relocation Commission (hereafter cited as NHIRC), *Interim Progress Report* (Flagstaff, Ariz., 1978), p. 1. The number of Navajos subjected to relocation grew dramatically as the NHIRC continued its enumeration. By the end of 1980, the commission had enumerated 2,801 Navajo households, comprising 9,525 Navajos residing on Hopi land; only 109 Hopis resided on land partitioned to the Navajos. See NHIRC, *Report and Plan* (Flagstaff, Ariz., 1981), p. 3.

26. Third Term Inaugural Address of Peter MacDonald, p. 4.

27. NHIRC, *Interim Progress Report,* pp. 11, 148.

28. Quoted in Jerry Kammer, *The Second Long Walk: The Navajo-Hopi Land Dispute* (Albuquerque, 1980), p. 219.

29. NHIRC, *Interim Progress Report,* p. 9.

30. Peterson Zah, personal interview, May 7, 1983; *Dineh.*

31. *Navajo Times,* January 20, 1982.

32. Ibid.

33. Ibid., February 10, 1982; Gallup *Independent,* February 10, 1982.

34. Thayer Scudder, *No Place to Go: Effects of Compulsory Relocation on Navajos* (Philadelphia, 1982), pp. 126–27. See also John J. Wood, Walter M. Vannette, and Michael J. Andrews, *A Sociocultural Assessment of the Livestock Reduction Program in the Navajo-Hopi Joint Use Area* (Flagstaff, Ariz., 1979); and John J. Wood and Kathy M. Stemmler, *Land and Religion at Big Mountain: The Effects of the Navajo-Hopi Land Dispute on Navajo Well-Being* (Flagstaff, Ariz., 1981).

35. *Navajo Times,* May 12, 1982; *Arizona Daily Sun* (Flagstaff), May 7, 1982; May 9, 1982.

36. *Navajo Times,* June 23, 1982; June 30, 1982.

37. Ibid., June 30, 1982; July 7, 1982.

38. Ibid., February 3, 1982; May 12, 1982; June 9, 1982.

39. Ibid., July 14, 1982; June 8, 1978.

40. Gallup *Independent,* August 12, 1982; *Navajo Times,* August 18, 1982.

41. *Navajo Times,* October 6, 1982; and October 14, 1982; Gallup *Independent,* October 28, 1982.

42. Gallup *Independent,* October 28, 1982.

43. Ibid., October 21, 1982; *Navajo Times,* August 25, 1982.

44. Gallup *Independent,* August 11, 1982; *Navajo Times,* March 23, 1983; and August 25, 1982.

45. *Navajo Times,* June 8, 1978.

46. Gallup *Independent,* October 6, 1982; *Navajo Times,* October 20, 1982.

47. *New York Times,* January 14, 1983; *Navajo Times,* November 10, 1982; Gallup *Independent,* November 3, 1982; and November 4, 1982.

48. *Navajo Times,* November 4, 1982; Gallup *Independent,* December 8, 1982.

49. Peterson Zah, Inauguration Address, January 11, 1983, p. 1.

50. Ibid., p. 2.

51. Ibid.

52. Peterson Zah, State of the Navajo Nation, January 25, 1983, pp. 2–3.

53. Gallup *Independent,* April 5, 1983; Peterson Zah, Report of Peterson Zah, "The First 100 Days," pp. 6–7.

54. Gallup *Independent,* February 22, 1983; *Navajo Times,* March 2, 1983; and March 9, 1983.

55. *Navajo Times,* March 25, 1983; Gallup *Independent,* March 2, 1983; March 24, 1983; *Qua Toqti,* April 7, 1983.

56. Gallup *Independent,* March 31, 1983.

57. Zah, "First 100 Days," pp. 9–10.

58. Ibid., p. 6.

59. *Arizona Magazine,* May 8, 1983, p. 11.

Essay on Sources

Twentieth-century Navajo history is covered in Peter Iverson's recent work, *The Navajo Nation* (Albuquerque, 1983); two chapters are devoted to the administrations of Peter MacDonald. The book contains an up-to-date bibliography, and students of Navajo history also should consult Iverson's volume, *The Navajo: A Critical Bibliography* (Bloomington, Ind., 1976). Iverson has contributed an essay, "Peter MacDonald," in *American Indian Leaders: Studies in Diversity*, ed. R. David Edmunds; he discusses "The Emerging Navajo Nation" in Vol. 10, *Southwest*, ed. Alfonso Ortiz, *Handbook of North American Indians* (Washington, D.C., 1983), pp. 635–40. Additional general works on the Navajo include Ruth Underhill, *The Navajo* (Norman, Okla., 1967); and Clyde Kluckhohn and Dorthea Leighton, *The Navajo* (New York, 1962). See also Broderick Johnson and Virginia Hoffman, *Navajo Biographies* (Rough Rock, Ariz., 1970); Robert W. Young, *A Political History of the Navajo Tribe* (Tsaile, Ariz., 1968); and Robert W. Young, ed., *The Navajo Yearbook*, vol. 8 (Window Rock, Ariz., 1961).

Comparatively little published material exists on Peterson Zah, although his activities as director of DNA are covered in *The Navajo Nation*. Zah's own essay, "A Personal Presentation and Evaluation of Community Development at Low Mountain," in *Indian Communities in Action*, ed. Robert A. Roessel, Jr. (Tempe, Ariz., 1967), provides an important perspective on that small, traditional Navajo community and its response to the changes that occurred after World War II. The documentary film, *Dineh: The People—A Portrait of the Navajo* (1976), produced by Western World Productions, is narrated by Peterson Zah and focuses on the Zah family at Low Mountain. The film is a sensitive portrayal of traditional Navajos living in this isolated area in the former Joint-Use Area. The impact of trading posts, energy development, and relocation all receive extensive coverage.

Much of the information on Peterson Zah must be gleaned from the pages of the *Navajo Times*, the Gallup *Independent*, and other regional newspapers, such as the *Farmington Daily Times,* the Flagstaff *Arizona Daily Sun,* and the Hopi weekly, *Qua Toqti* ("The Eagle's Cry"). Metropolitan daily newspapers in Arizona and New Mexico—the *Arizona Republic* (Phoenix) and the *Albuquerque Journal*—represent additional sources of information on the modern Navajo. The *Navajo Times,* which recently began daily publication, occasionally has defended itself against charges that its coverage of events on the reservation has favored the incumbent tribal chairman at the expense of others; indeed, a lengthy article in the May 12, 1982, issue is devoted to justifying its policies. DNA–Peoples' Legal Services (DNA) apprised reservation residents of its activities in the *DNA Newsletter* and in *DNA in Action.*

The Navajo-Hopi land dispute, the partition of the former Joint-Use Area, and the ensuing relocation program are the subjects of Jerry Kammer's book, *The Second Long Walk: The Navajo-Hopi Land Dispute* (Albuquerque, 1980), and Thayer Scudder's *No Place to Go: Effects of Compulsory Relocation on Navajos* (Philadelphia, 1982). For analyses of specific issues relating to relocation, see John J. Wood, Walter M. Vannette, and Michael J. Andrews, *A Sociocultural Assessment of the Livestock Reduction Program in the Navajo-Hopi Joint Use Area* (Flagstaff, Ariz., 1979); and John J. Wood and Kathy M. Stemmler, *Land and Religion at Big Mountain: The Effects of the Navajo-Hopi Land Dispute on Navajo Well-Being* (Flagstaff, Ariz., 1981).

Since its inception in 1975, following passage of the Navajo-Hopi Land Settlement Act, the Navajo and Hopi Indian Relocation Commission has produced a number of important documents concerning relocation of Navajos and Hopis. Its 1978 *Interim Report* (Flagstaff, Ariz., 1978) and the *Report and Plan* of 1981 (Flagstaff, Ariz., 1981) are lengthy publications that cover a variety of problems that have developed as a result of the 1974 federal legislation and the ensuing partition of the former Joint-Use Area. The NHIRC *Annual Reports,* beginning in 1976, also should be consulted. NHIRC periodically contracts for research reports on various relocation issues, and such material is generally available to researchers; see, for example, John J. Wood and Michael J. Andrews, "Characteristics of the Population Subject to Relocation by the Navajo and Hopi Indian Relocation Commission" (Flagstaff, Ariz., 1981). The commission also receives studies prepared by the Indian Health Service, Navajo Community College, and other agencies concerned with the relocation of Navajo families. Less accessible are the materials produced by the Navajo Land Dispute Commission; and consequently local newspapers, such as the *Navajo Times,* remain important sources of information.

Contributors

DAVID M. BRUGGE received a B.A. in anthropology from the University of New Mexico. He is presently Regional Curator for the National Park Service in Santa Fe, New Mexico. His major area of research is Navajo cultural history and ethnohistory. His publications include *Navajos in the Catholic Church Records of New Mexico, 1694–1875* and *A History of the Chaco Navajos,* as well as some co-authored volumes and articles and reviews in professional historical and anthropological journals.

RICHARD N. ELLIS is professor of history at the University of New Mexico. He took his B.A., M.A. and Ph.D. degrees at the University of Colorado. He was director of the American Indian Historical Research Project and has received awards as the outstanding professor of graduate education at UNM. He is the author or editor of a number of books including *General Pope and U.S. Indian Policy, New Mexico Past and Present,* and *The Western American Indian.* His articles have appeared in numerous scholarly journals.

LAURENCE M. HAUPTMAN is professor of history at State University of New York, College at New Paltz. He received his B.A., M.A., and Ph.D. degrees from New York University. He is author of *The Iroquois and the New Deal* as well as many articles in Iroquois and frontier history. He is co-editor of *Neighbors and Intruders: An Ethnohistorical Exploration of the Indians of Hudson's River.* His book *The Iroquois in Contemporary History: From World War II to the Era of Red Power* is forthcoming.

GEORGE M. LUBICK received his Ph.D. in history from the University of Toledo. He is director of the Historical Research Center of the Colorado Plateau, Flagstaff, Arizona. His major area of research is American environmental history. He is the author of articles that have appeared in *Montana: The Magazine of Western History, South Atlantic*

Quarterly, and *Teaching History,* and he has contributed chapters to anthologies on the history of the American West.

RONALD MCCOY received a B.A. from Arizona State University and an M.A. and Ph.D. from Northern Arizona University. He has been an instructor of history at the College of Ganado, Navajo Nation, Arizona. He is assistant director of research at the Paul Dyck Foundation-Research Institution of American Indian Culture in Rimrock, Arizona, and he is the author of *Tim McCoy Remembers the West,* as well as two novels, *Thieves' Road* and *Fandango.* He is currently completing a book on Sioux winter counts.

VALERIE SHERER MATHES received her B.A. and M.A. in history from the University of New Mexico. She has been a full-time faculty member of the history department of City College of San Francisco since 1967. Her major area of research is nineteenth-century Indian reform, and she has published over a dozen articles as well as numerous book reviews. She is currently a doctoral candidate in history at Arizona State University, and her dissertation topic is "Women Indian Reformers in California."

WILLIAM E. UNRAU received his Ph.D. in history from the University of Colorado. He is professor of history at Wichita State University. His major area of research and writing is Indian-White relations in the nineteenth and twentieth centuries. He is author of *The Kansa Indians: A History of the Wind People, 1673–1873; The Kaw People; Tending the Talking Wire: A Buck Soldier's View of Indian Country, 1863–1866; The Emigrant Indians of Kansas: A Critical Bibliography;* and co-author of *The End of Indian Kansas: A Study of Cultural Revolution, 1854–1871.* His articles and reviews have appeared in a number of professional historical journals.

H. A. VERNON received his Ph.D. from the University of Chicago. He is associate professor emeritus of history, State University of New York, College at New Paltz. His major area of research and writing is in Canadian and Iroquois history, and articles in these fields have appeared in *The Beaver, Niagara Frontier,* the *Bulletin* of the National Museum of Man (Ottawa, Canada), and in *American Indian Culture and Research Journal.*

Editors

L. G. MOSES, associate professor of history at Northern Arizona University, received his B.A. and M.A. degress from Sonoma State University and his doctorate from the University of New Mexico. He is author of *The Indian Man: A Biography of James Mooney* and a number of articles and reviews in professional historical journals.

RAYMOND WILSON, associate professor of history at Fort Hays State University, is the author of *Ohiyesa: Charles Eastman, Santee Sioux*, and co-author of *Native Americans in the Twentieth Century* and *Administrative History, Canyon de Chelly National Monument, Arizona*. His articles and reviews have appeared in several professional historical journals. After receiving his B.A. from Fort Lewis College and his M.A. from the University of Nebraska, Omaha, he earned his doctorate from the University of New Mexico.

Index